My (Underground) American Dream

MY (UNDERGROUND) AMERICAN DREAM

*My True Story as an
Undocumented Immigrant Who Became a
Wall Street Executive*

JULISSA ARCE

With MARK DAGOSTINO

CENTER
STREET

New York Boston Nashville

Author's note: Some of the names in this book have been changed to respect the privacy of those in my stories. While I have kept very detailed journals most of my life, this book was written mostly from memory. To the best of my ability, and with all my passion, I am sharing my truth and story.

Center Street
Hachette Book Group
1290 Avenue of the Americas
New York, NY 10104
centerstreet.com
twitter.com/centerstreet

First Edition: September 2016

Center Street is a division of Hachette Book Group, Inc.
The Center Street name and logo are trademarks of Hachette Book Group, Inc.

The publisher is not responsible for websites (or their content) that are not owned by the publisher.

Library of Congress Control Number: 2016944756

ISBNs: 978-1-4555-4024-2 (hardcover), 978-1-4555-4025-9 (ebook)

Printed in the United States of America

RRD-C

10 9 8 7 6 5 4 3 2 1

*For my dad, Julio, and my mom, Luisa, who
sacrificed everything for me.*

Contents

PROLOGUE

The Attack

I wasn't making the big bucks. *Not yet*, I thought. Still, as I sat there surrounded by unpacked boxes, drinking my ice-cold beer and watching TV on a humid July night, I thought about just how lucky I truly was.

In two weeks, I'll be on my way.

I was sitting with Robert, my on-again–off-again maybe boyfriend, in his new apartment at 45 Wall Street in the heart of a reborn lower Manhattan. It was a gorgeous night in that promising summer of 2005. We'd both landed big-city jobs and rented apartments in the same building on one of the most famous streets in the world. So what if we'd driven all the way from San Antonio in a Penske truck to save money on airfare? So what if Robert's roommate wound up making that drive with us at the last minute, the three of us all squished together and sweaty on a black vinyl bench seat, erasing all of my romantic road-trip dreams? So what if I was slightly annoyed that Mr. Third Wheel was cramping our space in that apartment in that moment, too? We were there. We were on our way.

I was just about to say something about how lucky we all were when I felt a sharp pain in my chest. I suddenly felt like I couldn't breathe. A tingling feeling crept down my left arm.

I tried to convince myself it was some sort of a head freeze. Maybe the beer was too cold or I'd pounded it too fast. After a few minutes of silent agony, though, my palms started sweating and the pain in my chest became searing.

"Guys," I said. It was difficult to speak. I could barely gather enough air to make words. "I think I might be having a heart attack."

"What?" Robert said with a little laugh. "Get outta here."

"No, really. My chest hurts, and my left arm's all tingly."

I was twenty-two. I couldn't possibly be having a heart attack. It'll pass, they said, and I wanted to believe them. But I felt like I was dying. *Actually* dying. The room closed in on me. Sweat started pouring out of every pore. I tried to breathe slowly and control the pounding of my heart, but I couldn't.

"I really think I need to go to the hospital," I said.

I couldn't call 911. I was too afraid to call any government numbers, and Robert was just about the only person who knew the reason why.

He looked into my eyes and finally seemed to get it.

"Okay," he said. "Let's go."

It was late. Wall Street was dead. Miraculously, a cab appeared. We told the driver to take us to the closest hospital, which was NYU Downtown, on William Street. It was less than a half mile away, but getting there felt like an eternity. I saw the buildings arcing in on top of us the entire drive, as if we were passing through a giant tunnel in slow motion.

"Everything's going to be okay," Robert said, but I could see he was worried now, too.

At the hospital I handed over my student ID and insurance card from the University of Texas. I'd graduated in May. I was pretty sure the insurance had expired, but that was all I had. I was sure I was about to collapse in full cardiac arrest on the hard, industrial-tile floor of that ER and suffer the embarrassment of making a scene in front of Robert. Somehow I was more worried about making a fool of myself in front of him than I was about possibly dying.

The person at the desk took one look at me, wrote down the information, and didn't ask any questions.

The nurses hurried me in and hooked me up to a dozen monitors. One of them handed me an aspirin to dissolve under my tongue while another drew blood and began a long list of routine questions. "Are you on any medicine?" "No." "Any chance of you being pregnant?" "No."

Robert looked at me. "You don't want to take a pregnancy test to be sure?" he asked.

I shook my head emphatically. "No!"

When the nurses left I shot him the side-eye. "What the hell, Robert?" I said, my voice muffled by a plastic oxygen mask. "Why would you say that?"

"Well, what if you are?"

"How can I be pregnant, Robert? We aren't even having sex!"

If I wasn't already aware of how complicated our relationship was, he made it painfully clear to me in that moment. *I should dump him*, I thought. But how could I dump him? He was there in the hospital with me, in the middle of the night.

We didn't talk much after that. I lay there for hours with doctors and nurses coming in and out until finally one doctor came in and told me that he had some good news. I wasn't having a heart attack at all.

"What you've experienced is a major panic or anxiety attack," he said.

I was confused. I wasn't the type of person to panic. I wasn't

someone filled with anxiety. There were types of people I associ-
ated with panic attacks, and I was certainly not one of them.

"What could cause that to happen?" I asked. "Because it doesn't
make any sense that I would have one."

"Sometimes they just happen," the doctor told me. He said I
would be discharged shortly and left the room.

I hated that answer. I hated uncertainty. I've always hated uncertainty. I like facts, which is why I've always loved math. There
is no ambiguity in math. If he'd told me I'd had a heart attack
and needed surgery it would have been better than walking away
without a concrete answer. "Sometimes they just happen" made
absolutely no sense to me.

It was early morning by the time they discharged me, and I
didn't express any of my worry and confusion to Robert as we
walked out the front door. I was too embarrassed, and we were
both too tired to speak.

The old streets of downtown New York are particularly beautiful
early in the morning, before the crowds and the cars take over. The
edges of the cobblestones were just catching flickers of orange light
from the rising sun as it poked its head up between the buildings,
and I could hear birds chirping in that rare Manhattan quiet as we
made the walk back to our shared building.

There was plenty of noise in my head, though. *Why on earth
would I have a panic attack?*

We were almost back when it finally dawned on me.

In less than two weeks there was more than a good chance my
secret would finally be exposed—the secret that could ruin my
life, that could send me to jail, that could end my career before
it ever began. The secret I'd been forced to keep since I was fourteen years old.

In less than two weeks I would report to work and be fingerprinted for a building ID. I would have to show two forms of government-issued ID to start on payroll. I had already passed a background check, miraculously, but there would be more background checks, this time from government agencies to obtain my various financial licenses. It was all standard protocol. To anyone else, that stuff might have been no big deal. The big deal would have been that they were starting their dream job at Goldman Sachs. To me, it was a big deal in a different way. I was two weeks away from walking into Goldman Sachs's New York headquarters to start my coveted career as a financial analyst, and I'd been so focused on the details of the move and trying to figure out this whole Robert situation that I hadn't stopped to consider the possibility that I might never make it past day one.

Since the age of fourteen, I had learned to live an alternate reality, an imagined reality in which my immigration status didn't matter. Denial had become the only way I could move through life. But on that day, everything I had pushed down inside of me, the potential consequences of my secret, came rushing to the surface without warning. The reality of my situation was suddenly undeniable. Everything I'd done in my entire life, every accomplishment, every dream could disappear the moment I walked through those doors.

PART I

"*Undocumented*"

CHAPTER 1

Home Alone

What the hell are you doing?" my grandfather yelled, spanking me just before I managed to get completely undressed.

"What did I do?" I cried, while everyone laughed and laughed.

It was Christmas Eve and I was three. I don't remember anything of my debut performance, but the story has been told to me many times. At some point during the festivities, I drank a little bit of someone's champagne, which, of course, I wasn't supposed to do. While it wasn't enough to get me drunk, the alcohol made me feel hot. So I started taking off my clothes, right there in my grandmother's living room—in front of my whole extended family.

I suppose it's fitting that I caused a scene that night my family would talk about for decades to come, because as a young girl I always wanted to be in the spotlight. I was sure that I would grow up to be a performer. I made myself the center of attention at every family gathering from that moment on by singing, dancing, or directing my cousins to act out plays in front of everyone.

It's even more fitting that it all started on Christmas Eve, because Christmas was my favorite holiday. I was pretty much convinced that the party was for me and not for baby Jesus, because every Christmas Eve my extended family, thirty to forty people, would gather at my grandparents' house for an evening filled with music and laughter and booze and presents, and I turned each one of those gatherings into the Julissa Show. My aunts and uncles and cousins all gathered around the living room, clapping and cheering and snapping pictures. Then I'd go to my home just down the street and wake up to dozens of presents from Santa Claus. Santa Claus didn't just come to my house, either. I collected presents on Christmas Day from every single one of my aunts' and uncles' houses, too.

The thing I loved most about Christmas, though, had nothing to do with being the center of attention or even the lucky recipient of so many gifts. What I loved most about Christmas was that I would get to see my parents. It was the one time in the whole year when I was guaranteed that my parents would come home to me in Mexico. They never missed a Christmas. Not one.

By the time I was born in 1983, my mother had started what would become a very successful business selling silver jewelry and merchandise from our hometown of Taxco (pronounced "Tas'-co") to buyers at trade shows all over the United States. Within a few years my parents set up shop in San Antonio, Texas. From that moment on, the two of them stayed in the United States pretty much year-round, working as hard as they possibly could to provide for their family in the hopes of building a better life for us.

While I grew up under the care of a nanny and my two older sisters in a house just five minutes from my grandmother's house, my parents grew their business, traveling to faraway cities with exotic names like Chicago, New York, and New Orleans. I would later learn that my parents were importing $300,000 worth of sterling silver into the United States each year when their business was at its peak in the mid-1980s. I was told that my mother was responsible for putting Taxco silver on the map all over the United States.

So, no, I was not the poor barefoot Mexican girl who sold gum on the side of the road or who didn't go to elementary school because she had to work. In fact, I had the sweet life of a spoiled brat.

My parents enrolled all three of their daughters in an all-girls Catholic school. I walked to school each day in a pristine, navy blue uniform with a white plastic collar, a big red bow tie, long white socks, and red bows in my very long, jet-black hair, which I would make my nanny braid again and again until it was perfect, with not one hair out of place. After school, I took piano, ballet, art, and karate lessons—anything that was offered in my small town of Taxco.

I was privileged to receive wonderful gifts bought in America all the time, too, never mind that the labels said MADE IN CHINA. I was the first kid I knew to have a Nintendo, and the only kid with a Barbie-pink lunchbox that had come all the way from a mall in San Antonio. None of the other kids believed it was from America, and none of the other kids liked me very much, either. "You're an orphan," they would sometimes taunt me. I did my best to ignore them.

Taxco is a small city full of picturesque Colonial stucco buildings and narrow, winding, cobblestone streets all arranged on a beautiful hillside. It sits about a three-hour drive south of Mexico City, and its spot in those idyllic hills means it pretty much enjoys perfect weather year-round. While Taxco is big enough to serve as a tourist destination and has been known for its silverwork for more than a century, it's still small enough to be marked by landmarks rather than addresses. If anyone asked where I lived I would say, "On la calle nueva"—that's "the new street," even though it's a really, really old street—"by the central market, in front of the tortilla factory, on top of the second Metales Aviles."

The fact that Metales Aviles was a recognizable landmark in Taxco is a big point of pride, because that is the business my maternal grandparents founded. My grandmother and grandfather both came from nothing. They sold pots and pans on the streets and at the market to get by in the early days. They moved on to selling conchas, or seashells, for use in jewelry, and they soon saw the need local jewelers and craftsmen had for supplies and tools that were difficult to come by in Taxco at the time. So they opened up Metales Aviles, selling tools and supplies from sandpaper to special pliers to thousands of minuscule earring backings in the Mercado Tetitlán (the central market).

They quickly grew Metales Aviles into a successful business, opening their own stand-alone shop in town and building their dream home within walking distance. It wasn't long before they bought another building and opened a second shop, just off La Calle Nueva, the busy street where dozens of eighteen-wheelers would park and dozens of men would carry fruits, vegetables, and other goods to the Mercado each morning. The new building had small apartments on the second floor, and one of those apartments would later become home to my parents, my sisters, and me.

After Papa Miguel, my grandfather, died, my maternal grandmother—or Mama Silvia, as all her grandkids called her—became the rock of the family. No one ever disagreed with her, no one fought in front of her, and no one so much as raised their voice around her. I wanted to grow up and command as much respect as she did. The words "I am going to tell Mama Silvia" made everyone in my family stop doing whatever it was they were doing. Even my tough-guy dad had the utmost respect for her.

Stepping through Mama Silvia's gate, past the huge bougainvillea tree bursting with color, up the steps made of tiny stones, I would run inside under the high ceilings as a child and feel like

I was home. That house has always been a retreat for me. I felt at peace there, even when I found myself arguing with Mama Silvia's cook or getting scolded by one of my older sisters for something I'd done. No matter what the temperature was outside, it always seemed to be the ideal temperature inside that house. And from the big windows on the first floor, up the spiral staircase to the second-floor bedrooms, to the giant terrace on the third floor, which was filled with big earthen pots of flowers and herbs, the house was flooded with beautiful sunlight all day long.

Mama Silvia kept a parrot for a pet. She really loved that big green bird, even though it would sometimes bite her when she fed it. "Stupid parrot who can't even speak!" she would curse. Yet she cared for it devotedly.

I also watched closely as she cared for her business. Metales Aviles carried a little bit of something for everyone, in addition to the craftsmen's tools and supplies. They kept a seasonal section in the store, and at Christmastime they would sell toys brought in from Mexico City. Once I was old enough to walk the streets of Taxco myself, Mama Silvia used to send me to do market research. I would go around to all of the big toy stores in town and see what was popular so we could buy and then sell those things, too. Then I would get to travel with her to Mexico City to buy the toys. It was one of my favorite things to do all year.

They sold incense at the store, too, and for fun I used to take a tray full of tiny bags of copal (a kind of tree resin) incense and sell them at the Mercado. I wore a jean apron that had a zippered pocket for money, and as a little girl I used to walk around that bustling market yelling, *Copal! Copal! Cinco pesos el copal!* I loved selling. Some people might have thought, *Poor thing. Her parents are making her work.* But that wasn't it at all. I wanted to work. I wanted to contribute. Whatever my mom and my grandmother were doing, I wanted to do it, too. So I was always coming up with new business ideas.

For instance, from the balcony of my home I could see men unloading all of the trucks at the Mercado in the early morning, and I started noticing that they didn't have any food, coffee, or water. There was no one there in the early morning to serve them. So I said, "We should sell them *tortas*!" I didn't even make sandwiches for myself at that age. I had a nanny to do that when I was hungry in the morning, and I figured all those men must get hungry in the morning, too. So I made my nanny get up extra early and make tortas at five o'clock in the morning, and I turned that into one of my first entrepreneurial endeavors: selling food and lemonade to the dozens of men who unloaded the eighteen-wheelers. But I hadn't yet learned the importance of recognizing and celebrating teamwork. I was too proud of myself to share the credit or profits with my nanny, who did all the work. Instead, I spent all the profits on candy. Over time there would be women selling breakfast food and coffee to the drivers and deliverymen in the early morning. But growing up, I had a monopoly on the fast-food breakfast business.

Everyone in my family was entrepreneurial, and even though I didn't get to see my mother nearly as often as I wanted, I knew how far she had come in life. I knew she was a force to be reckoned with in the business world, and I wanted to be just like her.

My mom, Luisa, was stunningly beautiful. She had long legs, shiny long hair, and delicate features. My grandparents didn't have money when she was growing up, so she really *was* one of those poor Mexican children who had to work in order to help support her family. She was the second oldest of six, and when her older sister married in her teens and moved out of the house, my mother was forced to drop out of school to become the primary caretaker of her four younger siblings. She never graduated from high school. My grandparents were busy building their business, and she had no choice but to give up her childhood. Her days included taking care of her siblings, working long hours, and being beaten by my grandparents for any offense. There were no time-outs, no "You are grounded." There were only beatings. My grandparents weren't bad people, she later told me. They loved their kids. "In those days beating your kids was common," she would say.

One night, after my grandfather beat her so badly she could barely walk, my mother made up her mind to leave home. She would later tell me with regret in her eyes, "In those days, a single woman living alone was unheard of, unless you were a woman of the street." So the only way for her to get out of her situation was to get married.

Enter Julio Arce Casimiro.

With her looks and the growing prominence of her Aviles family name, my mother had many suitors in her late teens. Yet none of them caught her attention the way Julio did.

My dad was shorter than my mom and darker skinned, with big, thick eyebrows, and bigger lips. He was the opposite of my mother in so many ways. He'd had his nose broken several times from street fights, but nevertheless, he looked so strong and handsome, with his head of jet-black hair. He had a tattoo on his bicep that read "Carmella," for some girl he'd met before he met my mom. The tattoo bothered me more than it ever bothered her.

After his father died in a mining accident and his mom remarried, my father left home to make a life of his own. He was twelve at the time. So, like my mom, he was one of *those* Mexican children. Yet even under those circumstances he still managed to finish high school by attending night school.

As a young man, he once ran away from a gang by climbing

on top of the eighteen-wheelers that were lined up in front of the Mercado and leaping from one to the other. The stunt earned him the nickname El Aguila (the Eagle). He certainly didn't run out of fear. He was tough. He *looked* like a street fighter, and he intimidated just about anyone he met (except for Mama Silvia). I swear everyone in Taxco knew the story of how he taught himself to box: he filled a big bag with dirt and stones and punched it until his knuckles bled.

One day, my mom's youngest sister introduced Luisa to Julio and, as the story goes, my mom was instantly smitten. My dad "couldn't sleep, couldn't eat, couldn't look at any other ladies" after he met my mom. It wasn't long before my mom confessed her situation at home, and my dad, the fighter, wanted to rescue her. I don't entirely believe the story of the night they ran away together, but this is how it was told to me at least three dozen times when I was a kid.

My dad would start: "Your mom and I went to a *tardeada* [a kind of high school dance], and we were having so much fun."

"Your dad actually danced," my mom would say with a smile, "and we lost track of time, and it got really late."

My mom knew that if she went back home to her parents after curfew, she was sure to get a beating—so my dad said she didn't have to go home at all. She could just run away with him. And she did. She was seventeen. They got married shortly after, and my grandparents didn't speak to or forgive my mom until after my sister, Aris, was born, almost two years later. At that point, in order to receive my grandparents' forgiveness, my parents were finally married in the Catholic Church, and all was right with the world.

My dad worked as a truck driver and a handyman when they first met, but shortly after Aris was born, in 1972, he landed a job as a deliveryman for Coca-Cola. That job provided a steady income. My mom picked up my dad's check every Friday, and she ran the house from the very beginning.

Being a truck driver's wife was not enough for my mother, though. She had her eyes set higher, and she was relentless in the pursuit of her dream. She wanted to build a house. She wanted her daughters to attend Catholic school. She wanted to see the world. Taxco was far too small for her.

Once her silver business took root and the two of them set off to make their fortunes in America, my parents started construction on a six-story house in Taxco. As my nanny braided my hair, I could see that big, empty building going up from the windows of our tiny second-story apartment. I wanted to live in that house so badly that one day I defiantly made my nanny move all my clothes into its unfinished shell.

I knew my parents were sacrificing for me, and that the biggest sacrifice they made was leaving their three daughters behind while they built a business in the United States. I heard it again and again. But more than anything, I just wanted them home.

Don't get me wrong. I was grateful for all that I had. I was thrilled whenever we got the chance to visit them. America was a place of wonder for me. I saw the riches portrayed in *Dennis the Menace* cartoons dubbed in Spanish, including one particular episode when Dennis put the mean neighbor's house on wheels, which I thought was the coolest thing ever. There was another episode that featured an RV road trip, and I briefly believed that everyone in America had houses on wheels that could go anywhere they wanted. When I was a little older, I sneaked into my grandmother's living room late at night to watch how Americans, who were all beautiful, rich, and white, lived on *Beverly Hills 90210*.

My sisters and I visited my parents in America often, too. One summer, my parents took my cousins and sisters and me on a road trip around the United States in an RV, and it felt like my house-on-wheels, rich-American dreams had all come true. I loved going to shopping malls. I marveled at the wonders of Sea World and Six Flags. But we were just tourists. I always came home to Taxco. And my mother and father would always go back to the United States.

Since Aris was ten years older than I was, she wasn't around that much during my formative years. I mostly saw her from afar, as this beautiful Barbie doll who seemed to have everything, including lots of friends and suitors, and in whose footsteps I hoped to follow. She was the girl who celebrated her *quinceañera*, that all-important Mexican rite of passage on a girl's fifteenth birthday, at a grand hotel with a party that seemed fit for royalty.

Our middle sister, Nay, was the one with whom I spent more time, and even though she was just five years older, Nay took on more of the day-to-day parenting duties in my life.

She was the sister who made sure I did my homework and ate my vegetables, even if that meant smacking me to get me to shape up. We ate our dinners at Mama Silvia's house, where she had a woman who cooked for us. I hated this woman. She was my nemesis. I am certain that she figured out what I didn't like and cooked that just to torture me.

One of the dishes I hated the most was a mushroom cream soup that she made all the time. One day, I finally put my little eight-year-old foot down. "I'm not gonna eat this. I can't eat this!" I yelled.

Nay, who was all of thirteen at the time, gave me her best stern parent voice: "You're gonna eat that soup, or I'm gonna smack you!"

Nay was a bit of a round-faced, chubby kid, and when she got mad, she looked like an angry Hello Kitty. It was really hard for me not to laugh. That particular time, I could hear in her voice that she really meant business, but I refused to budge. "I will not eat this soup!" I repeated at the top of my lungs, trying not to laugh at her funny, fuming face.

Finally, she stood up. "If you don't eat this soup, I will smack you for every mushroom you don't eat."

There were nineteen mushrooms in my soup bowl, and I got a spanking for every single one of them—laughing the entire time, which only made her angrier.

"Why are you laughing?" she yelled in exasperation.

My stubborn streak bore itself out in other places, too, particularly the classroom, where I always got in trouble for talking too much. I simply didn't like to keep quiet, and I didn't understand why my talking was a problem. My teachers said I asked too many questions. *How can it be bad to ask questions?* I wondered. I got good grades. So what if I caused a little commotion? *Why can't we talk and have fun in the classroom, too?*

My mother called us on the phone every single night. She told me over and over how important it was for me to do well in school, and to be a good girl, and to be a good Catholic, because that way I would have the opportunity to do whatever I wanted when I was older—opportunities she did not have as a girl whose only way out was to find a husband and have a baby at the age of nineteen. I would listen, and I would try to be good. But as the years went by, I saw less and less of her. The trips home became less frequent, and our trips to America became less frequent, too.

Every year my school held a big festival for Mother's Day, where we would all present our mothers with handmade gifts. My parents vowed to be around for my birthdays and holidays, and they really tried to be there. But one year, when I was eight, my mom couldn't come for Mother's Day, and my grandmother was working, so I wound up being the only kid in class holding a handmade placemat for no one.

At the end of the day, as I put the placemat into my backpack, one of my classmates asked me—again—if I was an orphan.

"No. My mom lives in the United States," I said. "And when she comes back, she's bringing me a lot of presents."

I wasn't trying to brag, more like justifying why my parents were not around. I was trying to make sense of my own existence—as if maybe it was worth it that my parents weren't in Mexico because they bought me nice things. I was sure none of these other girls had ever been on a Disney cruise. My mother had enrolled me in etiquette classes so I would know how to behave on the ship, choosing the right forks for dinner, and basically learning not to be rude or offensive in a world outside my own.

On the way home from school that day, I asked Nay if we were, in fact, orphans, and I'll never forget what she told me: "Of course not. We have parents, and we have aunts and uncles who love us. We have Mama Silvia, and we have each other."

Nay didn't seem to be bothered by the absence of our parents. I wished I could be tough like her. She was the closest thing I had to a parent, and besides a couple of girls at school, and my cousins, she was one of my only true friends. I appreciated her trying to prop me up, but those kids at school punched a hole in me, and the sadness of my parents' absence flooded in.

I tried to console myself with Nay's words. *At the very least, I have Nay, and we have each other*, I repeated over and over in my mind. Plus, my parents wouldn't be in America forever. Construction on our six-story house was nearly completed. I kept telling myself that someday soon all of us would be living together.

CHAPTER 2

The Last Drop

My positive thinking didn't work.

When I finally saw my parents that summer of 1992, they came bearing terrible news: I was about to get kicked off the donkey.

In Mexico, we have a saying that when you're the favorite child, you sit on the donkey, just like the Virgin Mary sat on the donkey while Joseph walked through the desert to Bethlehem.

My mom was pregnant.

I would no longer be the baby or the favorite in the family. I had sat on the donkey for almost nine years, and I wasn't ready to give up my place to a baby—especially to one who would get to live with my parents in San Antonio.

"I hate the baby," I told my mom as soon as she finished sharing the news.

Then, the news got worse. It's a big deal to have a boy in Mexican families. She tried to tell me it was a miracle; she and my dad had prayed for a baby boy for twenty years, and God had finally heard their prayers. All I could think was, *He'll live with my parents in the Unites States, and I'll be left behind, and my mom won't love me anymore.*

"I'm gonna throw the baby out the window," I yelled.

"Julissa! How dare you say something like that!" my mom said, looking absolutely horrified.

"Fine. I don't want the baby to die. But I am gonna throw him into a trash can. So he'll survive, but he'll be gone."

My mother was none too pleased, but neither was I.

That wasn't the only bad news they came bearing, either. My oldest sister, Aris, had been accepted to one of the most prestigious colleges in Mexico, they told me—in a city two hours away. She would be going to live there when the new school year started. And Nay would be going to live there, too, to attend a prestigious private high school.

"What will happen to me?"

"You'll live with Mama Silvia," my mom answered.

I loved Mama Silvia. I loved her house. I even liked the thought of living there. But I still felt I was being abandoned.

My baby brother, Julio, was born on Christmas Day. Not only was he a boy, but he was born on Christmas. In America. He was blessed, and there was no way I could deny it. Not only had I been kicked off the donkey, but I'd been kicked off the donkey by a *miracle baby*.

My love of Christmas suffered a terrible blow.

I continued to be jealous of this baby for an entire year. It didn't help that my sisters and everybody else in the family kept teasing me about being kicked off the donkey. And it didn't take long before all of my doomsday dreams of abandonment started to come true.

That following year, something bad happened. No one ever told me what it was, but suddenly my parents were under all kinds of stress. Something terrible rattled their business. Money was suddenly tight. I was warned that my parents wouldn't be able to make trips home quite as often. Construction on our six-story house came to a halt.

Of course, I blamed it all on baby Julio—and I wanted it all to get fixed.

I pleaded with my parents on the phone—"Please take me to live with you in San Antonio"—even though it was a plea I was torn about making. I wanted to be with my parents, but I wasn't sure that I would fit in. I wasn't white and blonde like all the Americans I had seen on TV. Plus, my sisters, who were away at school, couldn't come, and Mama Silvia couldn't come, and I wasn't ready to be separated from them. They were my family—the only real family I'd ever known. My parents for the most part were strangers to me. Still, I thought, wouldn't it be best for a girl to be with her parents?

It didn't matter. My parents said I could not come live with them. Everything in America was more expensive, they said. Plus they traveled all the time, and we didn't have family in the United States to help care for me.

So there I stayed, living with Mama Silvia and her stupid mute parrot and feeling abandoned by my mother, my father, and now my sisters, too. I knew their reason for working so much and being gone so much was to give me a better life, but I didn't see my life as better at all. I would rather have eaten salt tacos every day than dined on fancy mushroom soup that I hated. I would rather have gone to public school with the "hood kids" than a bunch of stuck-up princesses who made fun of me because my parents were never around.

I didn't say much of this to my parents, but it was clear to them I wasn't happy. I didn't take it out on Mama Silvia, either. I actually liked living with her a lot more than living with the nanny at our house down the street. Yet, clearly I was acting out, because

I heard Mama Silvia on the phone with my mother, saying that I didn't seem like myself. She was worried about me. My grades were slipping. I was getting in more and more trouble for my questions at school.

What worried my mom most were my slipping grades.

In Mexico, one of the biggest academic honors is to be part of *la escolta,* an honor roll of sorts. Only we did more than metaphorically parade our academic honors: we physically paraded them. The students who made la escolta marched around the school while the national anthem played, and the person with the highest GPA got to hold the flag, while parents and students all watched and cheered. Good grades alone weren't enough to make that parade, though. The grades had to be coupled with good conduct—the one thing that repeatedly kept me out of la escolta. My grades would have qualified me to hold the Mexican flag any number of times, so I didn't think it was fair to be left out for a little talking, but the rules were the rules.

So my mother made a deal with me: If I was able to get on la escolta, meaning if I was able to keep my mouth shut, not ask questions, and generally be a good Catholic student, she would fly down to see me march in the parade.

"I won't miss it for the world," she told me. "I will be there. I promise."

I hadn't seen my mother in months at that point. It was all I wanted. So I kept my mouth closed, I worked hard, and I made la escolta! I called my mother to tell her, and she was elated.

When the day finally came, though, she didn't show up. Instead, I got excuses. A delay at the airport. A snowstorm in the city where she was attending a trade show. Her flight was canceled. I couldn't understand it. I couldn't understand any of it. My mother had always kept her promises to me.

There are few things worse than a broken promise from a parent. I got all dressed up in my school uniform and walked in la escolta that day with tears in my eyes.

The applause, the national anthem, marching all around that school meant nothing without her there. *Why did she not fly down sooner?* I wondered. I knew she had a tendency to be late to things. I was old enough now to recognize that for all of her business smarts, my mother was messy, disorganized, and late. Her purse was full of restaurant sugar packets, and all sorts of old receipts and makeup and wrappers and things that looked like they'd been in there since the 1970s. *Was she late to the airport? Was that why she missed her flight? Or was it the baby who was slowing her down?*

I was tired of being ignored. I was tired of feeling abandoned. For all those years I'd gone off to piano lessons and karate lessons and art lessons for hours every day after school, I'd worked really hard because I wanted to make my parents proud. I could never be what a baby boy was in their eyes, but I could paint, play the piano, and kick some butt in karate. I was determined to have the best painting at the art show, the best piano performance at the recital, the most karate trophies. I wanted them to say to the other parents, "That's our daughter!" I wanted them to be proud of me. But then I would take a cab all by myself to my piano recital and play to an audience of strangers.

How can they be proud of me when they aren't even here?

Even when they *were* there, it seemed as if they were no longer standing up for me.

The next time my mother made it to Mexico we all went to my cousin's fourth birthday party, and at the request of my aunt, I put on one of my Julissa Shows. I jumped up on the dining-room table and began singing a rendition of "Voy a Traer el Pelo Suelto" ("I

Am Going to Let My Hair Down"), a song that was as popular in Mexico as Nirvana's "Smells Like Teen Spirit" was in the United States. The crowd loved it, singing along with me. I even saw my mom giving me two thumbs-up.

I was on my knees, swinging my hair when I felt a yank. My grandmother grabbed me by my long black hair and pulled me off the table.

"What are you doing?!" she cried. She was so embarrassed.

She wasn't embarrassed that I was dancing on my knees. What embarrassed her was that her granddaughter had climbed up and stood atop another woman's nice white linens. My mom did nothing.

"How could I say anything?" she protested after the incident was over.

Right, I thought. *You're right. After all, it's my grandmother who is raising me. Not you.* I went home with my grandmother. I didn't want to stay at home with my parents.

I only saw my parents twice that entire year, and I came to regret not going home with them that night, even if my mom had let my grandmother humiliate me in front of the whole family.

I didn't have luck making many friends at school that year, and I really missed Nay and her angry Hello Kitty face. One of the few bright spots for me that year was a crush I developed on an older boy named Enrique. He was in my art class, and he was *so* cute and *so* nice. Even though he was nice to me, he didn't really pay attention to me the way I wanted him to. The girls he paid attention to were his age, thirteen or fourteen years old, and they had *boobs*.

One day, I thought I found the perfect way for Enrique to like me. I stumbled across an old *Playboy* magazine in what used to be my uncle's room at Mama Silvia's house. I thought, "Enrique will think I'm so cool if I give this to him!" I wrapped it up in a newspaper and hid it. The next day I stuffed it into my backpack, ate dinner in haste, and skipped my homework. I was so excited about art class and giving the *Playboy* to Enrique. I hadn't even looked inside the magazine. I just knew it had girls with boobs in it, and I had figured out that all boys like boobs.

Enrique was sitting across from me that day. We were working with oil on canvas. I waited until the teacher wasn't looking and then ran around the table and whispered that I had something to give him after class. In my excitement, I knocked over my own painting, which was still wet, and it was pretty much ruined when it hit the floor, but I didn't care. Enrique would think I was supercool. I was sure of it.

After class, Enrique asked me what was up.

"Wait right here," I told him. "I'm going to get something for you."

I made my way to my backpack and took out my gift. I ran back to where he was standing and handed him the bundle of newspaper.

"What is this?" he asked.

"Just take a peek," I said, smiling ear to ear. He looked at the magazine, and his eyes got wide in disbelief.

"Mrs. Stella!" he yelled, and he suddenly turned with that magazine in his hands and ran all the way down the hall to the administrator's office. I didn't know what was going on. A couple of minutes later, Mrs. Stella called me into her office and I passed Enrique as I walked in. He looked shaken. His eyes were watery.

Wasn't he supposed to be excited? He wasn't supposed to cry when he saw boobs, and then tell on me.

What a wimp, I thought.

It didn't occur to me that the ripples of this event might be life altering. I never imagined that my bold gesture to Enrique would turn my world upside down. But suddenly, with one phone call to Mama Silvia, all hell broke loose.

My grandmother prayed three extra rosaries for me that night. My sisters were brought home in the middle of the week from their far-off schools. Within a few days, both my parents flew back to Mexico. Everyone told me they were sorry for leaving me alone. Everyone blamed themselves because apparently I was turning out to be some degenerate child.

I just wanted a cute boy to think I was cool. That was all. I didn't realize that slipping a *Playboy* magazine to my crush would change my life forever.

As I lay down to take a nap on the first afternoon my mother was there, I overheard her talking with one of her close friends on the phone. "All my daughters are so good," she said. "I don't know where we went wrong with Julissa."

A few days later, my parents went back to the United States, and I thought the whole ordeal was over, but I was wrong.

When summer came, I flew to San Antonio with my sisters to visit my parents, just as I had many times before. When summer ended, both of my sisters flew back to Mexico to start school, but I did not.

"When am I flying back?" I asked.

At first my parents seemed to avoid the question. Finally, after I nagged them enough, they gave me an answer I never expected: "You are not flying back," my parents told me. "You are staying with us."

CHAPTER 3

Strangers

My parents' two-bedroom, second-floor apartment was bigger than our apartment had been in Mexico, but it didn't feel like a home, and it certainly didn't feel like *my* home.

The view from the balcony wasn't of a bustling street, but of planes about to land at the San Antonio airport. There was no Mama Silvia's nearby, no tortilla factory across the street, no kids running around outside our windows.

Unlike in Mexico, we had no living room, no couch, no pictures hanging on the walls. Just a kitchen and dining room, with a table covered by my mother's supplies and paperwork from all the trade shows. The rest of her things were scattered everywhere. My parents shared their bedroom with my eighteen-month-old brother. I shared my bedroom with a fax machine.

When my sisters and I had visited San Antonio for a few weeks at a time, much of which was spent running off to Six Flags in between my mother's trade shows, I didn't care that I couldn't walk to Mama Silvia's house or to any of my aunts' houses. Suddenly, it mattered. I couldn't go anywhere without my parents having to drive me. I'd lost my independence. I'd traded my familiar world of cobblestone streets and my grandmother's bougainvillea tree for scorching Texas summer heat in a city built on concrete and pavement.

As the weeks went by, it became clear to me that my getting into trouble had been just the latest in a series of problems my parents were facing.

"We don't have money to pay for that," my mother would say.

"Well, whose fault is that?" my father would respond.

I would hear their raised voices through the door of my new bedroom. It would always start the same way, with something about some bill that wasn't paid or the debt they were in. Then came the blame: my father yelling at my mother for stopping the van to go to the bathroom; my mother yelling that it was he who made them stop at the diner too long because he was hungry. Then the words would get ugly. Sometimes, something was thrown. Something would break, and then the voices would stop.

My parents had lost everything in that past year, and the more I listened to their nightly arguments, the more I came to understand what had happened.

They had developed a fairly standard routine, shipping all of the sterling silver for their business from Taxco to Laredo, Mexico, where they would pick it up, load it into a van, drive it through customs at the U.S. border, and then bring it to San Antonio. They would carry tens of thousands of dollars' worth of silver in that van every trip, and from San Antonio they would repackage it and get ready to fly or drive to their next trade show. They had done this dozens of times without incident.

One day the previous year, during the trip from Laredo to San Antonio, they stopped at a diner. My mom wanted coffee, or to use the bathroom, or my dad wanted a sandwich—whatever the reason, they both went inside and left the van alone for no more than fifteen minutes. They said they could see the van from where they were sitting, but that fifteen minutes changed everything. When they came back to the van, they discovered that one of the windows that was hidden from their view had been cut out, and the silver was gone. All of it.

A fifteen-minute rest stop cost them twenty years of hard work.

The merchandise had been given to them on credit, and none of it was insured. Without that silver in hand to take to trade shows, they had nothing to sell, and no way to pay back their debt. My dad never got my mom to understand the importance of saving, so despite all of their success, the money went out as quickly as it came in.

At some point in the aftermath, they took out a mortgage on our six-story house in Mexico. They used some of the loan money to repay some of the debt and the rest to buy more inventory. They booked twice as many trade shows as they did before. But the profit margin was slim, and now they had a mortgage payment on top of their other expenses. They just couldn't catch a break. As soon as things were looking better, something else would happen. My parents were elated when NAFTA (the North American Free Trade Agreement) was signed in early 1994 because, in theory, the agreement was supposed to make cross-border business easier and more efficient, but that never happened. On December 20, 1994, on my dad's birthday, the Mexican government devalued the peso. Within days, the Mexican peso lost 50 percent of its value against the U.S. dollar. My parent's loan was in U.S. dollars, so their mountain of debt turned into a spewing volcano of woe.

Seeing my parents so stressed made me feel guilty about the trouble I'd caused. Living with my parents full-time for the very first time in my life, I couldn't help but feel that my presence only made things more difficult for them. I felt responsible for their inability to dig themselves out of their troubles. With me around they couldn't move about as easily.

When I was a little girl, my dad was always the fun parent. He was the one who bought me a retro-looking shiny red bike with gold handles and taught me how to ride it during one of his visits home. My mom tried to buy me a pink bike with a basket on it, but my dad knew that wasn't my style. He fought with my mother about it and won. I expected his role in my life to continue that way, and at first, it did.

Right after they told me I'd be staying with them for good, my mom flew off to another trade show, so my dad was the one who helped me get settled in. He took me to a local furniture store and bought me my first-ever matching bedroom set—a white dresser with pink flowers and antique-looking gold handles, and a twin bed with four posters. It was furniture fit for a queen, and I loved it.

They couldn't pay for it in cash, so my dad bought it on credit. He used every opportunity to teach me some sort of lesson, and when he bought me that furniture he told me, "In this country, you are nothing without good credit."

Since it was just me and my dad at home so often, my parents started leaning on me to help with Julio: feeding him, changing him, tending to him when he cried. Being around him made me realize he wasn't so bad. It was kind of nice to have a baby brother. I loved making him laugh, and so did my dad. I just didn't like having the responsibility of taking care of a baby. It made me feel like I was eleven going on thirty.

Caring for my brother wasn't my only responsibility, either. I also had to keep the apartment clean, which wasn't an easy task. Every time my mother came home it was as if the Tasmanian devil swept in. I had to ask her all the time to pick up her things in my room so I could have some space just to walk around my new bed.

With both of my sisters enrolled in top private schools in Mexico, paying tuition was one of the money issues my parents fought about. My mother insisted that we keep them enrolled in the best schools. There were other sacrifices they could make, she argued. She would not sacrifice their education, and she wasn't about to sacrifice mine. She enrolled me in a Catholic school in San Antonio.

"I don't even speak English. How can I go to school here? I won't be able to make any friends," I protested when she told me I'd be attending an all-English-speaking school.

"It's what's best for you, Julissa," she said. "You'll learn English soon enough."

I began to realize just how much I'd left behind in Mexico. I hadn't said good-bye to anyone. I worried that the few friends I had made back home would think I'd abandoned them. On the plus side, I imagined they probably didn't think I was an orphan anymore, but I felt bad that I hadn't given one last hug to Mama Silvia or any of my aunts or uncles or cousins.

"We'll visit at Christmas," my parents told me, but that seemed like a million years away.

Next thing I knew, my mother was taking me to my new school. My parents spoke enough English to get by, but they were by no means fluent. They had learned how to speak to their customers about sterling silver and always had a translator around when they attended trade shows. My mother would unabashedly use her hands and anything she could to communicate, but my father mostly kept quiet around anyone he didn't know, even if they spoke Spanish. That made the process of getting me enrolled a little confusing. This wasn't a Spanish-speaking school. They didn't offer ESL (or English as a Second Language) courses, and even if they did, my mother would never have enrolled me in such classes. There was and still is a stigma that if you don't speak English it means you aren't smart. This couldn't be further from the truth, of course, but perception is everything. Somehow *ESL* means "remedial" to a lot of people, when it should just mean "I speak one more language than you do."

I was about to be thrown into classrooms with all English-speaking students, but my parents were determined to set me up for success. They hired one of my teachers to tutor me every day after class and on weekends, so I could start to learn English as fast as was humanly possible. In their eyes this wasn't a matter of assimilation, it was a matter of survival.

I had taken some English lessons in Mexico, but they'd taught me nothing. I could sing one child's song in English. That was it. I was scared. I was terrified, actually. *How will I ever make friends if I can't talk to anyone?*

I didn't realize how terrified I should have been. As an eleven-year-old girl in a new country, I didn't know the first thing about immigration laws. All I knew was that my parents told me San Antonio was my new home. I had no idea that enrolling as a student in that American school was breaking the law.

My parents had brought me to America on a tourist visa instead of on a student visa. It didn't matter that I was enrolled in private school. Enrolling in school was a violation of that permit, even if I wasn't being educated by the state. If anyone found out I was going to school on a tourist visa, my visa could have been revoked and, presumably, I could have been deported. I was breaking the law in the eyes of the U.S. government and in the eyes of many U.S. citizens. Not by choice and not on purpose, but because I came to stay with my own parents, and they wanted to make sure I didn't lose out on my education while I stayed with them. They weren't looking to break the law by enrolling me in school; they certainly weren't looking for a handout. They just wanted to save me from a lifetime of sin and *Playboy* magazines.

The thing is, I don't think my parents ever expected to stay in America for good. The plan was to make enough money to build their dream house and move back to Taxco, and they were well on their way to accomplishing that plan before that shipment of silver was stolen from their van—not on the "dangerous" Mexican side of the border, but on U.S. soil.

My parents' business was completely on the up-and-up. They were registered with the state and federal governments. They paid all the fees and taxes that were necessary under the law. I know this because it didn't take long before they enlisted me—an eleven-year-old—to help them with the mountains of paperwork that buried our dining room table.

My parents both had Texas driver's licenses. All they needed back then was a passport and visa to get one. In fact, both of my parents also had social security cards that specified they were "NOT VALID FOR EMPLOYMENT." Those cards allowed them to pay their business taxes and open lines of credit in the United States.

The only "illegal" thing they did was to take me, their own daughter, to school—even though it was a private education, at no cost to American taxpayers and for which they paid top dollar.

Before moving to San Antonio, I imagined that classrooms in America were filled with only rich, beautiful white kids like I'd seen on TV. But San Antonio wasn't like that. There were lots of brown people with black hair who looked just like me all over the city. There were lots of people who spoke Spanish, too, although that wasn't the case in my particular school. Other than the language barrier, for the most part, I felt like I was pretty much like everyone else. As far as I knew, everything was normal. I was an eleven-year-old girl. Eleven-year-olds go to school. I went to school. No one asked me what type of visa I had, or whether I was supposed to be there, and I had no idea I wasn't supposed to be there.

My parents had valid Mexican passports with U.S. visas, and so did I. We could come and go across the border as we pleased at that point, as long as we had enough money to travel—which we didn't. Not for many months. I assumed that traveling back and forth with ease would always be the case, and that when I grew up and made my own money, I'd be able to go anywhere I wanted. I had traveled across the border for years, and I had no idea that my tourist visa had an expiration date. When I came to live with my parents, my visa had less than two years remaining. I suppose two years seems like a lifetime when you're a child, so even if I knew, I don't think I would have worried about it. I would have guessed, and hoped, that maybe we'd be back in Taxco permanently in less time than that. I assumed that my parents wanted that, too.

I had no idea what staying in this country beyond that expiration date would mean for me. I had no idea that I was running out of time.

⎯⎯✸⎯⎯

That sixth-grade year turned out to be one of the worst years of my life. My grades were terrible. I failed open-book tests because I couldn't read and write in English. All of the other girls made fun of me for having an accent, for having long hair, for eating hard-boiled eggs at lunchtime, though I didn't know what they were saying at the time. I would just laugh along with them, not even realizing that they were laughing at me.

Strangely, I was never embarrassed by it. Perhaps it was because my mother never seemed embarrassed by anything, because even though kids at school didn't like me, I didn't let their ridicule shut me down. I always wanted to shine bright rather than close myself off. I was never shy. I always raised my hand. I always wanted to speak in front of the class. Even when I could barely form complete sentences, I always had something to say.

There was one other girl who spoke Spanish in my class at school. She also happened to be a new student, so we bonded pretty quickly as the outsiders. This girl was from Spain, and she was going to be in our school for only one year because her family was moving somewhere else at the end of the school year. She let everyone know that. Maybe that was why our friendship never grew particularly close. Or maybe it was that she came from such a different world. This girl had rich parents. She lived in a mansion in a gated community that was unlike anything I had ever seen in my life. I never felt poor, even now that we were staying in that apartment with no living room. I had seen real poverty in Mexico, and I knew the difference. But being around her made me realize just how much I had been forced to give up by coming to America.

My parents didn't have a nice home. They couldn't afford the piano lessons, karate lessons, or art lessons I'd enjoyed in Mexico. They couldn't afford to buy me a new school uniform. My uniform came from a secondhand store. I don't think any of the other students knew, but I did, and it only served to make me feel even more like an outsider.

I suppose it was during that first school year in San Antonio when I realized just how important money really was and how badly I didn't want to struggle. I saw how hard my parents were working just to get by, and I knew, instinctively, that I had to accomplish something more.

The only other friend I made that whole year was a girl named Tiffani. Tiffani didn't really speak Spanish, but somehow we made it work. She was kind of short and had braces and curly hair, and like me, she was loud and really opinionated. The other girls at school didn't really like her, either, but she didn't care. She didn't let their teasing stop her. She was super-outgoing, and I liked that.

As the school year went on, I started spending a lot of time at Tiffani's house. Her parents were warm and accepting of me. As Tiffani and I grew closer, she opened up to me about some tough things that had happened in her life. In turn, I started to open up about some tough things that were happening to me.

I had early memories of my dad pushing my mom around a couple of times during their visits home. Domestic violence happens in every corner of the world, and growing up in Mexico I heard about it all the time. I didn't like seeing it, and I didn't and still don't understand it.

My father never hit any of his children, though. That is, he never hit any of his children until I came to live with him. I don't remember the first time it happened, but I do remember the first really bad beating. I was fixing a bottle for Julio, trying to open up a can of liquid baby formula. I was using a handheld bottle opener with the sharp puncher on one side for the first time, and when I tried to punch the top, the can slipped. The formula spilled everywhere. My dad was furious, and he hit me with a wooden spoon until the spoon broke.

I didn't know how to open a can like that. I had never done it by myself before then. I told him I was sorry, but it didn't help.

My dad apologized later that night. It didn't take long for me to figure out that after hitting me, he would always apologize. He would tell me he felt really bad about it, and I know he did. He would tell me he was sorry and that he'd never do it again, and I knew he *wanted* to never hit me again. He was my dad. I wanted to believe him. I loved him.

"Okay, Dad. It's okay," I would say. And then the next day, he would hit me again.

I tried to convince myself that it wasn't my fault. I tried to convince myself it wasn't his fault, either. He had a hard life growing up, way worse than getting made fun at school for not speaking English. I tried to convince myself it was the alcohol's fault.

When I first moved in with my parents, I noticed that my dad would have a beer or two every night. As the school year went on, though, my dad was stuck taking care of two children every time my mom traveled, and those two beers turned into a six-pack. Then more than a six-pack. He never drank during the day. He was never under the influence when he came to pick me up at school or anything like that. But pretty much every night, he got drunk.

When he drank, he kept his beer in a little cooler on the floor to one side of his chair. When he finished a beer, he'd crush the can and set it down neatly on the other side, and dispose of them all before he went to bed. But the more he drank, the angrier he became. And the more he yelled, the more he hit.

I remember telling Tiffani about being hit with the spoon. She never judged me, or my parents for that matter. She just listened. Opening up about our problems brought us closer—perhaps to the exclusion of everyone else.

As our sixth-grade year came to a close, that girl from Spain threw a big going-away party at her parents' mansion. The house was decorated like something out of a fairy tale. That girl changed into three different, beautiful outfits and made dramatic entrances in each of them at various points during the evening. Everyone had such fun!

I didn't witness any of this with my own eyes, though. I had to hear about it all from the other girls. Tiffani and I were the only two girls in the entire class who weren't invited.

When the last day of school finally came, I was just glad the year was over.

CHAPTER 4

Strangers No More

There was no summer vacation for me that year. Instead, my parents enrolled me in an intensive English program, spending more money they didn't have in an attempt to have me speaking English like any other American by the time I went back to school. So off I went from 9:00 a.m. to 3:00 p.m. every day, all summer long—not with other kids my age but with adults. There were eight levels in that English program, and thanks to all the tutoring I'd had, I tested into level five. I was glad I tested so high, because I didn't want my parents to spend more money. I hated seeing them struggle so much.

My dad drove me to the class and always made my lunch—cucumber salad with lime and salt, and two hard-boiled eggs. I would sit with all of the adults at lunchtime and eat my boiled eggs with salt on them. The mean girls at school didn't intimidate me, and a classroom full of adults didn't intimidate me, either. Actually, the adults seemed far shyer than I ever was. Whenever the teacher asked a question, I raised my hand, and those students all treated me like I was the mascot of the class. They looked out for me, and watched over me at the end of the day while I waited for my dad to pick me up.

I shared with my parents everything I learned that summer.

We'd practice the new words I learned every day. I wish my parents had been able to take those classes with me. It would have made life easier for them. But there wasn't enough money, or enough time, so everything they had they invested in me. They would have gone hungry if that meant their children were fed.

By the time I started seventh grade, I was pretty close to fluent. I even started dreaming in English, which was a total trip the first time it happened. Armed with my new language skills, my grades improved almost immediately—and I decided to take a new approach to making friends.

My natural inclination in seventh grade would have been to join the drama club. But the cool kids didn't do drama. They played sports. They were cheerleaders. So that was the path I chose. I suppose this was my first attempt at assimilation. I wanted to be cool and liked, and I thought that was what I needed to do to accomplish that lofty goal. As it turned out, I still didn't fit in and still didn't have friends, and wouldn't have any real friends other than Tiffani for the rest of my middle school years.

Looking back on it, it strikes me that I didn't spend my days thinking about whether I wanted to stay in America my whole life, or whether I wanted to move back to Mexico. I didn't really think much about that at all. I was a kid. All I thought about was how I couldn't wait to go to high school, how I couldn't wait to grow up, how I couldn't wait to fly back to Taxco to celebrate my quinceañera so I could finally be on my way to adulthood and all of the freedom I imagined that would bring.

All the while, my parents kept pumping me up on the American dream. "You can do anything you want here. You can *be* whatever you want!" they said, over and over, to the point where I had no choice but to believe it. Despite the setback of the silver theft, they had already proven to themselves that it was possible to come from nothing, work really hard, and make something better for yourself and your family in America. To my parents, everything was better in America. They would go on and on about the stores here, the things you could buy, the food. My mom raved about how much better *bacon* was in America.

They still saw America through rose-colored glasses—the America I'd seen when I came to visit: the shiny, sparkling dazzle of Sea World and Six Flags, in a land full of Happy Meals and Chicken McNuggets. Even as an eleven-year-old girl, I began to have doubts about this American dream, and whether it was really made for me. My daily life had been far better back home in Taxco, in lots of different ways. But their enthusiasm, even in the face of adversity, was contagious.

The fact that I was getting a good education gave me even more of a leg up in the world than they had, they insisted. So I had every reason to believe that if I kept going, if I kept doing the right thing by learning and getting good grades, I'd be on my way to whatever success I wanted for myself.

My parents never really talked to me about race or racism. I don't know if they never experienced it, or if they were naive about it or unaware of it, or maybe they thought I wouldn't face those barriers because I was growing up in America. I just don't know. As a result, being a young Mexican, a young Latina, wasn't something I thought about then, either. I was just a girl, about to be a teenager, who was starting to fall in love with sports, who was starting to get even more boy crazy than I had been for Enrique, and who wanted to fit in—not because my race or my immigration status made me feel like an outsider, but because I was like any other girl that age.

I didn't let go of my Mexican roots while I went to school and lived my American life. I jammed to Maná and José Alfredo

Jiménez , two of the most influential musicians in Mexican history. I loved Chespirito, one of the most important Spanish-language comedians. The Mexican revolutionary Pancho Villa was my childhood hero. I was happy I could still watch TV in Spanish and that there was plenty of Mexican food I could eat in San Antonio—although a lot of it was of a strange variation called Tex-Mex. I had never eaten let alone seen this huge thing called a burrito before I came to America. That was never a part of traditional Mexican cuisine at all. And hard-shell tacos? I didn't even understand the point of those. Still, I didn't think of myself as different from anyone else.

I learned about slavery and the civil rights movement in middle school, and it made a deep emotional impression on me. I'd share everything I learned with my dad on our rides home after school, and with my mom when she'd come home from her trade shows. "I can't believe they treated black people so badly," I would say with tears in my eyes. "I can't believe you brought me to a country that *owned* people!"

I assumed that racism was a dynamic exclusively between black and white people. I hadn't read anything about Mexicans or Latinos being a part of the civil rights movement, so I wrongly assumed that we weren't a part of it at all—and that racism wasn't something I needed to worry about.

In fact, since I wasn't black, I figured *that must mean I am white.*

As I finally began to settle into my new life I was, for the most part, blissfully unaware.

That all changed the moment I tested into an honors-level math class.

Throughout my sixth-grade year, math was the only class where I didn't feel stupid. Two plus two is four in any language, and most of the things they were teaching in sixth grade I'd learned way back in fourth grade in Mexico. So when the teacher announced the names of the students who would be placed in the honors math class, I was so happy to hear my name.

A boy named Justin was not.

"Why is *she* in the honors class?" he said. "She's *a Mexican*! She doesn't even speak English!"

The whole class laughed.

In a flash I realized that "a Mexican" was something less than desirable in his brown eyes. Everything in his voice and his expression told me I was an *other*. And it hurt. I have no idea how I kept myself from crying.

I wasn't just like everyone else. I wasn't white. I wasn't black. I was *a Mexican*.

Was *that* the reason I didn't fit in? Was *that* the reason I had such a hard time making friends? I might not have read about any other Mexicans in the U.S. history books, but I knew instantly that this boy saw me the same way so many people saw and treated black people in those books.

They were American. *They* were white. And I was not one of *them*.

That day I rode in the car with my dad and I cried, yet again—only this time it wasn't about something from a book: "I want to go back to Mexico where I can be Mexican along with everyone else!"

"Don't pay attention to that," my dad said. "It will all be all right. Don't pay attention to any of that." But once my eyes were opened, I could never close them again.

—————

My mother began taking me along to more and more of her trade shows as the year went on. I loved seeing her in her element.

Everywhere she went she was very outgoing, full of energy, and happy. And she never, ever gave up. Over and over again I watched my mother persevere and figure things out when others would have quit.

She and my dad had a friend who worked as their assistant, a balding man with glasses that made his eyes look really big. Sam had worked with them since the mid-1980s, and he had become a close family friend. He was around a lot, and I remember his frustration packing the van one time. There were boxes and boxes left that wouldn't fit. "There's no more room!" he complained. My mother wouldn't hear it. She went to the van, rearranged those heavy boxes all by herself, and got every single box to fit. Just like that. And that was how she approached everything.

She seemed to be able to talk her way into or out of things, whether getting to the front of a long line with her children, or getting a discount on almost every purchase she made. Sometimes her assertiveness would embarrass me. I wished that occasionally when somebody said no, she would just say, "Okay," and move on. But most of the time when we heard no, I shook my head and instantly knew: *Here we go.*

She would do quirky things, too. If we stopped at a coffee shop or a diner, she would almost always take a bunch of Equal packets off the table and put them in her purse. "Mom, please!" I would say, worried that we might get in trouble. There were times when she grabbed a whole bunch of napkins, because we needed napkins at home. All I could do was hide my eyes, silently saying, "Oh, my God. Mom!"

Sam had served as her translator and assistant at those trade shows for a very long time, but I think my mom enjoyed having me there to serve as her assistant and translator now, and I definitely enjoyed being with her. Traveling with her was the only time

I really got to see her. I asked her why she couldn't send Dad to do more of the trade shows, and she told me that she enjoyed being out there selling. I could also see that she was a much better sales-person, because she had so much more of an outgoing personality than my dad. So it made sense.

At times it felt as if my mother enjoyed her trade shows more than she enjoyed being at home with her children. I noticed that a lot of my friends were learning from their moms how to cook and apply makeup—all sorts of girl things I never learned from her.

The first time I got my period my mom was out of town, and it was my dad who had to buy me pads. From that moment on until I was living on my own, I would never go into the store to buy pads. I would just let my dad do it and wait for him in the car, avoiding having to face a clerk with what I viewed as an embarrassing pur-chase.

I shouldn't say I learned *nothing* girly from my mom. I have al-ways considered her stunningly beautiful, and I wanted to know how to look like her. So I paid attention. I noticed the way she took care of herself, and ate well, and dressed well. She washed her face every single night, no matter how tired she was, which is something I do to this day. She told me how she ate nothing but special Mexican chicken soup for forty days after each of her children were born, and she swore that was why her body bounced back. One look at her and who could argue?

She also said to me, "A girl without earrings is like a night with-out stars." And I believed her. I pierced my ears, even though I didn't want to at first. If I ever forget to wear earrings, even now, I feel like a night without stars.

Neither of my parents had that many friends, which made Sam's presence all the more significant in our lives. He was one of the few adults whom I would interact with outside of school on a regular basis. There were times when my parents were out running errands, and Sam would babysit my brother and me at his apartment. He was a trusted family friend, and to Julio and me, he was almost like an uncle in this place where we had no other family.

But he was nothing like my real uncle. I haven't mentioned him yet, but my mother's brother, my uncle Mike, was one of my favorite people in the world. He was the first in our family to go to college and easily the most sophisticated member of my family. He wore shirts with cufflinks. He took me with him to *charreadas*, the traditional Mexican parties with horse shows, mariachis, and the most amazing food. He read me books, and when no one else was there he would show up at my art shows. I thought I would see him at Christmastime, but we never did go home for Christmas. It was just too expensive. Another promise broken. I was thrilled that I got to see him the first time we got back to Taxco the following summer, though. I was happy to see everyone, and I swear just breathing in the air and feeling the sunshine at Mama Silvia's that year felt like the best present ever.

My uncle Mike was one of those uncles who liked to slip his nieces and nephews a little money when they visited, and during that first visit he gave me five hundred pesos to spend on myself. In the old days I would have run down the cobblestone street and bought myself some candy with that money, but after seeing my mother in action in the United States, I decided I wanted to invest those pesos rather than spend them. I wanted to turn my money into more money. So I decided to look for something I could sell at the trade shows. I sifted through the bins at Metales Aviles with the eyes of a saleswoman and found a collection of Mickey Mouse pendants. *Perfect*, I thought. I bought up all of the little pendants I could and then asked my mom if I could sell them the next time we went to a trade show together. She loved the idea, and so I set up a little corner on the table to sell my pendants. They were a big hit.

I forget how much money I made, but I do remember that my mom asked me if she could borrow that money at the end of that first day. I said yes, and I was really upset that she never paid me back. I told myself that I shouldn't feel bad, since she was my mom and she paid for everything. But it was *my* money—money that I invested rather than wasted.

I also came up with a bigger version of my breakfast-for-truck-drivers idea that had worked so well in Taxco. I noticed that the vendors at the trade shows didn't have any good options for lunch. All of those people were stuck inside all day selling jewelry, clothes, and gift items, and the only food they could find was the crappy, overpriced food at the convention centers. So my dad and I started selling Chinese food to the vendors. Whenever my mother did a trade show within driving distance, we would buy big helpings of chicken broccoli, lo mein, spicy beef, and more from the hot-food section at HEB, a big grocery store chain in Texas, and then I would go around taking orders from all of the booths. They were willing to pay $8 for every $4 worth of food I bought, which was good business. I wound up handing over all of that money to my parents, too, but at least it was fun. We made a profit, and the vendors were all thrilled to get some fresh food at lunchtime.

If life could have been all about the work, traveling with my mom, buying and selling, I think it would have been a whole lot easier. Because life at home was so confusing.

My dad paid such wonderful attention to me. In fact, he started teaching me how to drive when I was still in middle school. We had this Oldsmobile Bravada, and he let me drive it around the apartment complex.

"Never, ever, ever use your left foot because you can get confused on what pedal to use," he would tell me. "And keep both hands on the wheel!"

He was very patient when he was teaching me things, and I loved the fact that he wanted me to know everything a father would teach a son. "If you're gonna drive, you need to learn how to change a tire, and you need to learn how to change the oil, and you need to know what questions to ask a mechanic."

He took the time to teach me all of those things.

He was the one who took me to school, waking up at five so I could get to cheerleading practice by six. He was the one to pick me up after practice. He was the one who showed me how to cook. I wished he could have been like that always.

Instead, as I wrote in my journal at the time, "My dad hits me every day. Every day I feel like I'm walking on eggshells, not knowing what's going to set him off."

My mother hated it. In the beginning, I would run to her or tell her on the phone every time he hit me, and my parents would get in big fights about it. "Stop hitting her," my mother would order him, and my dad would answer in a shamed voice, "Yeah, I know." But nothing changed.

There was one time when I made eggs, and I burned them, and my dad was so mad he made me eat them.

"But they're burned!" I cried.

"Then you should have been paying more attention!" he yelled, forcing me to swallow the charred, blackened, disgusting mess I'd made.

Another time I was making eggs and the oil splashed on my forearm. Bubbles formed on my skin, but I didn't want to tell my dad because I thought he would get mad and hit me. So I hid the burn. It was one of those hot Texas summer days, yet I put on a long-sleeved shirt just to hide it from him.

Later that day, my little brother and I were playing outside at the apartment complex while my dad was grilling dinner.

"Why are you wearing that shirt? Aren't you hot?" my dad asked me.

"No, no, no. I'm okay," I said.

Then he touched my arm, and saw me wince.

"What's the matter?" he asked, and I showed him.

"Oh, my God. Why didn't you tell me?" he said, so concerned.

I started crying, "I thought you'd be mad at me."

"I'm so sorry," my father said. "Of course I'm not mad."

He cleaned my arm and put Neosporin on the burn and took care of my wound and was really nice about it. When I got up to wash the dishes after our barbecue, he told me to stay put. "I'll take care of the dishes tonight," he said.

There were many times when he was a great dad. He was always there to fix anything that needed fixing. He told us jokes. He danced around all goofy in his odd-looking uniform of short-sleeved shirts, short pants with long dress socks, and loafers, just to make us laugh.

He was really, really fun—until he wasn't.

For all of her ability to get things done and fix any situation, my mother never could get him to stop hitting me. Instead, she would come home from every trip with a big smile on her face and armfuls of presents for Julio and me. I know she thought she was meeting her responsibilities as a parent by providing food and shelter. I know she thought she was going above and beyond by buying us nice things. I know she believed in her heart that she was doing the best thing by working so hard to provide us with the opportunity to have a better future. But she didn't seem to understand it wasn't her presents that I needed. What I needed was her.

CHAPTER 5

You're an Illegal Now

My dad's childhood dream was to own his own mechanic shop, and I promised him over and over again that when I was grown up and rich, I would buy one for him. In the meantime, whenever my mom was out of town and had taken Julio with her, my dad and I spent time at his friend's shop.

It was there that my dad taught me to listen to the sound of an engine, to discern whether there was a pressure leak, a problem with the oil pump, or something else I should know about cars. I would help with the oil change on his truck, a 1988 Ford that had taken us from Mexico to San Antonio many times. Just as I loved seeing my mom in action at the trade shows, I also loved watching my dad in action at that shop. He was in his element. That shop was his happy place.

We would listen to old José Alfredo Jiménez cassette tapes whenever we drove somewhere in my dad's truck, and he and I bonded over all of those great *ranchera* songs that were such a part of our heritage. Those were good days, mostly.

After we finished the oil change one afternoon, I climbed into the truck out in the parking lot to do my homework and listen to the radio while my dad played cards and drank beer with his buddies inside. We'd done that before. He'd have a couple of beers, and then we'd swing by the 7-Eleven near our house, buy a six-pack of beer for him and an Icee for me, and then go home to watch *Sábado Gigante*, a popular variety show on Univision.

That day was different, though. He took too long to come back.

I walked into the shop and found him asleep on a chair. I had never seen him that drunk. There were new faces in the shop I had never seen before, and I didn't like the way they were looking at me.

"Papi, it's dark outside. I'm hungry," I said, shaking him awake and guiding him outside to the truck.

When my dad came to, he demanded to know why he was in the passenger seat.

"You drank too much, Daddy," I told him.

"I'm sorry," he said. "Aren't you hungry? It's dark out. Let's get you a pizza."

He reached into his pocket for the keys, and I reminded him that the truck was already running. "Smart," he said. "Running the radio for that long would have drained the battery if the engine wasn't on."

I smiled. He was too drunk to drive, but those new faces were making me increasingly nervous. I wanted to go home. I sat in the driver's seat for a while and finally made up my mind it would be best if I drove us home.

I was thirteen.

We've done plenty of laps around our apartment complex, I reasoned. *Surely I can drive us a couple of miles.* I leaned over and put his seat belt on. I adjusted the mirrors. I backed up just fine. I pulled out onto the road just fine. But the more I drove, the more scared I got.

My heart was pounding as we reached the first traffic light. It was red. I stopped and watched as a million cars zoomed by on the crossroad in front of me. I was trying hard to prepare myself to drive across the first major intersection I'd ever encountered from a driver's seat. That was when my dad opened his eyes and realized what was happening. I thought he would be furious, but he just told me to stay calm and started mumbling instructions as if it were any other driving lesson.

"Your left foot better be doing nothing," he muttered.

"It's not, Dad."

"That's my girl," he said, as he smiled and closed his eyes again.

The light turned green, and I pressed on the gas, and we made it across. Eventually, we made it home. I helped him to his chair in the living room and he handed me a wad of bills. "I won," he said. "Order some pizza."

It's difficult to reconcile those moments with the dad who was so overprotective of me that if he saw me so much as standing next to a boy, he would ask, "Why were you talking to that boy?" I mean, I still fold towels the way he showed me to do it. I pay my bills on time because he paid our bills on time. But whenever I started to let my guard down and to love my dad without caution, his disease would interfere.

The drinking got to be so much that my mother would occasionally lie to my father and say she was taking me with her on her business trips just so she could get me out of the house. I couldn't miss that much school, of course, so on those occasions I would spend a few days at Tiffani's house. Her family was wonderful to me. They would take me to school, and they welcomed me at their dinner table as if I were Tiffani's sister. I felt like a regular American teenage girl when I was with Tiffani's family, and between my father's drunken outbursts and the constant needs of my little brother at home, if it weren't for those escapes I might have gone mad. They even took me to our middle school football games on Friday nights, where I could cheer for our team; eventually I even joined the pom squad. I could also talk to all the boys I wanted without anyone questioning me about it.

It was during those Friday nights that I fell in love with football. I loved learning about the plays and the formations and the intricacies of the game—not just the cute boys. I was fluent in football before I was fluent in English. Friday nights were the only time in middle school when I felt like I belonged.

As I started high school, at a different but still small, private, college-prep Catholic school, I missed the freedom of my life in Taxco more than ever. I missed my sisters. I missed my aunts and uncles. I missed my grandmother. My mom was still traveling so much for her work at that point that I missed her, too.

I had no idea what my future would hold, so one of the few thoughts that cheered me up, and just about the only thing I looked forward to after three years in the United States, was something I hoped wouldn't happen on American soil at all. I pictured my older sister, Aris, in her pink embroidered dress, and I smiled just thinking about it—knowing that it would soon be *my* turn.

I knew that money was still as tight as ever, so I was afraid to bring it up, but one day shortly after my fourteenth birthday, I simply could not hold it in anymore: "Mom, we have to start planning soon," I said with a big smile.

I could tell my mother knew exactly what I was talking about.

I had dreamed about my quinceañera since I was three years old, as many Mexican girls do—envisioning a once-in-a-lifetime birthday celebration that would symbolize leaving childhood behind in order to become a young woman. I didn't just have to imagine what my quinceañera would look like, either. Pictures and memories from both of my sisters' quinceañeras served as constant reminders of how beautiful my big day would be.

Nay's party, which had happened five years earlier, wasn't so memorable to me. Nay wasn't all that interested a participant, and the festivities weren't as spectacular. The quinceañera I remembered, the one that was embedded in my heart, happened when I was only five years old.

Aris looked so beautiful. She's petite and was shaped just like a Barbie doll come to life. In fact, my mother went to great lengths to find a Barbie doll with black hair to put atop her cake on that magical day. It was the late 1980s, and Barbies of various ethnicities were not the norm. I kept that Barbie for years afterward, as if it had been mine all along. She even came with me to America.

I looked up to my sisters so much. Aris was a full ten years older than me, and seeing her celebrated like royalty on her fifteenth birthday made *me* feel like I was the one who was a princess.

The thing about money in a small city in Mexico is that if you had it, or people *thought* you had it, you had to show it. At least that was how it was back then. Nowadays, having money or people thinking you have money can be dangerous. My parents, who were doing quite well at that time, hosted Aris's quinceañera at Hotel de la Borda, a hacienda-style hotel with a beautiful swimming pool surrounded by a courtyard adorned in strung-up lights that seemed to twinkle like stars. The hotel was built in the 1950s, in the finest location in the city, with sweeping views of the seven hills that surrounded my little corner of the world. It was well-known that a former American president, John F. Kennedy, and his bride, Jackie, had spent one night of their honeymoon in a suite at that very hotel.

My mother wore a dress that was custom-made for her. Nay and I wore custom-made matching dresses as well. My parents had roses trucked in from some faraway city—more roses than I'd ever *imagined* let alone seen with my own eyes. There were even doves at this party.

The planning that went into that day was not unlike the planning one might expect for a huge wedding. The location, the dresses, the search for just the right Barbie to go atop the cake, all of it stretched back to when Aris turned fourteen and had spanned that entire year. I actually think my mom had been planning that party since the moment Aris was born.

The night of the festivities felt like *my* night. I popped my smiling face into just about every photo, my early version of a photobomb, and pretended that I was becoming a young woman myself. I danced with all of Aris's *chambelanes*, the specially chosen young male escorts with whom she shared a series of choreographed dances—dances that had taken her most of that year to master. I'll never forget the sight of her practicing and practicing, filled with anticipation. Yet I danced even more than she did on her big night, probably because I wasn't wearing a corset or heels.

Aris's hair was so big and beautiful. She looked straight out of one of the fashion magazines we would see at the newsstand. Her dress was soft pink and embroidered by hand. It showed off her shoulders and it was floor-length with a big, full skirt. I watched her twirl and curtsy with that smile on her lips, and I dreamed of the day when it would be my turn, when it would be my party, when *I* would be the one in the beautiful pink dress. And now that time was less than a year away!

"We have time, we have time. We'll talk about it later," my mother said.

I was all too familiar with my parents' finances, and I was sure that their stretched budget was the reason she didn't want to talk about it. I remember thinking, *Isn't America supposed to be the land of opportunity? Why is money still such a problem now? I've watched them work so hard for the last three years laboring to unbury themselves from the debt of the stolen silver.*

I tried not to let it bother me. I was sure my mom would figure something out. She always figured things out. She had promised me a party like Aris's, and she always kept her promises. Well, except for that one time when she didn't show up at my school for la escolta. But that was a long time ago.

I didn't push back when my mother put me off. I trusted we would start planning soon enough. I also got the bright idea that I would use the time in between to help put some of their financial worries at ease. Without either of my parents knowing, I got on the phone to discuss it with some of my relatives in Mexico. I imagined how pleased my parents would be when they found out I'd figured a way to help save them some money to pay for my party.

The weeks went by and my mother never brought it up. So the moment she walked in the door after one of her sales trips, I started talking.

"So, I've been thinking, I really want to have my quinceañera in Mexico, since that's where all our family is. Maybe even at Hotel de la Borda, like Aris, since it's so beautiful there. And—"

"I am tired; not right now, okay?" she said. "You know we don't have that kind of money anymore."

"I know, but I was thinking that Uncle Mike and Mama Silvia could help."

"Your grandmother and uncle already do enough by helping with your sisters," she said.

"I already called them and they said they would help!" I replied.

"Ay, *mija*," my dad sighed.

My mother closed her eyes and pressed the palms of her hands against them. She looked so sad that I regretted saying anything at all.

"I promise we can do this without spending a lot of money," I said.

"Your mother said she doesn't want to talk about this right now," my father said.

"I'm willing to help," I pleaded. "And I know the whole family will help. I just know it. My dress doesn't have to be—"

"You cannot go to Mexico," my mother said as she pulled her hands away from her eyes and looked right into my own.

"What do you mean?"

"If you go to Mexico, you won't be able to come back."

I couldn't understand what she was saying or why she looked so sad.

"Look, I didn't want to get into this, but your visa is expired. You can't go back to Mexico, and you cannot have a quinceañera."

"What?!" I screamed. I could not believe my ears. "What do you mean?"

"I am sorry, but there is nothing we can do. You cannot have a quinceañera. I am so sorry."

It felt like she'd cracked my chest open and ripped out my insides.

"I hate you!" I screamed. "I hate it here!"

"Julissa, sit down!" my father yelled.

I stormed into my bedroom, yelling, "Why did you ever bring me here! I want to die!" I slammed the door and cried like I'd never cried in my life. I'd been looking forward to my quinceañera for as long as I could remember. And now they'd taken that away from me, too.

I didn't understand the true ramifications of my mother's words. All I'd heard was that I couldn't have my party, and I knew this wasn't a party that I could throw myself when I was all grown up and rich. It wasn't a moment I could re-create. It would be gone forever. I was simply too young or maybe too naive to understand that on that night my mother had shared a secret that would define and haunt me for years to come.

The next day at school, I told Tiffani. She knew just how devastating that news was, because I'd been talking her ears off forever about the details of my magical evening. She didn't even need to say anything. I could see how much she cared. In many ways, she'd very quickly become almost like a sister.

"How can I not have a quinceañera? How can they be this mean to me? I hate my parents right now."

"I'm so sorry," Tiffani said.

"I wish I could come live with you. Your parents are so nice."

We both laughed, but that night as I lay in bed, after coming home to find my parents had nothing more to say about the matter, a whole series of new questions and thoughts entered my consciousness: Why could I never go to Mexico again? And if I did, was it true that I could never come back to America? My mother couldn't have meant it that way. It didn't make any sense. My family was in Mexico, but my parents were here. My life was in both places. There had to be some way around it. Why couldn't we go back to Mexico and renew my visa? The answer to that question was simple: I had already violated my tourist visa, and there was a high chance it would not be renewed, especially since my parents' financial situation had changed so dramatically. What if I really could go live with Tiffani? What if Tiffani's parents could adopt me? I figured that would make me an official American. Certainly that would that take care of my visa problem. Just as I saw finding money for my quinceañera as a problem I could fix, I started to think about my expired visa as a problem I could fix, too.

I decided to speak to Tiffani's parents the next time I saw them—to ask if they might adopt me.

Tiffani's parents would have adopted me if my parents had agreed. That was how kind they were. That was how much they cared about me. They listened to my pleas and said that if my parents would agree to talk to them about it, maybe something could be done. My parents listened to me present the idea, but they were too proud to have their daughter adopted, even if it was just for papers. They didn't have any other solutions for my visa situation. They didn't explain anything more about it, and I don't think they fully realized what it would mean for my future. And yet, I started to figure it out pretty quickly.

I had heard people talk about "illegal" immigrants. We lived in Texas. It was a pervasive topic. I often heard people refer to them dismissively with just one word: *illegals*. I was smart enough to know that now as a fourteen-year-old high school freshman I was one of them. I was no longer just "a Mexican," which seemed to be bad enough in certain people's eyes. I was an "illegal," or worse, an "illegal alien"—like some thing from another planet that wasn't even human. I couldn't reconcile what I saw on the news with what I saw in the mirror. The news reported on the illegals the way they would report on a murder or a grand theft. And yet I was merely a fourteen-year-old girl worried about not having a pretty pink dress.

When I thought about criminals, I didn't picture somebody like me. I pictured people who robbed, or stole, or killed. Yet people seemed to throw that word *illegal* around with the same disdain in their voice they would use to describe a thief. *Is that how people would treat me if they knew?* I'd moved seamlessly from middle school to high school just like any other student. I didn't think anyone suspected anything. I didn't *feel* illegal. Having an expired visa didn't make me feel less human. It certainly didn't make me feel like a criminal. I had a transcript full of good grades, my ac-

cent wasn't apparent anymore, so no one questioned anything—
and it very quickly became clear to me that that's the way it had to
stay.

"You just keep quiet about it," my mother told me. "If anyone
finds out, you could be deported."

Making sure I never said anything about my visa or my status
became front and center in every conversation I had from that moment forward. I didn't want to be deported. I didn't want to be
separated from my parents. As rough as things were sometimes,
they were my parents and I loved them. I didn't want to be separated from my little brother, either. America was my home now.

Then, before anyone else had the chance to turn my immigration status against me, my own parents started using my
immigration status as a threat: "Don't you go breaking any
laws, Julissa. You'll get deported." "Don't you even think about
drinking alcohol or doing drugs. You get caught and you'll get
deported, for sure!"

When I was little, they use to threaten me with La Llorona,
the Mexican female version of the boogeyman. As I got older I
realized the Llorona wasn't real, but the *Migra*, the INS or ICE,
wasn't something mythical made to scare children. The Migra was
real, and scarier than anything I had ever heard of.

The rites of passage of American adolescent rebellion suddenly
felt like a privilege I wouldn't be afforded. I couldn't believe it. I
was finally in high school, and suddenly I felt like I had less freedom than ever.

I still wasn't making new friends at school. I thought starting
high school at a different Catholic school—a high school that was
co-ed—would be so much better. But it wasn't. And with all of
this new pressure and disappointment, I could feel myself becoming ever more distant from my classmates.

I simply couldn't fathom the idea that I was somehow illegal. What had I done? Especially when I knew of people who had very clearly broken a just law yet faced no punishment whatsoever.

I forget what city it was in, but my mom took me along to one of her trade shows that was far enough away that we had to fly. This was back in the day when the airlines weren't so strict with the carry-on luggage, so whenever my mother made one of these trips, she and her assistant, Sam, would bring four carry-ons between them filled with all her silver. Sam didn't go on this particular trip, which was why my mother brought me in his place. He did help us pack, though, and took care of our itineraries. This was a big show, and we brought a lot more silver than usual, which meant we had to check one large bag full of jewelry.

The trip went well, but once we were back in San Antonio, by the time we deplaned and made it to the luggage area, everyone's luggage from under the plane was already going around on the conveyor belt. We waited and waited as everyone else grabbed their bags and left, but our bag—that large bag full of thousands of dollars' worth of silver—never showed up.

My mother was in a panic.

I quickly put two and two together.

"Mom, do you think it's just by coincidence that your bag full of silver disappeared?" I said. "Someone had to know what to look for to pick up that bag."

We checked with the airline, and they were positive the bag came off the plane. It wasn't lost. It wasn't diverted to another airport by mistake.

"Mom, the only person who knew when we were coming in besides Dad was Sam," I said.

My mother stared at me in complete disbelief. "No. He would never do that," she insisted.

"Mom," I said. "No one else knew. This wasn't a mistake. Someone didn't just take the bag by accident."

I finally convinced her to do something about it. We called the cops. We filed a report. Eventually, they went to Sam's apartment to investigate—and they found a whole bunch of my mother's jewelry.

Sam turned over what was left, but many pieces were gone. He had sold them off cheap, and he couldn't repay her for them. Yet my mom refused to press charges. He was a friend, she said. "A *trusted* friend." She insisted she couldn't do that to him. Sam was gay, and my mother told me later that she was terrified to think what might be done to him in prison. I thought it was the least he deserved.

Slowly, it dawned on both my parents that Sam may have been stealing from them all along. He knew their travel routines. He knew everything about them. It was extremely likely that he, or someone he worked with or hired or collaborated with, was the one who broke into the van when they stopped at the diner. It wasn't random. It wasn't like someone threw a brick through the window and grabbed a few pieces and ran. They cut that window out precisely and made off with every single box. It *had* to have been premeditated. It *had* to have been Sam's doing. I started to wonder how much inventory had disappeared in smaller amounts over the years. Who knew what deals he had been cutting for himself or what money he'd been making on the side since he'd begun working as my parents' translator?

I was furious that my mother just let him get away with it.

Uncle Mike flew up to help my parents sort through it all, and he agreed with me: "You should press charges!" he told her. But my mama said, "No." And that was that. I was so frustrated with her, but at the same time I was so taken by her compassion and her ability to forgive.

Sometimes when I look at old pictures and see Sam with my family, I want to tear those pictures apart. Did he ever think about what he had done to them? To me? To all of us? Did he consider for one second the hardship he put them through? Did he know how much stress he caused them?

Sam deserved to go to jail, and it stung more every time my father's stress bubbled up through the alcohol in a new fit of rage. I swore to myself I wasn't going to take it anymore. I started threatening to call 911 when my dad would get out of control. But I used 911 in the same way they used La Llorona. I didn't think I would actually ever do it. He was my father and I loved him unconditionally despite his disease. It was just an empty threat. But for a while at least, that threat made him back off.

Instead, he started to turn his anger elsewhere.

CHAPTER 6

Decisions, Decisions

Change came in fast and furious my first two years of high school. I bugged my parents all the time about wanting to move to a house with a yard, in another part of town—far from Sam—and they finally relented, moving us into a three-bedroom rental in a decent neighborhood. Julio now had room to play in the backyard, and I had a first-floor window that I could climb in and out of when I wanted to escape.

My sister Aris had gotten married by then, and she and her husband moved from Mexico and in with us. They took one bedroom, my parents had another, and I shared a room with bunk beds with Julio. My brother and I actually got along really well as he got older. I watched out for him, like any big sister might, and I would soon come to see that he watched out for me, too.

Aris's moving in didn't change the dynamic in the house that much. She and her husband had their own lives to lead. In fact, the thing I remember most about 1999 is that it was the year the San Antonio Spurs won our first championship. Yes, *ours*.

One thing I truly loved about San Antonio was how the whole city rallied behind the Spurs. It made it easy to fall in love with the team. My love of football expanded beyond Friday night games as I came to worship the Texas Longhorns. Sports were my way into

America. Sports bring people together in a way that nothing else can. Even music. Music brings people together, too, but music can sometimes be segregating in itself. If I liked rap too much, I was trying too hard to be black; if I liked country, I was trying to be white; and if I liked Spanish music, I was too Mexican. There is sometimes a cultural divide when it comes to music. Sports, on the other hand, bring all people together, from every socioeconomic or ethnic background.

My ability to talk about the Spurs with my classmates in high school along with Friday night football games gave me a sense of being a real American and of fitting in with my peers. I couldn't talk about many pop culture references. I never watched TV shows like *Full House* or saw the movies that my classmates grew up watching. I wasn't allowed to watch MTV. But I could talk about Avery Johnson, Sean Elliot, Timmy, and "the Admiral," David Robinson. I knew which teams we were playing and who talked trash about whom.

As my parents' financial situation improved a little bit, I was even able to go to a few Spurs games and sit in a stadium full of thousands of people and feel like part of a community. The fact that the Spurs would bring home our first championship in the first year I was able to attend games only solidified my undying love for them.

After Sam's theft at the airport, my mother stopped selling jewelry wholesale. She couldn't get another meaningful loan to buy more inventory. Instead she began attending fairs and festivals, where she sold retail. That led to her selling tacos at the fairs to make up for the lost revenue from the trade shows. My mom didn't care if she was a walking stereotype—a Mexican woman selling tacos—we were making money and that was what mattered. It was manual labor, and I knew my family in Mexico were all talking about it like it was a bad thing: "Luisa is now selling *tacos*." As if it was some kind of failure. My mom didn't care; she was providing for her family. Nothing was ever beneath my parents. That's one of the many things I especially love about them. They were hard workers. They would have scrubbed toilets if that was what they needed to do to provide for us.

A lot of people get it wrong when they look down on immigrants for scrubbing toilets and doing work "no one else will do." My parents' priority was to provide for us, to put us on a path for success. As long as they were earning an honest living, they didn't care what the job entailed. That's how it is in Hispanic families: we'll do whatever we need to do to take care of our own.

Seeing the profits that could be made in a day of selling food, my parents decided to invest in a funnel cake stand. My mom had seen how much funnel cakes sold during our trips to Six Flags and decided to add them to the menu of food items she would sell. I've always been so impressed by my mother's ability to figure things out. Those were the days before Google, so she must have had to search the Yellow Pages and then drive around to track down the wholesalers for the dough, the Fryolator, and all the equipment needed to make funnel cakes. We didn't have enough money to buy a real food truck, the kind that is so popular and trendy these days, so we bought only a Fryolator, and we would load it into the back of my dad's pickup truck for every festival. Later, my mom would also invest in a roasted corn machine. Dough and corn were inexpensive inventory to purchase, which meant every item sold was at a high profit margin, but we had to sell a lot to make any real money. That meant long hours, greasy-smelling clothes, and occasional burns from the oil in the Fryolator. None of that stopped my parents.

The fairs and festivals could be hit or miss, so my parents started looking for more regular locations. It didn't take long for them to establish a couple of regular spots in San Antonio. The first was in a public square where the city held an open-air market every weekend. The second was just outside of the PX on the grounds of Fort Sam Houston military base, where they set up on weekdays. That meant my mother didn't have to be on the road as much, and that made me happy.

Things improved for my parents once they started that funnel cake stand. They weren't rolling in money or building a six-story house like they were back in the 1980s, but we all felt like we could breathe a little. My dad had always dreamed of owning a Cadillac, and after our Oldsmobile was totaled in an accident, he used the insurance money to buy a big, old, ugly white Cadillac to call his own. I was happy for him, even if I was embarrassed to be seen riding in his new prized possession.

There was one time during that 1999 championship season when my parents splurged and let me take Julio to a Spurs game. I actually stole a little money from the funnel cake stand's cash register before the game so I could buy us better seats. I know it was totally wrong to do that, but after my dad dropped us off, Julio and I wound up sitting three rows up from the bench. *Worth it!* I thought.

At one point, Julio got so into the excitement of the game that he took off his favorite David Robinson jersey and started swinging it over his head. Somehow in the midst of the crowd, his jersey got lost. In a normal seven-year-old reaction, he started crying at the top of his lungs. When the game was over we stayed as everyone filtered out, looking everywhere for that jersey. Finally an usher saw Julio crying and asked what was wrong. When I told him he said, "Come with me." He wound up giving us a brand-new shirt, and then took us down by the locker room. We had to wait almost an hour for the players to shower and come out, and the whole time I was thinking, *Dad is gonna kill me. He's probably sitting out there worried about us. I'll never go to another Spurs game again.* But then we got to meet David Robinson, Sean Elliot, and Tim Duncan. David Robinson even signed my little brother's shirt.

Okay, I thought. *I think God forgives me for stealing that money.*

I wish smartphones had existed back then so I could have taken a selfie!

When we finally got outside to my dad's car, he was fuming.

"I'm so sorry, but look!" I said, showing him my brother's newly signed T-shirt. Then my dad became just as excited as Julio and me; everyone in San Antonio loves the Spurs.

I hung on to moments like that—those fleeting moments of pure shared joy. I had to, because my life at school was totally miserable. I was surrounded by a bunch of snooty girls who had nothing better to do than to pretend they were cool while they called me fat. I wasn't fat. I was never superskinny, but I certainly wasn't fat. The teasing never ended, though. It continued as if we were still in middle school.

There was one girl who transferred in during my sophomore year, and she went around telling everybody that she had been bulimic. I was really nice to her, and I tried to be understanding, thinking she could probably use a friend if she was suffering from an eating disorder. Then one day in the hallway, in front of everybody, even *she* called me fat! I shot back, "Excuse me. I may be fat, but at least I'm happy. When you were fat, you decided to puke up your food." Then *I* got in trouble. I was the one who got sent to the principal's office for bullying a girl who had an eating disorder. I complained, "Just because she had an eating disorder doesn't give her the right to call me fat!"

After that, I came to the conclusion that private school was not for me. "I've got to get out of here," I begged my mom. I think my mom had this idea that if I went to public school I was going to end up pregnant. I knew that wasn't going to happen. I had a little brother who gave me a glimpse of what life would be like with a child, and I wanted nothing to do with that. Also, the public high school I would attend was a great school; they offered more AP classes than my college-prep high school. I even tried to convince her by showing her how much money we would save by switching me, but she still tried to fight it. My education and getting ahead in life were way more important to her than the money it cost them, she said.

In the end, my parents saw how unhappy I was at that school and they let me enroll at Theodore Roosevelt High School the summer before my junior year. I decided to start things off on the right foot. Rather than trying so hard to fit in with something that wasn't really my thing, I decided to be myself. That summer I auditioned for the school dance team. I'd been singing and dancing my whole life, and my natural inclinations kicked in at that audition. I made the team, and when I met all the girls before school even started, they immediately embraced me. They were so nice and so accepting that it was apparent to me right away that this whole experience was going to be different from Catholic school.

I was with that group of dance-team girls the first time I laid eyes on Chris. He was half white and half black, and he had this curly hair that was frosted yellow on top, and I remember he was wearing a red mesh backpack. (Clearly he made an impression!) I stared at him and leaned over to ask a girl named Latoya, "Who is *that*?" She said, "Girl, everybody and their mama likes Chris." I immediately fell back on my insecurities, thinking, *Well, he'll never like me then.*

A couple of weeks later, on the first day of school, I was blown away by the public school experience before I even made it through the front door. It was obvious that school wasn't just full of rich kids. There were poor kids, there were *really* rich kids, and there was everything in between. There were people who rode the bus to school, and there were also a few Range Rovers parked in the student parking lot. There were kids of every race and color, too. I felt at home. Instantly.

Then it got even better.

About ten minutes into my history class on that very first day, a student walked in late. I looked up and saw it was Chris—and he looked as fine as he had the first time I'd laid eyes on him that summer. There were a bunch of seats open in the classroom, yet he came and sat down at the desk right in front of me.

At that moment, I was positive that going to public school was the best thing that had ever happened to me.

Long story short, Chris *was* interested in me, and he very quickly became my boyfriend. My parents wouldn't allow me to go on dates, so our relationship mostly consisted of phone calls and whatever time we could get together at school, but we made the most of it. I was so happy. Getting handwritten, perfectly folded love notes in my locker between classes was better than I ever could have imagined. Chris was on the baseball team, and he was funny and a bit of a bad boy. People liked him. I *really* liked him.

Chris had lived a tough life. He lived with his grandmother because his dad was in jail and his mom had died of cancer when he was little. I wanted to open up to him about my own past, and my uncertain present, but I felt I couldn't. I kept hearing my mother's words: *You'll get deported.*

Sometimes Chris and I would skip school and just go hang out at his grandmother's house during the day so we could see more of each other. I wanted to hang out with him all the time. At night, I would sneak the phone into my room so I could talk to him. Because our phone was in the kitchen, I had to wait until my parents were asleep, then run the cord out the sliding door into the back-yard, all the way around the house and in through my bedroom window. Julio never told on me when I did that. Not once. Like I said, he had my back.

One time, Chris invited me to meet him at a friend's party. It was on a Friday night, and I told him I really wanted to go but my parents wouldn't let me.

As the school day went on, I got angrier and angrier about the fact that my parents were so strict. Here I was a junior in high school, living in America, and I felt as if I was penned inside a golden cage. I needed to break free. So I asked a friend of mine if she was going to the party.

"Yeah," she said. "Why don't you just come hang out with me at my house after school, and then we'll go over together."

I skipped dance practice that day and left with this girl after school without saying a word to my parents.

My dad picked me up every day after dance practice. I knew he would show up, and I wouldn't be there, and I basically didn't care. *This night is for me—whatever the consequences may be*, I thought. I figured the worst that would happen was I would get a beating. I'd gotten beaten before for no good reason. At least this time it would be worth it!

When I got to my friend's house I called my mom. I didn't want her to think I'd been kidnapped or something. But it was too late.

"You're dad is going crazy. He was so worried about where you are. He couldn't find you at school, and you didn't go to dance practice. What is wrong with you?"

I said, "Mom, I'm okay, but I'm going to this party and then I'll be back home later tonight."

"No, you're *not* going. Where are you?" she said in her sternest voice. "Give me the address. We're coming to pick you up."

"Mom, I'm not telling you where I am, but I'm okay. I'm not running away, but I knew you wouldn't let me go to this party, and I really want to go, so I'm going," I said. Then I hung up.

My parents had caller ID on their phone, which I didn't think about, so they kept calling back. My friend and I just unplugged the phone. By that time there were couple of other friends with us, and they were concerned. "Are you sure? Are you sure this is okay?" they asked me.

"Trust me," I said. "Chris is going to be there and I want to go to this party."

We wound up getting to the party pretty late. By the time we walked in, there were tons of people there—including Chris. He looked *super*cute. He lit up with a big smile as soon as he saw me. I had never been a kid who was invited to the parties at any of my other schools. Now, I was invited to *all* the parties, and for the first time, I was actually *at* one. Then, as if to cap it all off, one of my favorite songs, Lil' Troy's "Wanna Be a Baller," came on the stereo.

Every time I hear that song it takes me back to that day. Chris and I started dancing, and I just felt on top of the world. Super happy. And right in the middle of it, the cops showed up.

It was like a scene straight out of one of those teen comedy movies. Somebody stopped the music dead and yelled, "Run!"

All of a sudden everyone scattered. Chris and I ran into the backyard, which was more like a field. It was huge. We ran and ran until we reached a fence and he helped me up over it. We turned down an alley and finally looked back and didn't see anyone chasing us, so we slowed down, but I was in a panic.

Chris didn't understand why I was so worried. "It's no big deal. The cops would just give us a ticket. You show them some ID. Worst thing that happens is they might call your parents," he said.

Inside, I was like, *I'm going to go to jail and I'm going to get deported and my life is going to be over.*

I never told Chris any of that. I just said, "I cannot get a ticket."

Chris didn't have a car, but he managed to find us a ride, and he dropped me off at the corner near my parents' house. I wouldn't let him drop me off right in front of that house. I was afraid my dad was going to run outside and kick my butt in front of Chris.

The thing is, if I'd been caught that night and deported, it would have been worth it to me. I'd spent nearly two years having to be conscious all the time about every single thing I did and said, so that no one would find out I was illegal, and it was driving me nuts. It colored everything. My parents never let me forget that any wrong move I made could be *the one*. So when I took that risk, it was almost like a calculated bucket-list risk. I made up my mind that there were going to be times when I just had to live. And in those moments, I knew: If I got caught, I got caught. If I didn't take the risk, then I wasn't even living, and I couldn't even feel like I was alive.

I knew I would make those kinds of decisions again in the future. A conscious choice. A decision to break out of my big golden prison. I didn't know then that with each passing year, the decision to break free would get harder and harder, because I would always have more to lose. With each passing year, I retreated deeper and deeper into the cage.

I don't recall if I got a beating that night. If I did, it was just like any other. I was used to them. The only thing I remember is how good it felt to experience that freedom, to call the shots on my own, and to be with Chris at that party, on top of the world. It's still one of my favorite memories, cops and all.

I wound up having one of my favorite memories with my dad over the holidays my junior year as well—even if the holidays themselves had me feeling empty and left behind.

My mother decided to spend Christmas and New Year's in Mexico with Julio and my sisters. I couldn't go because of my lack of a visa, and because I would need to stay behind with my father and work the funnel cake stand on New Year's Eve—a potentially huge money-making night with all of the festivities happening in San Antonio, and a work night we simply couldn't afford to skip.

Christmas, which used to be my favorite holiday, had become almost meaningless. My parents were so busy they barely took time to decorate a tree. My birthdays weren't much better. There were a couple of times when they didn't even remember to get me a card, let alone any presents, let alone throw me a party. But having to spend Christmas alone with my father while my whole family celebrated together at Mama Silvia's seemed particularly cruel.

My father was tense heading into New Year's Eve. He complained about how expensive the permit was for that one event, and how we'd have to sell a lot of funnel cakes just to break even. He kept saying how we needed to earn enough money that night to pay Julio's private-school tuition for January and to pay our rent. He kept telling me how busy it might get and how hard it would be to handle the crowd with just the two of us and no one else to help.

Then finally the big night came, and business started really slowly. I could see my father's blood boiling as he stared at the dozens and dozens of passersby, none of whom seemed to want what we were selling. I could feel my own blood boiling, too.

Then, almost like magic, people started lining up for funnel cakes.

Within minutes, my dad and I couldn't keep up. I quickly went from being afraid of not making enough money to being scared my dad would blow up because the line was too long and I was too slow. We desperately needed more help. There was no way the two of us could handle the crush. We needed someone at the counter. But it was too late. There was no one we could call. People in line started shouting at us: "What's the holdup?" "Come on!"

I ran back and forth from the Fryolator to the counter, wiping sweat from my forehead, spilling powdered sugar everywhere, making greasy, floppy messes of the dollar bills I handed back as change.

That's when I noticed a familiar face in the line: Tiffani! I hadn't seen her once since I'd switched schools, but she smiled and started waving at me and pushed her way to the front. "You look like you need help," she said.

"Hi! Yeah, we can't keep up," I said, turning away quickly to flip the funnel cakes in the fryer before they burned.

"I'll be right back!" Tiffani said, and off she went. I saw her talking to her dad and then making her way back toward the stand, pulling her hair up into a ponytail as she elbowed her way through the crowd.

All of a sudden she walked right into the stand with us.

"Okay," she said. "I'll put the powdered sugar on the funnel cakes and charge people. Julissa, you make the funnel cakes, and Julio, you make the mix."

I looked up at my dad, worried to death that he would be upset that Tiffani had come barging in ordering us around like that, but to my surprise, he welcomed the help. "Okay," Dad said with a big smile. "Thank you."

I wanted to hug her, but the line was too long to stop.

Tiffani spent the next three hours with us, knee-deep in customers and suffering from the heat of the Fryolators. We fell into a rhythm like a well-oiled—or at least, well-greased—machine. With Tiffani's help, I was sure we'd sold far more funnel cakes in a single night than we'd ever sold before, even with Mom.

At the stroke of midnight, Tiffani grabbed a fistful of powdered sugar and threw it up in the air. "Happy New Year!" she exclaimed. My dad laughed and gave her a hug.

Shortly after midnight, Tiffani's dad came by to pick her up. "Thank you, thank you. I love you. Thank you!" I said to them. It felt good to see the two of them and to reconnect at the start of a brand-new year. There simply weren't enough words to express my gratitude, and my father thanked them, too.

Once again, Tiffani was my savior. She would always be my American sister, even as the years passed and physical distance took us farther apart.

It took my dad and me two hours to clean up that night before we loaded the truck and drove home, and my dad seemed happy the whole time. I made him play one of the old José Alfredo Jiménez cassettes again as we made the long trek home. It was the fifth time that day we had listened to the tape, but it fit the celebratory mood. There was something magical about the start of a new year and the successful night we'd just had.

Once we were home, the two of us were far too wired and wide-awake to go to sleep. We were excited about counting the day's spoils.

My dad sat on a chair and gave me a nervous smile as I laid out rows and rows of $1, $5, $10, and $20 bills neatly on the bed. I was still wearing the same clothes and smelled of powdered sugar, funnel cake mix, and grease—but the smell of those green bills overpowered everything.

"I don't think we've ever made so many funnel cakes in one night," I said.

"No," my dad said. He seemed happy. Calm. I hadn't seen him like that in a very long time.

I usually had a pretty good idea of what we made on any given day, but at $5 for a small funnel cake, $6 for a large one, and $2 extra for strawberries, I had completely lost track that night, and counting those bills gave me quite a shock.

"How much?" my dad said.

"Hold on. I have to count again," I told him.

The anticipation was killing him, I could tell. He seemed like a kid waiting to open his Christmas presents.

After I finished counting for the fifth time, I finally asked him, "Guess how much money we made?"

"How much?"

"Come on. Guess!"

"A million dollars?" he said slowly and with a smile.

"Close," I said. "Ten thousand!"

My dad's eyes got really big. He stood up. He grabbed a pile of bills and threw them in the air. "We're rich!" he yelled. He laughed. My father was laughing! "Ha-haaaaa!" he yelled, jumping up on that bed full of money and holding out his hand for me to join him.

It was such a rare moment of joy with my father that I threw myself into it like I had when I was a child. I jumped up on the bed with him and we spent the next few minutes throwing bills in the air, laughing, and proclaiming, "*Somos ricos! Somos ricos!*"

Of course, our family was not rich. That money would disappear nearly as fast as it had arrived. But smelling that money, feeling that joy and excitement, thinking about the power of money in America and what it could mean reaffirmed my desire to make it to the top. It reaffirmed this naive idea that if I had money, I could fix everything.

CHAPTER 7

The Accident

As the second half of my junior year got underway, that night full of laughter when we jumped on the bed in a whirlwind of dollar bills became a faint memory that I would cling to, wishing and hoping and praying that I could keep it alive.

That night was the way I wished my father could always be, and that I could always be with my father.

One night a few months later, my dad totally lost it. I don't remember what it was that set him off, but instead of directing his anger toward me, as he would have when I was younger and before I started threatening to call 911, he directed it at my mother.

He pushed her. Then he hit her. I threatened to call the police if he didn't stop. My seven-year-old brother screamed at him to stop, too, but he didn't.

I picked up the phone.

"No! Don't, Julissa!" my mom yelled. "What if they ask to see your ID? What if they ask questions? We could all get in trouble!"

I was far more afraid of what would happen if I didn't call 911 than I was about anything else.

I didn't really want to call the cops on my dad. I didn't want to dial. It was almost like an out-of-body experience and before I knew it, I dialed 911.

"My dad is drunk and hitting my mom," I told the operator. I kept a cool, calm voice that surprised even me. Julio was crying in the background.

"Is he armed?" the operator asked.

"No, he's just drunk. He's hitting my mom."

She told me to get to a safe place and that the police were on their way. My bedroom had become my safe place with the door closed and my dresser pushed up against it so my dad couldn't get in when he was angry. Julio and I slept that way most nights. But I wasn't going to run and hide from this. I couldn't abandon my mom.

By the time two cops knocked on our door, my dad had calmed down—not necessarily by choice. He was almost ready to pass out. I regretted calling the police the moment I laid eyes on them, and I'll regret it forever. The cops took my dad away in handcuffs. He didn't resist. He also didn't look at me. He looked defeated, broken, and I felt it was all my fault.

How could I have called the police on my own father?

What I was about to fully understand for the very first time is that for people in our situation, every single decision has potentially life-altering consequences. Nothing is ever as simple as it appears. There are always more complications to be faced. I had done the right thing by calling the cops; I had also done a terrible thing by calling the cops, and the fallout would be shattering.

My dad was in jail for one night. My mom bailed him out. When he came back, he gave me an honest apology and said, "Please, don't ever do that again." I think under any normal circumstance, life might have improved after that night. The threat of going to prison, an arrest record, the embarrassment and shame of it all, might have been the rock-bottom that turned my dad around. But our situation was anything but normal.

What I didn't know when I called 911 is that he would be deported. He had a valid visa, but for legal reasons I could not understand he was forced to leave the country for six months.

With a single phone call, I turned my mother into a single mom. I hardly remember what those six months were like without him except for the fact that everything got harder for her. My dad was the one who took Julio and me to school. He picked us up, cooked us dinner, drove me to my basketball games, or to dance practices at 6:00 a.m. My mom did the best she could to make up for his absence, but she wasn't organized the way my dad was. The house was a constant mess. I was late to every practice. I didn't have to put my dresser behind my door, but that didn't mean I didn't want and need my dad there.

I just wished that my dad could have loved me the way a dad is supposed to love a daughter. I wished I hadn't grown up afraid of him. I also wished he'd just been mean to me all the time, so that hating him wouldn't have hurt so much. That wouldn't be the only time I would realize that people are rarely total saints or total monsters. People and circumstances would rarely be white or black in my life.

My mother wasn't blameless when it came to her temper, either. There were times when my little brother hit me with a toy sword or something, and I'd hit him back, and she immediately turned around and beat me for hitting my little brother.

I resolved to spend as much time as I could out of the house. School became a sanctuary for me. I buried myself in my studies and activities, knowing that they were my only ticket out. I started reading up on colleges all over the country, in faraway places, believing in the American dream—that if I worked hard enough and got good grades I could get into one of those schools and leave that house.

I worked with my teachers and guidance counselors relentlessly to file early admission applications to colleges far away from San Antonio.

I was ready to escape, and by then it was about much more than just the escape from my unhappy home life. Going to college was the next step in the American dream I'd been taught to chase. I thought constantly about what it would feel like to be someone important, successful, and powerful. I wanted to make all kinds of money, so I could solve all our problems. I would finish the dream home my parents had stopped building, pay for my father to go to rehab, and pay for Julio's education. I would resolve my immigration status so it wouldn't be an issue anymore, and I would rise above all the challenges my family and I faced to live the great promise that America gives to so many. *If I were successful and rich, why would anyone want to turn me away?*

My hopes were high that by October of my senior year I would have a pretty good idea of what school I might be going to, and what area of the country I would finally escape to. It wasn't until the first few rejection letters arrived that I began to realize just how hard it might be to get there.

I went into that school year with nearly straight As. I was in all college-prep and AP classes. I had glowing letters of recommendation from my teachers. Yet the letters I received back from the schools I had applied to all included the phrase "We regret to inform you." Every one of those schools wrote back to say they could not process my application for early admission.

I remember picking up the phone and calling the admissions office at Colorado College. I just wanted to find out what was holding me back from having my application processed, and the person I spoke with on the phone pointed out that I had left my social security number blank on the application.

"Oh. Is that a problem?" I said.

"Well, without a social security number we can't process anything in terms of financial aid," she told me.

"So, if I don't have a social security number I can't go to school?"

I wasn't sure if the woman on the other end of the phone knew what I was implying or not, but the whole conversation made me feel like I was standing on shaky ground.

"No, I don't think that would matter," the woman said. "You could come to school, assuming you were accepted, but you'd be entirely on your own when it comes to paying tuition."

Tuition was something like $30,000 a year. There was no way my parents or I could ever come up with that kind of money. I also couldn't take out student loans given my immigration status, and my parents couldn't cosign, either, because they were not permanent residents or U.S. citizens.

I realized that the application forms for every school I'd applied to included a box for a social security number—and that I'd left that spot blank on every single application. I had no choice. There was no way I could change that.

Would that mean I couldn't go to college?

I tried to push that thought out of my mind.

Chris and I had broken up by then, after he left for another school, and I'd started spending a lot more time with a boy named Troy who became my best friend. Like Chris he was a bit of a rebel, but in a different way. He was handsome and really artistic. He wrote me poems and really long letters. I felt like I could tell him anything. Our friendship developed into a romantic relationship, and I started escaping through my bedroom window to spend time with him at night after my parents fell asleep. There were times when I'd get into my dad's Cadillac, put it in neutral, roll to the end of the driveway in silence, and then take off in that car to go see Troy under the cover of darkness.

Even when he caught me climbing back through the window in the middle of the night, Julio never told on me.

I didn't have a driver's license, which made my escapes twice as risky as any other teenager's. I couldn't get a license for the same reason I couldn't apply for financial aid on those college applications. That blank box, the lack of those nine numbers, held me back.

I remember being really down about it one day as I sat with my favorite teacher, my pre-AP physics teacher with the long Greek last name, whom we all called Mr. G. He was this super quirky teacher whom everyone loved, and I was definitely the teacher's pet. I had a free period during the last period of school, and because I was a senior, I could have gone home early, but I didn't want to. Mr. G let me come to his classroom to help him grade tests, or sometimes just work on my homework.

"I don't know if I'm going to be able to go to school," I told him that particular afternoon. I didn't explain the whole thing, but I said that because of my parents' situation we weren't able to apply for financial aid. I'm not sure if he understood what I meant by all of that or not, but it didn't seem to matter.

"Well, don't give up just because of that," he told me. "You should still apply to college. Just apply. Apply everywhere you can. See what happens. I'll write you the best letters of recommendation and they're going to *have* to let you in."

With his encouragement, I applied to schools like Georgetown and Dartmouth. He insisted I had the grades and the drive to get in, and I'll never forget when he wrote me a letter of recommendation for Dartmouth. He wouldn't let me read it but he said, "If this letter of recommendation doesn't get you in, then the world is doomed."

He also encouraged me to apply to the University of Texas at Austin. I told him I wanted to go someplace very far away from Texas, but he insisted: "It's a great school. It's one of the top schools in the country. Don't dismiss it."

I agreed to follow his advice, but then I put off actually submitting the application. I just didn't feel like it was the right school for me.

My mother kept insisting we would find a way to pay for the best school I could get into. She promised we'd make it work, and I believed her. Given her track record for making things work in every facet of our lives, her encouragement, her optimism, and her never-ending work ethic gave me hope. I filed applications, and hoped, and waited.

My father, back home after six months in Mexico, picked me up from school every day like clockwork during my senior year, so I was surprised to see Aris waiting in her car at the curb when I walked out on November 17. Aris had never picked me up at school before, ever.

"Hey," I said as I opened the passenger door. "What are you doing here?"

"Mom's been in an accident," she said.

"What?"

I could see that she had been crying.

"She was setting up at the PX and the fuel tank on the gas grill—it exploded."

"Oh, my God."

"It blew her right onto the sidewalk. She's not burned. It's a miracle she's not burned, but..."

Aris turned away and started to cry.

"Is she okay? Oh my God, Aris, is she okay?"

"She's at the hospital," Aris said. "They don't know if she's going to wake up."

The next thing I remember is standing at a window in a bright hallway with ugly white tile floors, staring at my mother in a hospital bed. She had a tube in her throat to help her breathe. She had tubes and wires all over her. Her beautiful hair was all shaved off. She looked frail. She looked like a deflated shell of the mother I knew.

Then all of a sudden I was standing with a doctor, with my dad and my sister behind me. My dad didn't speak English. Aris didn't speak English. So the doctor looked to me.

"She's lucky to be alive at this moment," he said. "She suffered very severe head trauma. All we've been able to do at this point is try to contain the swelling. There's not much more we can do but wait and see how she responds. We have every reason to hold out hope, but I have to let you know there is a very real chance she won't make it."

I wasn't prepared to hear those words. I wasn't prepared to translate those words to my family. But there was no one else to do it.

Phone calls were made. My mom's sister, my uncle Mike, and my other sister, Nay, all boarded planes to San Antonio the very next morning. Before any of them arrived, I got a phone call from the hospital telling us that they needed to do emergency surgery on my mom because her brain was swelling too much. The plan was to cut out a piece of her skull to allow for more swelling. The skull is a finite space; it can't expand. The only way for the brain to not explode is to cut small pieces out and hope it stops swelling. There was bleeding, they said, so their goal was to drain it. If that didn't contain the swelling, they would have to cut more pieces out, and the more they cut, the more damage it could cause. I was trying to absorb all of this while translating it to my dad in real time because they needed his permission to move ahead with the operation.

"You have to tell us now," they insisted.

I didn't even finish explaining it to my dad before I answered: "Yes. He says yes. Operate on my mom."

I made that decision myself, and as I hung up the phone I realized whatever happened next was on me.

We managed to get everyone in from the airport, and we all made our way to the hospital. It was a long, long surgery. Thankfully the accident happened on the military base, and a world-renowned neurosurgeon treated her at that hospital. We all felt lucky that he was the one operating on my mom, and we hoped that it was God's way of watching out for her.

My Christian upbringing and the power of prayer had never played a strong role in my life until that moment. I felt a little selfish praying when I hadn't spent much time in church and hadn't prayed for others very much before that day. But I prayed anyway, promising God that I would be a better Christian from that day forward while begging for my mom to live.

When the doctor finally stepped out of the OR, he told us that my mother had made it through the surgery, but that the only way they could keep her alive was by putting her into an induced coma—a coma from which she might never wake up.

He went on to explain that if she did wake up from that coma, she might be like a child again. She might need to learn how to walk, and talk, and she might not remember us. No matter what, she would need a lot of care.

"It may be years before she's back to normal, if she's ever back to normal," the doctor explained.

His words felt like a giant door closing on me.

I'm the one who's going to have to take care of my mom.

I'm not sure why I felt that all of the responsibility would fall on me. I have two older sisters, after all, and she had my dad, not to mention our extended family. But that was my thought: *I'll have to take care of my mom forever.*

With my mother in my life, I felt I could do anything. I could solve any problem. I knew nothing was impossible for her, and therefore nothing was impossible for me. She would figure it out. Somehow. Some way. She'd make it happen. How was I supposed to figure anything out by myself without her? She was the one who assured me that we'd find a way to send me to college. How could I do that on my own now? How could I possibly do that while also figuring out how to take care of her?

I felt selfish again, thinking of myself when all that mattered was for my mother to be okay. I couldn't help it, though. I was a senior in high school. This was a pivotal year for me. My entire future was at stake—a future that I could no longer even try to imagine. It seemed impossible for me to develop any long-term view of life at all. That view kept getting interrupted. All I could see was the next step, and the next step was college, and even that step now seemed out of reach.

A whole month passed. I quit the dance team. My mom had kept a jewelry table in a local souvenir store, and I had to go work at the shop after school every day now. I had to work the funnel cake stand every weekend, too. My dad and Aris needed the help, and we couldn't afford to stop working. We needed the money, and now we needed it more than ever as we faced gigantic hospital bills for my mother's care.

I prayed every night for her to wake up. I prayed for the night-mare to end.

A week before Christmas, it did. My mother finally opened her eyes. I was so relieved to see her awake the first time I walked up to her bed that I couldn't stop sobbing. But it didn't take long for reality to set in.

My mother was no longer everything she had been. She had no motor skills. She could barely talk. When she spoke, she said all sorts of things that didn't make any sense. She couldn't tell time. She didn't know that it was the year 2000. She knew her name and she knew that she had three daughters and a son, but she didn't know that I was in high school. She didn't really recognize me at my current age at all.

For days she kept asking if the baby survived. It finally occurred to us that she thought she was still pregnant with Julio. Her sense of time was completely gone.

The doctor insisted it wasn't permanent. "Over time, that gets better," he said, but I don't think I really heard him. All I could see was that my mom was completely *off.* She looked old, too. I'd always thought of my mom as this very stunning, beautiful woman. Her beautiful head of hair had been shaved off and now she had these little gray hairs growing back. She had aged dramatically in a short period of time. It made me so sad.

Some of our support system disappeared once my mom was awake. Her sister flew back to Mexico. Eventually, so did Nay. Uncle Mike stayed, though. He insisted he would stay with us for as long as he was needed. He promised he would make sure my mother was okay and that the burden of caring for her would not fall on my shoulders alone.

"Keep applying to colleges. You've worked too hard not to. Your mother would want you to," he said to me.

So that was what I did. I kept working hard at school, putting long hours into everything, getting my As, and applying to every college I could find, while my uncle became our lifeline. He took it upon himself to drive my mother back and forth to therapy every day. He started driving me to school and picking me up, too. He even threw me a big birthday party at an Olive Garden and invited twenty of my friends. Because of him, I started smiling again.

But I had learned the hard way that smiles don't last long.

I frantically filled out dozens of applications for schools I'd barely even heard of, in any faraway location that might take me away from everything I was dealing with, and the rejections kept coming, over and over and over again.

I kept applying anyway.

CHAPTER 8

The Wall

So, did you apply everywhere you wanted to apply?" Mr. G asked me one day in January, when we were sitting in his classroom grading papers.

"I think so," I said. "I applied pretty much everywhere!"

"Including UT?" he asked me.

I looked down at the desk and didn't say anything.

"Julissa! I'm telling you, it's a great school. It could be perfect for you. If there's still any time to get your application in, I really think you should apply," he said.

"All right," I said. "A lot of schools are already past deadline, but I'll look into it."

I looked into it and realized that the deadline was the very next day. That night I started filling out the rest of the application, and the next morning my uncle Mike drove Troy and me to Austin to drop off our applications in person. I finished the rest of the application in the car. I remember picking the business school as my first choice because it was ranked in the top five in the country, not so much because I knew I wanted to major in business. I was still pretty sure I didn't want to go there, but I also didn't want to let Mr. G down. He'd done too much to help me.

My mother made remarkable progress those next few months. I

shouldn't have been surprised; my mother is like the Phoenix, being reborn over and over. By the spring of 2001 she was walking again, and talking, and someone who didn't know her might have thought she was back to normal. I think she felt that way herself at times, too, because as soon as she started feeling better she wanted to go back to work, even though we all recognized that she couldn't. She would get tired. She needed to rest a lot. And those of us who were close to her could see that she was still not back to normal. She would be okay one minute, and then she would say something that didn't make sense, and her short-term memory was terrible. She would ask me something and I'd answer, and then five minutes later she'd ask me the same question. She was forgetful enough that we didn't feel it was safe for her to be around the funnel cake stand. The thought of what more could happen if she were left in close proximity to the Fryolator and the gas grill terrified us.

She exhibited some rather strange behaviors, too. There were times when we would take her out to the mall and she would panic over stepping foot on the escalator. It terrified her the way it might scare a young child.

"Mom, just get on the escalator! Stop being like that!" Nay would yell.

That made me angry. "Stop it, Nay! She doesn't want to get on the escalator," I'd yell back at her. "There has to be an elevator somewhere. We'll meet you upstairs. Don't pressure her to get on the escalator!"

I worried what would happen to my mother if I weren't around. How would she be treated if I ever got into college and moved away? Every time I tried to imagine it, I simply stopped thinking about it. I could not let myself think long-term or make long-term plans. I could never allow myself to dream that big, because when

I did, when I actually took a step back and I thought of the future, all I saw was uncertainty.

Troy was empathetic about all of it. He kept asking what was bothering me all the time, and one day I decided to tell him. I just blurted out, "I am in the country illegally."

Troy didn't seem upset by the fact that I was in the country illegally. Instead, he seemed upset that I hadn't trusted him enough to tell him sooner.

"You have to understand how hard this is," I told him. "I can't tell anyone. I can't let anyone know. I can't risk someone slipping up and saying something at the wrong time to the wrong person or I could be deported. Do you understand how serious that is?"

He said he did, and so I went on to explain the whole thing. I told him how I'd come here as an eleven-year-old, and how my visa expired without me even knowing, and how the fact that I didn't have a social security number might mean that I couldn't go to college.

Troy and I had always had a bit of a tumultuous relationship—one of those high school things where we would break up and get back together all the time. But when it came down to it, he was my best friend and he wanted to help me. In fact, he wanted to help so much that he suggested a way for me to get a social security number and get into college: "Why don't we just get married?" he asked me one day.

"What? You're crazy!" I said.

I wasn't ready to get married to anyone, but I could not deny that the thought gave me hope. I'd heard that getting married could mean an instant green card and a path to citizenship to anyone who wanted it. I assumed that a green card would allow me to apply for financial aid. But it was all just talk and rumors, things

I'd picked up from watching TV and movies. I didn't actually know how any of it worked and neither did Troy.

So one day the two of us decided—perhaps foolishly—to walk ourselves into an INS office and find out. We skipped school and Troy drove us. We went up to the front desk as stupidly and naively as could be and started asking questions: "We're wondering, for our *friend*, what you need to do to get a green card through marriage?"

Luckily the clerk didn't ask us any questions or ask to see any ID. I'm not sure what we would have done. Instead, the clerk gave us a whole bunch of paperwork and we read it over in Troy's car in the parking lot. It wasn't as simple as they made it seem on TV and in movies. In order for a marriage to qualify someone for a green card, the American spouse has to meet certain standards of income to ensure that he (or she) could fully support the couple. That was just one of the problems. The process was also very lengthy and the application fees were very high.

"Well, we don't qualify anyway," I said, putting off the whole marriage idea pretty easily. Thank God, too, because I did not want to be married, especially not at eighteen. Yet because he was my friend and I had told him about my status, I found it easier to stay in a relationship with him than to deal with any new crush. I just couldn't imagine getting into a new relationship with anyone else knowing that I would once again have to wrestle with telling them the truth about my life.

At times, I wondered if I would ever trust anyone else enough to tell them my secret.

My parents forbade me to go to the prom, but I saved some money, bought a dress, and sneaked out anyway. It was another one of those moments when I simply needed to *live*. I didn't come home until five in the morning, when the sun was coming up. I knew that whatever consequences I faced were worth it. I came in through the window and Julio woke up, shocked to see me coming in at that hour. I quickly changed and went to the bathroom to wash my face before I went to bed. On the way back to my bedroom I ran smack into my father.

"Did you just come in?" he said.

I didn't respond right away.

"Are you just getting home from somewhere?" he said, his voice rising in anger.

That's when Julio stepped out from the bedroom.

"No, Papi, she's been here all night," he said.

"Oh," my dad said. "All right, then..."

I will owe Julio for that one forever.

By the end of the school year, I'd received rejection letters from every college I'd applied to, except one: Hendrix College, a liberal arts college in a tiny town in Arkansas that I'd picked out of some college book. (Like I said, I applied everywhere!)

I couldn't afford the tuition.

I tried to stay positive. I kept moving forward as if going to college were an actual possibility. I had a phone call with the girl that Hendrix selected to be my roommate. We talked about what we would bring to set up our dorm room. And the whole time, I knew that I wouldn't be able to go unless some lottery-sized miracle came along to give my family and me a whole new start.

I talked about it with Mr. G and he suggested that I enroll at San Antonio College (SAC)—the local community college.

"Are you kidding me?" I said. There was a phrase among college-bound students at Roosevelt High: "Those who can't hack it, SAC it." Enrolling in a two-year school after all the work I'd put in seemed so unfair. But when it came down to it, I couldn't even afford to SAC it.

Without a social security number, I couldn't apply for financial aid. The deadline for making down payments on tuition at Hendrix came and went.

I walked in cap and gown at my graduation with absolutely no idea what my future would hold. I graduated in the top 5 percent of my class. I was all smiles. My whole family was proud of me. And all of us were worried.

I stood there that weekend after graduation with powdered sugar in my hair, covered in a layer of Fryolator grease, sweating in the scorching Texas sun, thinking, *Is this what my life is going to be now?*

I tried not to get down about it. I tried to take on my mother's attitude: "I'll find a way. I will!" But every time I tried to think about my future, it was like looking through a haze of powdered sugar. I couldn't see the life of wealth and happiness that I'd been imagining and working toward for so long. Not even a life of scraping by to make ends meet. I could see nothing at all.

I'd been driving forward for so long thinking only about that next step, about getting into school and moving away from home, that maybe I didn't see the reality of what was happening. It was almost as if I'd looked away for a second and then woke up after a horrible accident. *Had I lost control of the wheel? Was I even the one driving? What the heck happened?*

I thought I had everything going for me: I was a high school graduate, an honors student, a hardworking kid with good friends and mentors and the support of her family. Yet I had absolutely nowhere to go. Nowhere. Somehow, when I wasn't looking, my American dream had crashed into a giant wall.

PART II

The Road to the Street

CHAPTER 9

Opportunity

Uncle Mike handed me a piece of paper with a phone number on it and a name: Rick Noriega.

"What is this?" I asked him.

"Julissa, you have to call the number! Right now. Try now, before the offices close. This could be it! This could be what we've been waiting for!"

It was July. I was hot. I was tired after making funnel cakes all day. I looked at him with a blank stare.

"They passed a bill allowing students that don't have papers to go to college here in Texas!" he said.

"What?" I said in disbelief. Despite the fact that San Antonio is a very friendly city for immigrants, we still lived in Texas. The same Texas where some ranch owners near border towns use intimidation tactics to "monitor" the border.

"It was on the news. That number is for the office of the state senator who helped pass the bill. Call!" he said.

I was stunned. I wasn't aware that a bill like that was even in the works. A part of me wondered if my uncle had made a mistake and misheard something on the news. I didn't know what else to do except call the number. They put me through to Rick Noriega's office, and all of a sudden I was on the phone with a woman named Linda Christofilis, the state senator's assistant. I told her that I wanted to find out if I might be eligible to go to college under this new law my uncle had heard about.

"House Bill 1403, yes," she said. "Well, why don't you tell me a little bit about yourself, and we'll see if we can help."

I'd learned never to speak to anyone about my immigration status, especially someone in a government position, but there was something about Linda's voice that made her sound friendly and safe. So I started talking. I told her about when I came to the United States, how I came here, and that I'd just graduated high school in the top 5 percent of my class. She asked for all of my information, and I gave it to her: address, phone number, everything.

"Well," Linda said, "you're exactly the type of student this bill was written for."

"Really?" I said, my voice cracking.

Then I worried that it might be too late for the coming school year.

"I applied to UT. I applied to all these schools," I told her, "and they all rejected me because I didn't have a social security number. But the applications were all filled out, with recommendations and everything. I had my heart set on going to college this year. So, is there any chance that this bill is retroactive? Or will I have to wait until next year to apply to school again?"

There was silence for a moment.

"You know, that's a good question. Hold on a second," she said. She put me on hold for what felt like forever.

"Hi," she said, "yes, it is retroactive and could be applied to your applications to schools for this current year, for sure."

My smile got so big I thought my cheeks would break.

"That's amazing!" I said. "What do I need to do? How can I make this happen?" I wanted to know the exact next steps.

"Where else did you apply in the state of Texas?" she asked.

"Only UT Austin. I—"

Before I could explain, she said that was fine. She would type up a letter for the senator to sign, and they would send it to the UT admissions office and ask them to reevaluate my application.

"Really?"

"Yes, and if your grades are what you say they are and everything else is in order, I think you'll have a very good shot at getting in— and you'll qualify for the Texas grant."

"My uncle said something about that, too. How much is that grant for?" I asked. "Because paying for school is definitely going to be an issue for me. I—"

"It's for $5,000," she said, "so it'll cover a significant portion of your in-state tuition."

"Oh my God. That's fantastic!" I said.

"It's needs based and also merit based. So you'll have to keep your grades up if you want to hold on to that grant once you get it," she said.

"That is *not* a problem. I will work hard, I promise!" I said.

I was ecstatic that finally my grades mattered.

"Well, good!" Linda said with a little laugh. "The senator will be excited to hear about your case, and I'm just so glad you called today."

She was glad that I called that day!

"I don't even know what to say," I said. "Thank you so much!"

"Thank you, Julissa. I hope this all works out for you. We'll be in touch soon."

I got off the phone and noticed that my parents, my brother, and Uncle Mike were all gathered around expectantly waiting for me to tell them what I learned.

I covered my face with my hands and cried a little. Then I

looked up and said, "They said this bill applies to me, and the senator is going to send a letter to UT asking them to reevaluate my application!"

Then we all cried. My mother kept saying, "I knew we would find a way."

House Bill 1403 was better than winning the lottery. The chances of a law being enacted at that exact moment were proof, I believed, that God existed and that He loved me.

Texas became the first state in the United States to allow undocumented students to attend public universities, pay in-state tuition, and receive state financial aid. In the fifteen years that have passed, only twenty states have enacted similar laws. In places like Georgia, South Carolina, and Alabama, the laws that have been enacted are to ban undocumented students from pursuing a higher education. I can only imagine what a student in one of those states must feel when they learn of the laws in their state.

I was overwhelmed with joy, but I also had some lingering doubts. Perhaps UT was fully enrolled and wouldn't have room for any students that late in the summer. Perhaps I'd have to wait a year, but at that moment I could breathe a little. I could start seeing my future again.

I started checking the mail every day. Every day I would run out from my house to the mailbox and sort through everything, looking for a letter from UT. Finally, a couple of weeks after that first phone call, I recognized the logo in the upper-left-hand corner of the envelope. I didn't even wait to get back inside. I tore open the envelope—and I started to cry. Standing right there on the street, tears streamed down my face.

I can't believe it, I thought. *I can't believe this is really happening.*

I ran inside and I told them all, "I got accepted to UT. I got in!"

My mom and dad hugged me and then they hugged each other,

and my uncle told me something I've never forgotten: "Congratulations," he said, "but remember that you earned this. Nobody gave you this."

He had always called me his bright star, and of course he was happy for me, but he wanted to make sure I didn't think of my acceptance like winning the lottery or a handout because someone felt sorry for me. He wanted me to stay focused on the fact that this wouldn't have happened if I hadn't worked so hard. He wanted me to recognize that in life you need two things to be successful: preparation and opportunities. My mom and dad and my entire family had been helping me prepare my entire life, and now the State of Texas was giving me the opportunity I needed.

"This is just the beginning," he said. "This is just the first step."

By the time I received my acceptance letter, there were only two weeks left before the start of the school year. We hopped in the car and made the ninety-minute drive to Austin the next day. Of course there was no more student housing available, so my uncle and my mom and I had to search around town. We managed to find an off-campus dorm. We signed up and put a small deposit down, but as we drove away, it was clear to all of us that the rent was going to be more than my family could afford on top of all of our monthly expenses.

"We'll find a way," my mother insisted.

If my mom had spoken that sentence—"We'll find a way"—as part of some movie scene, that is where the sad music would begin to play, where unbeknownst to the characters something awful was about to happen.

My mother was still not well. In fact, it wasn't too long before all of this good news unfolded when my mother suffered a seizure one morning. Thank God my uncle was there and we were able to rush her to the hospital. But I could see that the constant care-giving was taking a toll on him. He'd left everything behind in Mexico and had been with us for eight months.

A few days after we came back from Austin, my uncle sat us all down and said he'd made a decision: he was taking my mother and Julio back to Taxco. There, my mother would have the help of Mama Silvia and the rest of the family. San Antonio was close enough to Austin that I could make the trip every weekend to work the funnel cake stand and use the money to pay for my college expenses.

My dad's feelings weren't really considered in that decision. But my mother agreed to it, and Julio was too young to have a say. They all agreed that my dad would stay behind to tie up loose ends with the house and our belongings and then join them in Taxco.

It all happened so quickly that I could barely wrap my head around it. In no time at all, I was packing up my things and moving into a dorm: the Madison House on Twenty-Second and Pearl, in West Campus, where all the fraternity and sorority houses were located.

I moved from a crowded house full of family to a crowded dormitory full of strangers. The place I rented was part of a suite with three bedrooms. Each bedroom housed two students, and then there was a common area that we all shared. Just like that, I was shaking hands with a girl I'd never met whom I would be sharing a bedroom with, saying hi to our suitemates—and saying good-bye to my parents and Julio as they headed back to San Antonio without me.

I was so excited and nervous, and at the same time I felt completely unsure about what the future would bring. Every other kid I saw in those first few days around campus seemed thrilled to be away from home, thrilled just to be there and to have some freedom, and all I kept wondering was, *When am I ever going to see my mother and brother again after they leave for Mexico?*

When it came to my immigration status, there was no light on the horizon for me. I was unaware of any bills in Congress, nothing being talked about, that might offer someone like me a chance to fix her immigration status and get on a path to citizenship. There was literally nothing I could do to change the situation I was in. There was no waiting line. My options were to continue pursuing my dreams or to give up. I could have given up my grant, given up the opportunity to receive a great education, moved back to Mexico with my parents, and thought about coming back to the United States at some later date. But I knew that as soon as the discrepancies in my visa showed up and it became clear that I had been living here undocumented for any period of time, I would instantly be banned from entry to the United States for a full ten years. *Ten years.* I couldn't wait ten years to go to college. I wasn't going to skip the opportunity to go to UT. I'd worked too hard; my parents had sacrificed too much. America was my home. I wasn't going to banish myself from the country where I'd done most of my real growing up.

So I went about my business knowing that one day in the very near future, I would see my parents and Julio off at the airport, and I would never, ever be able to go visit them. My own parents. My baby brother. That was the price of my college education. That was the price of beginning my American dream. My family would be gone. I wouldn't be able to see them, and knowing what shape they were in financially, there was a good chance they wouldn't be able to visit me, either.

I suppose it could have driven me crazy; instead it made me angry. I was angry that my dad didn't stop drinking when my mom was in the hospital. I was angry that she got into an accident. I was angry that life had been so tough on them. I had grown up watching my parents work hard, seeing the sacrifices they made, seeing how much they gave up to send me to private school most of my life and pay for the clothes on my back, and I got it into my head that I was going to use my college education to accomplish two very big goals: I wanted to bring my brother back to America, where he was born, so he could go to college here, too, when the time came, and I wanted to make enough money to provide for my mom and dad, so they wouldn't have to keep working so hard their whole lives.

Being responsible for parents in their old age is a big part of Mexican culture. Our parents take care of us when we're kids, and then when we get older it's our turn to take care of our parents. That's just what you're supposed to do in life. My parents never asked me to make it my goal to care for them; they would never put that kind of pressure on me. But in my family, there's simply an unwritten rule that we help each other out, no matter what. We would never put our parents in a "home." I never even heard of homes for elderly people until I came to live in the United States. The very idea of it seemed cruel to me. Still, by the time I started at UT, that desire to help my parents had developed into something more for me. It was a fire now—a drive to be wealthy and powerful and to fix all the things that were wrong.

I never remember a single time when my mother went out and bought herself a dress or a pair of shoes. Same with my dad. I don't remember him ever buying stuff for himself (except for the Cadillac, a used car, when we needed a car to get around in). After seeing that sort of sacrifice growing up, I knew that I never wanted to struggle like that. Now, with a chance to go to one of the best business schools in the country, I set my sights high from the very start. I decided I wanted to be a powerful businesswoman. I wanted to travel the world. I wanted to buy a mechanic shop for my dad and a jewelry store for my mom. I wanted to take them on vacations. I wanted my little brother to not have to worry about all of the things that I had to worry about. To me, *that* was the American dream. My parents had forever drilled this belief into me: "School is your salvation. Education is your salvation. Education is your way out."

There was never a time when I needed to believe that more than on the emotional day in that early fall of 2001 when I took my mom, Julio, and Uncle Mike to the airport.

There were people everywhere, rushing around as they always do, trying to get cabs and manage their luggage and hear themselves think over the never-ending announcements from the airport loudspeakers. We were running late, of course, and it all just seemed to go too fast.

"I love you," I said to Julio as I held his little face in my hands. "Behave, okay? Be good with mom."

"I will," he said.

I hugged my mom for a long time, but it wasn't long enough. I just held her and held her, and I can't even remember what we said to each other. I'm not even sure we said anything. I just remember that I soaked the shoulder of her shirt with my tears—and she soaked my shoulder, too.

"Mama Silvia and I will take good care of her," Uncle Mike said. "I promise."

"I know you will. I know," I said.

I watched them walk down the jetway until they disappeared around the corner, and onto the plane—not knowing when I would see them again.

CHAPTER 10

Normal-ish

From the outside, to anyone who didn't know my story, my freshman year experience looked just like the ones thousands of other kids have every year at schools all over America.

My roommate, Kim, was a sophomore, a year older than me. She was a military brat, and her last residence had been in San Antonio, so we had that in common. The other suitemates included a girl who I assumed was white (I would be surprised much later to learn that she was Hispanic, too), a half-Arab–half-German girl named Nadia, and an international student from Mexico.

Madison House was a small off-campus dorm, so we all got to know each other really well—not just my suitemates but everyone who lived in the building. We bonded over our love for the taquitos, the mouth-watering, deep-fried corn tortillas stuffed with cheese that were served on Wednesdays. There were movie nights during the week and other dorm-wide activities. All the normal stuff that a college-age student might expect and, most important to me, about a million things that I didn't have to worry about anymore. My dad wasn't screaming at me. I didn't have my mom being sick at home. I didn't have to help my little brother with his homework. I started to realize even in the first couple of weeks of school that I'd always felt like I wasn't allowed to feel whatever it was I was feeling. I'd always felt guilty about something, even if no one was making me feel that way. I was used to sneaking in through the window at night, and now I could always walk in through the front door. It was so good to just be me, to be selfish, to only worry about myself. To be normal.

Then Friday came around and I was reminded how *not* normal I was. As everyone else started in on their weekend plans, I boarded a bus for the ninety-minute ride back to San Antonio to sell funnel cakes so I could pay for school. I was instantly reminded of how much my mom, my brother, and my father were giving up just so that I could go to college. How could I not feel like I owed them everything?

I saw my father briefly over the course of the first few weekends. I was thankful to have him there to help me lift the Fryolator and get everything set up at the outdoor market. I was glad to still have him in San Antonio. I was happy to see him. But I didn't stay with him. I stayed with my sister, who by that time was living with her husband in their own place, with a new baby. It was crowded at her place. I didn't have my own room, and I felt horribly guilty about staying there instead of at home with my dad. He was sad about it and tried to convince me that he wouldn't drink if I came to spend the night, but I wouldn't give in. I left him there to drink alone in his chair every night.

Soon enough I was saying good-bye to him, too. I loved my father, and I had so many mixed emotions of love and regret, of forgiveness and bitterness. Like with my mom and Julio, I also wondered when I would see my dad again. Maybe next time I saw him, he'd be like the dad who came to visit me in Mexico when I was younger—funny and kind, and *only* funny and kind.

And then, it was just me working the funnel cake stand. Making the ninety-minute Greyhound bus ride back to the Forty Acres (the nickname for the UT campus) every Sunday night with a backpack full of cash. Sometimes it was thousands of dollars, mostly in small bills. I knew it was dangerous to carry that much money, but what else could I do? I couldn't open a bank account. I had no driver's license, no social security number, and therefore no options. I would stuff all the cash under the mattress or into the pillowcase on my bed in the room I shared with Kim. It wouldn't stay there long. I'd use it to pay tuition and rent, and buy food and supplies.

Then I'd jump right back into "normal" mode on Monday mornings. I went to classes, I went to the library, and I spent tons of time studying. One of the only things that felt odd was that the university enrolled me as an international student. Because the law that allowed me to go to school had just passed that summer, the school had to do some fast thinking as to how to accommodate students like me—who were Texas residents, American in many ways, but didn't have papers. So they lumped me in with kids from Thailand and Mexico and other countries who were in the United States on student visas. That meant I had to go to the international student office whenever I had questions or needed help with things. The classification offered a good cover, but I never spoke about it with anyone. I made a few friends through that "international" connection, but I definitely didn't feel "international." When people asked me where I was from, I simply said, "San Antonio." That *was* where I was from, after all.

Being classified as an international student didn't bother me too much, though, because soon enough I found a place where I felt I belonged. I think it was only a couple of weeks into my first semester when I attended my first HBSA meeting. The Hispanic Business Student Association was billed as a professional organization that would help students build the skills necessary to thrive in the corporate world. I joined the meeting having no idea it would be a transformative experience.

I figured it would just be a small group with a few nerdy members or something, so I was shocked to walk into a big auditorium filled with two hundred or so people at that first meeting. And then the president of the organization got up to speak, this charismatic, handsome older student in a business suit. Just before he started speaking I heard somebody whisper, "Here comes Scotty Too Hottie." Among all those Hispanic students, male and female, all dressed in professional-looking suits, Scott definitely stood out. He commanded the room. He spoke like a man in charge. Before that moment, I don't think I had ever encountered a Hispanic man, besides Uncle Mike, who spoke with that kind of presence. I thought to myself, "I want to be *that*!" Commanding, professional, and charismatic.

I signed up for HBSA on the spot, and I would never feel I fit in more than when I was among HBSA classmates. HBSA threw parties, so I went to the parties. They had mixers and professional development seminars of all sorts, too, and I went to every one of them. For a lot of people, college is where you go to find yourself and your groove. It's the formative years. And for me, HBSA was where I was shaped and molded and polished.

Most of its members were Hispanic, so they knew my culture and my first language, and many of the HBSA members came from lower-income households and had worked their butts off to make it into the business school at UT.

I didn't dare tell anyone I was undocumented. I didn't let anyone in that group know that I'd been accepted into school only a couple of weeks before the semester started. All they knew, and all I felt, was that each of us had found our tribe.

Back in high school, I had always thrown myself into extracurricular activities that strengthened my academic record. I didn't just take Latin while most kids were taking Spanish. I took Latin and then cofounded and became president of the Greek and Latin Society at our school. In addition to enjoying it, I knew how good those types of positions would look on a college application. Now that I was in college, I figured those sorts of positions would look good on a résumé, too. Since I was a business student, I decided to take a shot at becoming the freshman representative for the Undergraduate Business Council. It was an elected position, so I went out and printed some flyers, and I got up early on a Tuesday morning to go pass them out around campus.

I was standing with some friends when we noticed some people running out of one of the buildings. There were concerned looks on people's faces, and people started forming groups and talking to each other. A guy named Logan, who had red, curly hair, came running over to us. I'll never forget the look on his face. He had the most awful expression. "The Twin Towers have been hit," he said.

I didn't know what he meant.

"They think it's terrorists. We're under attack."

It made no sense to me. In San Antonio the Twin Towers was the nickname for the powerhouse duo of Tim Duncan and David Robinson, the basketball players who gave such strength to the San Antonio Spurs.

"The Twin Towers?" I said. Everybody else seemed to know: the Twin Towers were the World Trade Center in New York City. The Twin Towers stood over lower Manhattan at the center of the Financial District and were, in essence, a symbol for everything we were learning about in one of the top business schools in the country. It soon became clear that those towers had been hit by two commercial airplanes. People on the planes and in the towers had been killed. And it was only getting worse.

More and more people started running out of classrooms. Campus security swept in out of nowhere. Jenna Bush, the president's daughter, was enrolled at UT at time. Security began searching for her in such a frenzy that it scared every single one of us.

The president's daughter is here. What if the terrorists attack us because of that?

They shut down the school. I went back to my dorm and watched the events unfold on TV with my suitemates. I cried. We all cried. I watched those images of what would forever be known as 9/11 again and again and again in the coming days. I couldn't turn away. I could not believe this had happened.

One of the images that stuck in my mind the most was of bodies falling out the windows above the fire where the planes hit. The TV channels quickly turned away from those images; the magazines and the papers rarely showed them. It was hard to watch a person jumping out of the window to a certain death. I couldn't imagine how difficult it must have been for a person to make the decision that jumping was better than dying inside those buildings. I could only imagine how hot it must have been inside. I could imagine the questions they must have asked themselves. I could empathize with that kind of desperation that leads a person to jump.

Then, I watched the tremendous American fortitude and spirit that came out of that horrible event, and I felt that I was part of it. I felt the anger that united us. Someone had invaded *our country*. Someone had killed *our people*, innocent people. I felt for the people who lost their lives, and felt that I was an American as much as anybody was an American. What I did not know on 9/11 was just how deeply that horrific day would affect my life. In reaction to that tragedy, our country's immigration system would be forever changed.

On August 1 of that year, Senators Dick Durbin and Orrin Hatch had introduced legislation in the United States Senate that was aimed precisely at immigrants like me. The legislation was called the DREAM Act, which stands for Development, Relief, and Education for Alien Minors. There was that word again. *Alien.* As if I were some thing from some other planet. The proposed bill would create a process for undocumented immigrants who were brought to the United States as children through no fault of their own to begin a path to permanent residency and eventually citizenship. The bill argued that these children, like me, had grown up American and they had earned the right to be citizens of the country they called home. There would be all kinds of background checks and reviews, and even a provision dictating that immigrants like myself show "good moral character" in addition to a high school diploma or GED, and more. It wouldn't be easy. But I wasn't looking for easy. I was just looking for a path I could take, any path that would allow me to continue to live, and work, and go to school, and be a part of this country I now considered my home.

A part of me wanted to run out and join the movement, to show my support for that legislation. But I couldn't. What if that legislation didn't pass and I'd already outed myself? I felt like a coward. I heard my mother's voice ringing in my ears: "You'll get deported." So instead, I watched the news, and read the papers. Knowing that HB 1403, the bill that allowed me to attend college, had passed made it seem absolutely possible to me that the DREAM Act might pass, too.

After 9/11, the DREAM Act, which gave me so much hope, would soon fail. And it would fail again and again each time it was reintroduced. As I'm sitting here writing this book, all these years later, it still has not passed.

There was an air of sadness around campus the rest of the semester, but we all tried to get back to our normal way of life. The terrorists would not win.

I met my five best friends through HBSA that first semester. They had met each other during summer orientation programs, and I felt a little like an outsider at first, since I hadn't been able to attend those summer sessions with them. But in no time at all we formed our own little six-pack. We'd go to the library and study together during the week. I'd go to parties with them when I could, although the fact that I was only in town Monday through Thursday nights made that difficult. I couldn't really study during the weekend at all because I was selling funnel cakes all day long, so everything that had to be done, all of my papers and research, all of it, I had to finish Monday through Thursday. That didn't leave much time for hanging out, or making friends, or dating—even though I had my eyes on lots of different boys.

One of those boys was a boy named Robert. Robert wasn't very tall or incredibly good-looking, but he had these pretty, sad-looking eyes that drew me in. Out of the blue, he asked me if I wanted to grab lunch after class one day. I had just pierced my tongue for no good reason other than because I could, and because no one would be able to be mad at me for it. My tongue was still swollen and healing and I mumbled, "I can only eat soup." So we made our way off-campus to a nearby mall to eat ramen together.

From that moment on, even when I didn't have time, I some-how made time for Robert.

We hung out after class pretty much every day for the rest of the semester. We went on long walks while he smoked, and I pretended to smoke. We took rides in his two-door red car. He paid for my lunch, laughed at my jokes, and his sad eyes kept drawing me in.

We talked about what we were studying, and about what we wanted to do when we grew up. We talked about high school and God and religion and music. He was into Nine Inch Nails, and I was into hip-hop, but we both loved Tupac. We didn't have a lot of the same interests, but we were able to have really good conversations and we laughed a lot, so much that my stomach would hurt. Neither of us is a funny person nor what anyone would call a class clown, but we laughed at each other's humor. We really got each other. We were sarcastic to each other. We found we both liked eating good food and drinking good drinks. I could spend all of this time with him and not worry about a curfew and not worry about my dad. When I was with Robert, I wasn't an international student with no papers; I was just a college girl with a crush. Other guys showed interest in me over the course of the semester, but I seemed to be falling for this one guy who was the opposite of the type I thought I liked. We never kissed. We never talked about being boyfriend and girlfriend. Maybe we were just going to be really good friends. I wasn't sure. He just got me, and I wanted to be with him all the time.

Then one night near the end of the semester, after a ride in his two-door red car, we stopped in the parking lot of his building— and he leaned over to kiss me. And then, he asked me to go down on him.

I was so naive and sheltered, I really thought that once you kiss a guy, he's automatically your boyfriend. I really liked him, and I wanted to be normal. I was so confused. *Don't normal college girls go down on their boyfriends?* I had never tried doing that thing to anyone. Maybe my tongue ring was a misleading indicator. Maybe that gave him certain ideas. It felt very abrupt, but I tried to ignore my hesitations. In my mind, normal college girls did all sorts of things in the backseat with boys they liked. I had flashes of the film *American Beauty*, with all of its twisted views of love and sex and needy relationships.

Robert was a good guy. He was chivalrous. He was a gentleman who always paid and always opened doors for me. I noticed the way he walked with me on the curb side of the street. All these things were running through my mind as I did this thing that he wanted me to do. But I couldn't get over the fact that we had never once talked about our relationship.

I stopped. I looked up at him.

"So," I said. "What are we?"

"Are you kidding me?" he said. He groaned as he pushed my head down.

It felt all kinds of wrong.

"I can't do this," I said. I sat up and looked out the window.

"I'll take you home," he said in a half-disappointed, half-angry voice.

I didn't feel normal anymore. I wanted to know what we were, what we would be. He made it clear that we weren't going to be anything more than what we were—friends who had lunch and took long walks and rides in his two-door red car.

And this? I thought.

I got out and walked home. I never wanted to see him again.

Back in my dorm room, I felt embarrassed. I felt dirty. I felt used. The next day I brought it up to my six-pack friends and even the guys thought it was weird that Robert treated me that way. Kevin and Ivan, who were very protective of me, threatened to go beat him up!

That made me feel a little better. My new circle of friends had my back, and they let me know that my instincts were right. The semester was almost over and I only saw Robert in class a few more times, exchanging nervous glances but never exchanging any words.

I got over my disappointment with Robert a lot quicker than I ever thought I would. Maybe it was the fact that I had to worry about finals while juggling the three-hour commute to sell funnel cakes. I couldn't wallow in my broken heart when I was worried about a few slow weeks at the funnel cake stand. I spent Christmas break in San Antonio with my sister and her husband, feeling sad about not spending Christmas with my parents and Julio.

It was the second Christmas ever that I spent without my parents. The first was when Julio was born, but I had spent that Christmas with Mama Silvia and my sisters and all my cousins. This Christmas was different. There was no Christmas tree, no feeling of celebration. There was no birthday cake for Julio. Even though I was with my sister, my brother-in-law, and my baby nephew, and they tried everything to make me feel included in their little family, it was one of the loneliest days of my life. Perhaps it was my first realization of just how lonely my existence in this country would be.

But there was no time to worry about my feelings. I had to focus on making money at the funnel cake stand. The weeks leading into the holidays had been slow, and my second-semester tuition wasn't going to pay itself.

Luckily, after another highly profitable New Year's Eve, the second semester started off great. The whole six-pack enrolled in the same calculus class, so we started hanging out more than ever. One night we all decided to go to a crazy foam party. It was gross. Just the worst—all of these strangers dancing in a room that filled up with bubbly foam like the top layer of somebody's dirty hot tub. We decided to split early and had a good laugh over it all as we walked back to Kevin's car. Kevin was the only one of us who had a car, a green Firebird, and we were halfway back to it when this crazy drunk guy on the street started yelling at us and calling us names. That was when our friend Annie decided it would be a good idea to talk back to the guy.

"Oh, my God, Annie, what are you doing?!" I said. Annie was tough, but the guy was big and drunk.

All of a sudden the drunken guy started charging at us like he wanted to kill us.

"Run, girls!" Kevin yelled. Ivan and our other guy friend, Israel, stood there to block the drunk from getting to Annie. We looked back over our shoulders as the crazy guy reached them, and Ivan took one big swing and knocked the guy flat. He laid him out cold with one punch.

"Ivan, you're our hero!" we said as we jumped in the car and took off. I felt safe being around this group of people, and it came from much more than having a little muscle in the bunch. Kevin, Ivan, Israel, Delma, Annie, and me—we all looked out for each other. We shared notes when we were studying, and we covered for each other if someone had to miss class. Kevin lived in an apartment with his older brother, and we'd all go over to his house and take turns cooking. I remember one time I tried to cook rice and it came out like soup, so they all made fun of me. They still make fun of me. They're always asking, "How's that rice soup you make?"

I solidified my friendships with other people that second semester, too. There was Jessica, an officer in HBSA who had her sights set on becoming the group's president. Another girl named Tiana was the most laid-back and fun person I'd ever met. I also met my partner in crime, Clarissa. I spent a lot of time hanging out with my roommate, Kim, too, who accidentally discovered the stash of money under my mattress one day. "Oh, I just haven't had time to get to the bank yet," I told her as I thought of new places I could stash my money and not get caught. I'm sure she thought I was dealing drugs or stripping on the side, what with all those dollar bills. She never asked about it again, though.

I managed to make enough money that semester that I not only paid for tuition and books and rent, but I was able to help send my dad to rehab. Rehab was much cheaper in Mexico than it was in the United States. So I sent some extra money to my sister and we got my dad into a program. In time, it would work.

Making money was doing just what I thought it would: making everything better.

I even managed to save enough money to buy my first car, a 1998 Dodge Neon. That meant I didn't have to carry my cash in a bus full of strangers anymore. I could keep it in the backpack on the seat next to me, safe and sound. I still couldn't get a driver's license, though. So every single time I got in my car I had to tamp down a very real fear that I might get pulled over and get in serious trouble. I didn't speed. I always used my blinker. I always came to a complete stop at stop signs. I adhered to the rules of the road far more strictly than the average driver out there, simply because I couldn't risk getting caught. The consequences of something as simple as a traffic ticket were just too high for me. But all in all, my life was smooth sailing.

It's funny, though: life always seems to find a way to rip a hole in your sail just when you finally think you've got your bearings.

CHAPTER 11

Walking Papers

Right in the middle of my second semester, the City of San Antonio decided that the plot of land where the vendors set up shop for the open market on weekends should be put to better use. The powers that be decided to take that prime piece of land and use it for the building of a new museum. Just like that, my funnel cake stand lost its home. And I lost my only source of income.

One small part of me was glad. I was tired of making the three-hour round-trip commute every weekend and losing out on so many moments with my friends. I never made it to a Texas football game that first semester because I was always working on Saturdays. But the rest of me was a nervous wreck. I knew that I needed to find a job fast. And I knew that without the proper papers, there was no way anyone would hire me.

One of my suitemates had a boyfriend who was Mexican. He never said anything, and neither did she, but from talking to him I just figured that he was probably undocumented. I was desperate. So I went out on a limb and told her about my situation.

She talked to her boyfriend, and a couple of days later he put me in touch with a woman who could supply me with fake papers.

When I called, the woman gave me the address to her apartment. I took a few hundred dollars from under my mattress and made my way to a normal Texas apartment complex. The transaction was completely mundane. I handed her the money. She took my picture. She wrote down the correct spelling of my name and my date of birth, and two weeks later I received an envelope from her. Inside were a fake green card and a fake social security card with my name on them. I had never held a real green card or social security card in my hands before. They looked like government documents, I suppose, but I had no idea if they were good fakes or not. I had no idea if the paper was the right thickness, or if the typeface was correct or if they would fool anyone. All I had to go on was the fact that my suitemate's boyfriend had bought papers from this woman and that he had used them to get a job. I hoped those papers would allow the same thing to happen for me. All I really had to go on was faith. If it didn't work, that would be the end of the road for me. If I got caught using them, I'd likely be deported. I'd lose my grant. I'd probably lose my friends. *I'd lose everything.*

I saw no other way to move forward. Getting those papers and putting them to good use was the only path available to me at that moment. Period. Anything else would have meant giving up and I wasn't going to let that happen.

I knew that Ivan was making good money working in the call center at a prepaid credit card company. I was pretty sure he was making somewhere between $12 and $14 an hour. I knew he'd helped Kevin get a job there and some other friends, too. So the next thing I did was to go to Ivan: "Hey, I need a job because my funnel cake stand closed. Can you hook me up?"

"Yeah, of course," he said. "We're still hiring. I can get you in for an interview." He had no idea that I was undocumented. None of these people that I considered my best friends in the whole world knew my secret.

In all those HBSA meetings and mixers I'd gone to, I'd learned a few things about the corporate world. I learned how to dress the part. I learned how to give a firm handshake. I learned how to make eye contact and speak with some confidence. My grades spoke for themselves. The fact that I'd received a grant that was paying for my education said almost everything that a potential employer might want to know about the kind of hardworking person I am. Having a recommendation from an employee inside the organization went a long way, too.

I aced the interview. I got the job. Then I had to walk into human resources on my first day there and fill out a W-9. For the very first time in my life, I had to fill in a social security box, knowing it was a fake number—and not knowing whether or not it would be obvious to anyone else that my number was not real. It was one of the scariest things I had ever done. Then it got even scarier. I had to hand my fake social security card and my fake green card over to the woman in that office so she could photocopy them for their records.

I was absolutely terrified as she put her hands on my papers. What if they felt strange to her? What if something obvious was wrong about them and I didn't even know? Would she scrutinize them? Was there some magic pen, like the ones they use at grocery stores to make sure you're not passing them fake money?

I wasn't just worried about getting caught. I was worried about the repercussions. *What if I get caught and then Ivan gets in trouble because he recommended me? What if Ivan then tells all of my friends? What if I lose them? What if I lose this job opportunity and can't find something else and can't pay my tuition, or rent, or anything else? What if they confiscate the papers and then I can't even try to get another job somewhere else?*

The woman took those papers, put them on the photocopier,

and I watched the light beam stream out on the edges as it moved back and forth under the cover. I watched as the black-and-white pictures of my social security card and green card emerged on a sheet of paper on the side of that machine. I watched her pick that paper up, look at it, and then lift the cover and pick up my cards once again. I hoped she couldn't tell that I was shaking. She walked toward the counter, looked at those cards again—and then handed them back to me.

"All right. You're all set," she said.

She didn't scrutinize my papers at all.

As I walked out of that office, I felt dizzy. I had literally held my breath the whole time.

Well, I thought, *that worked*.

I started to think about what had just happened. I realized that there was no good reason why anyone would scrutinize my papers at all. I was a freshman at UT with a 3.8 average. Everything I'd done to get me that far was proof that I belonged right where I was. Why would anyone question it? There was no one raiding the UT campus looking for illegals. Most people didn't even know that people in my situation could go to college. When people thought of illegals, they weren't picturing me. So why would anyone in the corporate world expect a UT student to be undocumented? They wouldn't. Collecting my papers and making photocopies of them was just like checking a box on a form. It wasn't a test. It was a formality.

So I started working at my first real job—and I worked just as hard as I worked at everything else. I took every available shift I could get. Right off the bat I started averaging thirty hours a week on top of my class schedule. Saving that three-hour ride to San Antonio and freeing my weekends of greasy long days gave me what felt like loads of extra time to get my schoolwork done, and to get together with friends and go to parties and anything else I wanted to do. I would have worked even longer hours if there had been more shifts available.

I was so thankful to have that job, but the money I was making wasn't as good as the money I had made selling funnel cakes. Some weeks I'd work only twenty hours, and that wasn't enough money to pay for tuition, rent, books and everything else. I was desperate.

I had stayed in touch with Linda Christofilis, the woman from Senator Rick Noriega's office, and I called her to tell her my situation. I don't remember if I asked or if she suggested it after hearing my predicament, but regardless of how it happened, Linda cosigned a $10,000 loan for me. I have never understood the kindness it took for her to do that. She hadn't met me in person. We had only talked on the phone a few times. Yet she was willing to take a risk on me. She knew that there was more than a big chance that I wouldn't be able to get a job after college, and that I might never be able to pay back the loan. In that case, all of the financial responsibility of the loan would have fallen on her. Still, she cosigned.

God kept looking out for me, sending me angels.

Once again, things felt like they were falling into place, and new opportunities started opening up to me. That very year, Wells Fargo Bank made a deal with the Mexican consulate to allow Mexican citizens to open bank accounts in Texas using a Mexican-issued ID called a *Matricula Consular* (consular ID card). Suddenly, my new Mexican ID was all I needed to have checking and savings accounts just like anyone else my age. I had paychecks coming in that I could sign, cash, or deposit without any worries or all of the expensive fees that come when cashing a check at one of those predator-like check-cashing places with a staff that sits behind windows of bulletproof glass.

The more we settled into our college lives, the more my friends started talking about the chances we would all have to study abroad, or even to take a semester at sea, and I knew I couldn't participate in any of those amazing opportunities because I couldn't travel internationally. But I didn't let it get me down. I poured myself into work and school. If there was anything I wanted that cost a little more money, I'd just work harder. I'd do almost anything I had to do to make an extra buck.

I heard that you could make good money selling hair to wig manufacturers, so I did that. I made more than $200 for my long, dark, never-dyed hair. And then I went and dyed my new, short hair bright red—just because I could.

I sold my plasma for money, too, but that didn't pay nearly as well as my hair.

There were times when my bank account got down to five bucks between paychecks, and I would look at that balance and think, *Oh, good! I can go out tonight!* I would go to Ladies Night on Sixth Street and know I could buy beers for a dollar if some boy wasn't buying drinks all night. That meant I'd have enough for a slice of pizza when I got hungry.

Even when my bank account got to zero, I was positive that I could find a way to make more money to do the things I wanted to do and pay for the things I needed. Having a steady paycheck as a base was hugely freeing. By the end of my freshman year, after a whole school year away from my parents and all the money problems that I'd grown up with, making money was still always on my mind.

It just didn't worry me anymore.

Instead, I started focusing on all the money I was going to make someday.

At that time, I was pretty sure I wanted to be a sports agent. I'd seen the movie *Jerry Maguire* back in the late 1990s like a lot of people, but it wasn't about that. For me, the Spurs fan, the football fan who felt like sports was the one thing that brings everyone together, making the big bucks as a sports agent was the ultimate dream job.

The first step toward landing my ultimate dream job was to land an internship. I'd learned through various developmental organizations at school that one of the best ways to move toward *any* career is to land an internship in your chosen field.

Through HBSA, where I became an officer in my sophomore year, I learned about the Hispanic Alliance for Career Enhancement, or HACE. They brought a program to campus that allowed me to go through Dale Carnegie training, which is basically like the Bible camp of how to succeed in business. Having that training under my belt gave me another leg up as I made my way forward, and it put me at the front of the line for any internship programs that were affiliated with HACE.

The day I met the CEO of HACE, I casually said, "Do you know any sports agents that are looking for an intern?"

He said, "No, not really, but we do have a really great relationship with the people at the Chicago Fire, the MLS team in Chicago, and they have a Hispanic marketing team. That may be a great opportunity for you."

Major League Soccer wasn't the NBA or the NFL, but it *was* a professional sports league, and in true Dale Carnegie fashion, I reacted positively on the spot. I was like, "Yeah, that would be wonderful. I'd love to get connected!"

I went online and learned as much as I could about the Chicago Fire. The MLS wasn't FIFA, but it also wasn't the minor leagues. The Chicago Fire had several players who played on the U.S. Men's National Team, including DaMarcus Beasley. I was thrilled at the prospect of working for an organization like that. I followed up with the CEO of HACE and he put me in touch. I applied, and the team made me an offer. The internship wouldn't be paid. All they could give me for monetary compensation was a $100 transportation stipend. I would have to move to Chicago for the summer, which meant leaving my job at the call center. I didn't see how I could possibly do that. Without a job, I'd have no way to pay for housing in Chicago.

At that point, I was pretty delusional. I knew my immigration status might be an issue. I knew financially I couldn't afford to live in Chicago. But I forced myself to live in an alternate reality. I forced myself to live in a little bubble where none of those obstacles mattered, where everything always worked out.

And it did.

During one of our regular phone calls I told my mother and Uncle Mike that I'd landed an internship but had no idea how it was all going to work. All I was looking for was a little cheering up, but much to my surprise they said, "Oh, we have family in Chicago. We'll call them. I'm sure you can stay with them."

What? I had no idea I had family in Chicago. I got excited, and then I stopped. I let myself worry that no matter how we might be related, they wouldn't want a perfect stranger to come live with them for the summer. I quickly realized I shouldn't have worried at all. We're Mexican. Family helps family. End of story. Those distant relatives whom I didn't even remember offered to put me up so I could live rent-free and keep pursuing my dreams.

I still wasn't sure how I'd survive with no income the entire summer, so I mentioned my dilemma to the folks at HACE—and they offered me a part-time internship in their own Chicago office for the summer, too. A part-time *paid* internship.

So off I went to a brand-new city to hold down two jobs for the summer. I worked every day from 8:00 a.m. to 2:00 p.m. with the Chicago Fire, and then went to work for HACE from 3:00 p.m. to 6:00 or 7:00 p.m., or basically however late they needed me after that. HACE put on a big career fair that summer, and I helped by stuffing envelopes and anything else they needed. Like my parents had shown by example, no honest work was beneath me. My extended family lived way out in the suburbs, and I had to take two trains and a bus to get to work in downtown Chicago every day. The commute was an hour and a half each way. But it felt like the opportunity of a lifetime, and the hard work never bothered me. I *wanted* to work hard.

In fact, I put my time on those buses and trains every day to good use. That was when I read Dale Carnegie's life-changing book, *How to Win Friends and Influence People*. In the book, Carnegie suggests you read each chapter twice before moving on to the next chapter, to let it really sink in. So on my morning commute, I would read one chapter, and then I would read the same chapter again on the way back.

I knew in my gut that all of that hard work would get me one step closer to the thing that I wanted. I didn't want a career in soccer. I didn't want a career in marketing, either. But taking that internship allowed me to make connections in major league sports, and I knew that having that on my résumé would be really helpful.

The amazing thing was that with every small step I took toward my dream of success, the more I was able to develop a long-term view and focus on long-term goals. I started looking at things for more than just what they were in the moment. I often asked myself, *What is the long-term potential of this opportunity? What's the real benefit? Is there a drawback? Maybe the real benefit isn't what it seems.* Now that I was established in my college career, I dug deeper when looking at opportunities that came up: *What does this mean for my life and career?*

I think a lot of that was instilled in me from the start. My whole family was like that. Every person in my family had a really strong work ethic. My grandmother instilled so much of that in all of us, even my mom. Uncle Mike would always say to me, "Do things with excellence. If you're not going to do them with excellence, don't do them at all." They instilled in me this idea that everything you do is a reflection of who you are. If you turn in a sloppy paper or if you turn in incomplete homework, that says everything about *you*. If you don't want people to think you're a haphazard, sloppy person, then don't turn in haphazard, sloppy work.

I applied that to my internships at every turn, even though they were getting all of the benefit of my work for no pay whatsoever. I didn't approach it with a chip on my shoulder and think, *Well, why should I work hard when they're getting me for free?* I worked hard because it was a reflection of me and of whom I wanted to be.

I also went above and beyond because I wanted to make more money. The Chicago Fire had a partnership that summer with the Monarcas Morelia, a Mexican soccer team. An opportunity came up to step in as the Monarcas Morelia mascot, and I took it. I put on a hot furry costume of a monarch butterfly. I grabbed the team flag and went out there and ran all over the field to get the crowds fired up with all of the old middle school and high school dance and cheerleading skills I could muster. Everyone in the organization picked on me for being the shortest mascot ever, but I didn't care: That mascot work paid $20 an hour! There was an added benefit beyond the money, too—from that point forward, dressing up as the mascot always provided a conversation starter when recruiters saw it on my résumé.

Putting the mascot money I earned aside and combining it with some of what I'd been able to save during the school year allowed me to have some fun that summer, too, and one of the best moments of all was taking my first-ever trip to New York City.

Back in high school I'd met a group of three guys, Ade, Kevin, and Andrew, from a fancy Washington, D.C., school. We met during the National Junior Classical League Convention, a sort of Olympics of Greek and Latin grammar, oratory, history, and dramatic interpretation.

We'd stayed in touch, and I knew that Kevin had landed an internship in the financial world of New York City, at a firm I had been hearing all sorts of glowing things about in business school. In fact, it wasn't just *a* firm. It was *the* firm: Goldman Sachs, the firm everyone at school seemed to believe was the absolute pinnacle of the business world food chain. So the fact that Kevin landed an internship in the fixed-income trading division at Goldman Sachs was beyond impressive to me.

Like many other things in my life that should have been routine and mundane, boarding a plane was scary and risky. I'd found out my freshman year when I boarded a plane for the first time in a post-9/11 world that showing my Mexican passport with no visa at all and a UT student ID was all it took to get me past the TSA at the airport. Knowing that my Mexican passport worked didn't make going past TSA en route to New York City any less nerve-racking, though.

Kevin was going to be at work when I arrived at LaGuardia Airport early in the morning, so I made plans to go hang out with Andrew at Columbia University when I first arrived. I flew into LaGuardia and took the M60 bus from Queens to Columbia. Money was tight and a cab ride was out of the question.

It was amazing to see Columbia, which was its own sort of urban oasis in a city that made Chicago look like a small town by comparison. Andrew took me to a real New York diner for lunch, and I fell in love with Greek coffee shops then and there. After lunch, I went downtown and met up with Kevin, who was dressed in a business suit. The lobby of his building was in a high-rise full of all of these Wall Street interns in their suits and ties, and the girls in suits and high heels. The hustle and bustle of it all was intoxicating.

Over the course of that long weekend, Kevin showed me the scope of the dreams that New York City has to offer. I remember going to Times Square at night and all the lights. It was the first time I'd ever been to a place like that, and I stood there looking up, and thought, *Wow. This city is amazing.* We ate New York–style pizza. He took me to see *The Lion King* on Broadway. We went for dim sum in Chinatown, and even though I didn't like that food very much, I ate up the conversation when he started talking about life at Goldman Sachs.

He told me that he worked incredibly long hours, but he didn't mind that hard work because he was getting a fabulous education. "I barely sleep, but I'm learning so much," he said. "Everyone there is *so* smart."

I already thought Kevin was one of the smartest guys I'd ever met. He was thinking about going into medicine, and to him an internship at the most powerful firm on Wall Street was just a stop along the way, the way my soccer internship was just one stop on the road to whatever career I was aiming toward, I thought—because at that moment, I started to develop all sorts of dreams that had nothing to do with being a sports agent at all. I suddenly imagined myself working in a place where everyone was as smart as or even smarter than Kevin, and where everyone was as driven and successful as Kevin, and that thought got me drunk with excitement.

Kevin could have shown me a lousy time and maybe I wouldn't have liked New York City at all. He could have *not* planned that amazing trip for me. He could have made no plans for when I was there, and we might have sat around his apartment, watched TV, and drunk beer. I wouldn't have been any the wiser. But he *did* make plans, and he showed me a world of possibilities that I never knew existed. I'm not sure if he knew what a big impact that weekend had on my life.

I wanted to be rich, and here he was, already living a very rich life. *Could that happen to me in a year?* I wondered. Then I thought about everything I'd learned, and everything I'd read on those long bus and train rides through Chicago, and I corrected my thinking. I changed my question to a truthful statement that I reminded myself over and over again: *that can be me a year from now.*

By the time that weekend was over, I knew two things: I wanted to come to New York, and I wanted to work at Goldman Sachs.

My mom used to say to me, "Tell me who your friends are and I'll tell you who you are." Who you surround yourself with is important; it matters who your friends are and who's influencing you. I stayed in touch with successful and driven students that I had met through my academic extracurricular activities, and that had a direct impact on my life. I could only imagine how powerful an effect it would have if I could surround myself 24/7 with people who'd made it to the absolute top of the financial world.

Back at UT, I had heard about an organization called SEO, or Sponsors for Educational Opportunity. SEO recruits and trains outstanding minority college students for summer internships. Not just any internships, but power internships that lead to full-time jobs with investment banks, corporate law firms, and other top companies. One of my HBSA friends had landed her internship through SEO.

Coincidentally, I had made contact with SEO during the second half of my sophomore year. Through HBSA, I'd met a recruiter from Goldman Sachs as well. I didn't think a whole lot of it at the time, but I had dropped Kevin's name to that recruiter. It was a casual thing. "Oh! I have a friend who's going to be interning at Goldman Sachs this summer," I said.

Amazingly, he had met Kevin. He knew him. So we had a connection in common.

The groundwork was already laid, I thought.

CHAPTER 12

Race to the Offer

I went back to UT at the start of my junior year more determined than I'd ever been. But before I could start on my master plan to make it back to New York, I had to figure out how I was going to pay for tuition and rent that semester. I hadn't made or saved very much money during the summer in Chicago. So I picked up the phone and, once again, Linda Christofilis saved me. She told me about the Texas Conference for Women scholarship. The scholarship wasn't intentionally opened to undocumented students, but the eligibility requirements didn't specify immigration status. So I applied—and I won. I received a $10,000 scholarship that would be awarded to me in a public ceremony by none other than Rick Perry, the governor of Texas, himself.

As I walked on stage to receive the plaque and shake hands with the governor and his wife, all I kept thinking was, *I wonder if he knows he's shaking the hand of an undocumented immigrant?* I wondered if it would matter to him. After all, he had signed HB 1403 into law, and now he was handing me a check for $10,000. The plaque had an inscription that read, "Today you are setting a record of success that is an example for your fellow Texans. As your achievements and accolades grow, remember always that you are the Texas of tomorrow and one of our great state's brightest rays of hope for the future."

An undocumented immigrant, *me*, was being called a ray of hope for Texas's future.

I took it to heart. I became president of HBSA that year. As president I planned all the weekly meetings, and every week, we brought in a corporate sponsor. Every week there was a speaker to talk to us about something to do with jobs, internships, and different career paths you could take at their companies or elsewhere. We had all sorts of companies that wanted to recruit from HBSA. One of the groups I made sure to bring in for a presentation right away that year was SEO. As president of the group, I managed to get extra time with the recruiter, a Puerto Rican man named Rafael. We started speaking about the possibilities that SEO offered for someone like me, and he said, "You should definitely apply. You should apply first round." So I did. I applied for what amounted to an early-admission membership in SEO.

When it came time for my phone interview, I was pumped. And when the interview was over, I was completely deflated.

It was a pressure interview, and I had never experienced anything quite like it. They would ask a question, and then right in the middle of my answer, in the middle of a sentence, they would ask another out-of-the-blue question like, what's seventeen times fourteen? When I hesitated for a few seconds to do that math in my head the interviewer said, "Oh, you don't know that? You don't know that? That should be easy!"

It kept happening. I kept stumbling. I managed to keep my composure. I didn't show any temper. I just rolled with it the best I could. When I hung up the phone I thought, *There's no way I'm getting an internship at Goldman or into SEO. This time, if I don't get the job it will be my fault. It will not be because I am not eligible; it will be because I am not qualified.*

I called my Goldman contact directly to try to work that angle and maybe save myself, and I admitted to him that I didn't think I was going to get into SEO.

"Well, if you thought you aced that SEO interview, then you'd have an even bigger problem. No one thinks they did well on the SEO interview. That's just the way it works," he told me.

I couldn't let it go. I worried that maybe I had set my bar too high. I let myself think that maybe I wasn't good enough or smart enough, despite my GPA and the fact that I'd had so much success at UT.

Part of me wondered if I should take a step back and try to get some other internship through the business school.

There was a Hispanic woman who worked there, and I assumed she would be helpful to someone like me. She was one of the few Hispanic women who worked at the business school. I think there's a part of being a minority that makes you believe that we're all in this together. We're going to help each other out. But it doesn't always work that way; sometimes even your own people try to put you down. I'll never forget the way she looked at me when I walked into her office with my résumé for the first time, with my dyed-red hair and my tongue ring. I knew it wasn't professional, which was why I took out the tongue ring for every HBSA meeting; I also put my hair in a bun so no one could tell it was red. She practically scoffed at me. And then? She did absolutely nothing to help me figure out what I could do to get a head start on lining up a career once I graduated. I was nineteen years old, excited, ambitious, looking for help, but it seemed that all she could see was red hair and a tongue ring.

By the end of my freshman year, I had decided to move past her and find other ways to get ahead. *I don't need her*, I told myself. Yet now, I wondered if I'd been too rash.

With all of that in mind, I still was thinking I'd blown it with SEO. I was preparing myself to suck up my pride and have some face time with her.

But before I did, I leveraged another offer. Just the way I had applied to a million colleges, I submitted my résumé to various companies and snagged an early offer from General Motors. I can't stress enough how much in denial I was. I didn't really stop to think about my immigration status, about the fact that my papers were fake. I just kept forging ahead, focusing only on the things that I could control. I couldn't control Washington; I couldn't control if the DREAM Act would ever get brought back to life and make it through Congress. The events of 9/11 caused all sorts of mistrust about border security and a fear of terrorism that dashed prospects of any kind of relief for the immigrant community. I simply couldn't worry about it. I could only worry about landing my internship with SEO. The rest wasn't up to me.

I called Rafael at SEO and told him about my offer from General Motors, information he shared with the rest of the selection committee. Before I had a chance to walk my résumé into the Hispanic woman's office, Rafael called me back: I was in! I didn't know at which firm they would place me, but I knew from that moment on that I was about to make some of the most powerful connections the industry has to offer. By the end of my first semester of junior year, I knew that I was going to land a killer internship the very next summer. Every business student at UT knew that the internship you land between junior and senior year was the most important of all. That was the big one, because that was the internship that could very well land you a full-time job offer before you even completed your senior year.

I was flying.

It couldn't have been more than a week later when I found myself on a bus to campus, and I looked up and saw Robert. I hadn't run into him or really even thought about him since that night in his red car my freshman year. He saw me, too. He said, "Hi." I said, "Hi" back. We started talking. I told him about my internship in Chicago, and my success with SEO. He told me he'd been applying for internships unsuccessfully through career services. I asked him how his grades were. He had a 4.0, so I pressed him further and found out he wasn't involved in any student activities at all. He hadn't landed a sophomore internship the way I had. "Well, that's going to make it hard to land an internship," I told him. Next thing I knew I was giving him advice, inviting him to come join HBSA, telling him how to apply to SEO, and offering to help him out.

What can I say? Those pretty, sad-looking eyes of his caught me off guard and drew me in, the very same way they did way back when we first started going for long walks and talks together after class as freshmen. By the time I reached my stop, I was pretty much a goner. I stepped off the stairs onto the sidewalk, and as the bus pulled away, I thought, *Oh, crap.*

Since I'd walked out of Robert's car three years earlier, I had built new friendships, had new experiences, and generally moved on. I could have never imagined that one conversation on a random bus ride would lead to Robert being part of my life again. Yet in no time at all, that was where we were: back to taking walks, grabbing meals together, having deep conversations, and laughing. It was just like old times in other ways, too: I was never quite sure if he was my friend, my boyfriend, or something else entirely.

We realized that we both had moved to the same part of town

and had shared that bus route for an entire semester. By the time our second semester started junior year, we were taking several classes together. He also joined me in HBSA and had been accepted to SEO.

Everything seemed to keep falling into place.

After my own acceptance into SEO, I called the Goldman recruiter I'd made the connection with the previous year. I let him know that I had been accepted to SEO and that I would love nothing more than to do my internship at Goldman—and with that one phone call, I secured my spot at Goldman Sachs.

Robert landed an internship at another firm in New York City, and with our junior year behind us, we both flew to New York on the very same day. We had both arranged to live in New York University dorm rooms that summer, but we were placed in different parts of town. My dorm was near Union Square, but I called him as soon as I landed and took the train to meet him at a McDonald's near his dorm in Chinatown. The front had an ornate awning and brightly lit wall menus printed in both English and Chinese. This was my first meal as an intern, an all-American lunch in the middle of Chinatown; it couldn't have gotten more New York than that.

I'm not sure if it was the odd setting, or the newness of it all, or the excitement of the big move for the summer, but as we sat there over Big Macs and Chicken McNuggets, Robert started opening up to me in a way he never had before. It's not my story to tell, but Robert had experienced some dark times in his life, and I never felt more close to him than when he decided he trusted me enough to share them with me.

I figured that cleared the way for me to open up, too. I told him about my father. The drinking. The beatings. The good, the bad, and the ugly of that relationship that still broke my heart.

I didn't say anything about my immigration status. I could still hear my mom's voice in my head: "You'll get deported." It was easier to open up about the most personal details of my relationship with my father than it was to share that I wasn't really supposed to be in New York City, interning at Goldman Sachs. I hadn't told anyone about my status since I'd purchased my papers. Not a soul.

The experience of sharing our painful childhood and family memories bonded us more than ever, just as it had with Tiffani way back when I was in middle school. But it still didn't help to define our relationship.

The entire summer would be a series of split experiences: split between my time with Robert and time with the new friends I would make through SEO and Goldman Sachs. It was almost like living in two separate worlds, which would only occasionally connect.

On the first day of SEO training, a Saturday, I rode the subway to Columbia University early in the morning. It was easy to spot other SEO interns on the street that day: young people in their power suits, with excited faces and fearful eyes.

As I walked into a room full of four hundred smart, driven, and intelligent minority students, I was instantly wowed. The SEO chairman at the time, Walter Booker, gave a speech that both terrified and inspired me. His remarks can be summed up like this: *You are amazing. You have the opportunity of a lifetime. Don't mess it up.*

Before the end of the first day of training, I met a crew of guys with whom I would really hit it off: Kelvin, Steve, and Tyler, as well as a bunch of other really cool, driven people who all seemed to revel in the achievement we shared by getting into SEO. Only a handful of people from UT made it that year. But now, the competition part was over. We were all there for the experience of a lifetime, to help each other out, and to get ahead.

On top of setting us up with our internships, SEO set up a series of seminars with major players that summer, including partners and CEOs from every big-name financial firm in town. They taught us how to act professionally at those seminars, having us prewrite questions and insisting that every single one of us raise our hands during the Q&A portion of any talk. They even gave us specific instructions on how to act at parties and mixers where we would be expected to get face time with those big-time players. They taught us *little* things, like to never eat the shrimp. We weren't there to eat, they said. We were there to network, and it was up to us to stay focused. They taught us not to drink at those parties, either. There wasn't usually any alcohol, because most of us were still underage, but even if there was, they said, you don't ever want to risk taking your eyes off the prize. Your hands need to be free for shaking hands. Parties with big players in New York City are business opportunities. Period.

We had to find other times for fun. Kelvin, the self-appointed head of the party planning committee, always had plans for us after the seminars. Kelvin, Steve, Tyler, and I, along with a couple of other guys from the summer crew, would always start the night at a spot called Dallas BBQ. The food wasn't particularly good, but they took our fake IDs, and with a $6 Long Island Iced Tea we were set for the night. (Yes, I had a fake ID in college like so many other students. I wanted to go to bars. I wanted to buy alcohol. Of course, the consequences of getting caught could be a lot steeper for me than for most college students. Still, showing that fake license wasn't anywhere near as scary as showing my fake social security number and green card to anyone.)

Even as I spent more and more time with those friends, things with Robert kept moving along. One night we walked back to his dorm. We kissed. I spent the night. He told me he loved me. He also told me that he wanted to wait to have sex until he was married or at least until he knew for sure he'd met the woman he wanted to marry. We never talked about it again, but we started doing more couply things: watching movies together, holding hands while we watched movies together, showing more physical affection for each other.

Looking back on it now, I have no idea how I had time to deal with any of that with the demands of the internship and the amount of time and energy I poured into my efforts to stand out from the crowd. The most important thing in the world to me that summer was landing a job offer. That was my one and only priority. That and figuring out how to live and work in the metropolis of New York City. I swear, every time I got on the subway I went in the wrong direction, or took the express train instead of the local train, or missed my stop, or something. I would go down the stairs, buy a MetroCard, swipe it *just* right so the machine would let me through the turnstile, then board the train and sit there happily until all of a sudden I'd see sunlight. *Crap. I'm in Brooklyn again.* So I'd get off and make my way around to the other side of the tracks, sometimes having to pay a second time to get back into the station to make the return trip to Manhattan. Then I'd get out at the wrong square.

"No! I'm in Times Square. I was supposed to get off at Union Square! God. Will I ever get this stupid subway thing right?"

I had to leave extra early all the time just to make up for my subway mistakes. SEO taught me that being on time is being late, and only by being early can you be on time.

After two weeks of SEO training on everything from financial modeling to how to dress for the workplace, after they'd inspired us to be the first one into the office and the last one to leave, and to give handwritten thank-you notes to our bosses and colleagues, the transition to actually starting at Goldman Sachs felt like a breeze.

I wore a black skirt-suit on the first day and made my way to Jersey City, where training would be held at 30 Hudson. Construction on the newest Goldman Sachs building had just been completed. It wasn't the iconic, conspicuously unmarked building in the fast-beating heart of downtown Manhattan, but, regardless, I was full of pride. *This is where I belong.*

By the time I made it to Jersey City, I was drenched in sweat. New York is hot and humid in the summer. Wearing a suit in the subway is torture. I cleaned myself up, and then made my way to the conference room where all interns would begin a week of training and presentations. It was there that I got my first introduction to the various groups within the private wealth management (PWM) division of Goldman. The two standout speakers were Dave Coquilette, who gave a presentation about the markets coverage group, and Eric Lane, one of the youngest partners at GS, who ran all the special and alternative investments, as well as the markets coverage group. I immediately recognized those were men I wanted to learn from, and I did my best to set up coffees and meetings with them so they could get to know me in the coming days. It was a lot of networking that first week, meeting people from different groups, going to dinners, schmoozing, and always remembering to *never* eat the shrimp.

Then we got down to business. The summer would be split in two: four weeks with one private wealth management team and four weeks with another. The way it works is that each private wealth management team is tasked with managing clients' money. They go out, they find new clients, and they bring them on to be Goldman Sachs clients. The team then acts as those clients' private wealth advisers. The PWM teams mostly followed the Investment Strategy Group's philosophy, but they could implement their own individual approaches to earning the most money for their clients.

A white man, a white woman, and an Asian man ran the first team I was placed with. The Asian guy was really nice and really helpful, but the woman was intimidating. She was older, and I just found myself scared to even talk to her. Still, that didn't stop me from offering to do anything and everything I could to make their jobs easier. I was just glad I wasn't being hazed like some of the interns in the sales and trading division.

I'd heard a story about an intern at UBS who worked on the trading floor. The UBS trading floor is huge; it's the size of two football fields combined. This intern was a bit chubby, and his team had a field day with him one afternoon. The head trader sent the intern on a quest to find an "uptick" around the trading floor.

"Go find me an uptick and don't come back unless you have one," the trader told the intern.

"Where do I find one of those?"

"Do I look like I have time to explain? Go find me one!"

One of the junior traders told the intern he could find one with the guys at the interest rates desk. Before the intern reached the interest rates desk on the other side of the floor, the head trader had called them and told them to send him to another desk. Pretty soon the whole trading floor was in on it and everyone watched as this chubby intern ran from one side of the floor to the other. Finally, the intern ended up with the technology help desk, out of breath, with his white shirt now drenched in sweat. "Please, please, where do I get an uptick?" he said.

"We don't have one of those!" responded the IT guy, trying hard not to laugh.

What the hapless intern didn't realize was that an uptick is a small increase in the price of a stock. It wasn't some physical object he could find on that floor no matter how hard he looked.

The moral of the story was that you'd better know your crap or you'll get crapped on.

Besides the normal intern routines, like getting coffee and lunch for the bosses, they also gave me the task of reading the news every single day and, basically, trying to find new rich people for them to prospect. Like, if someone was mentioned in a story because they owned a $20 million yacht, it was up to me get their name and try to find out more about them, because chances were that if someone owned a boat like that, they were worth pursuing. I'd imagined that many of our clients would be professional athletes and famous people, but to my surprise I quickly learned that few of those types of people actually have enough investible assets to be clients. They may make $10 million a year, but after taxes and their high expenses, they don't meet the Goldman Sachs minimum of $25 million of assets that can be invested. Most of our clients were actually business owners of some sort.

I would compile lists of potential clients and then do Power-Point presentations. There were lots of those. And I spent forever putting every presentation together so there would be no mistakes. Punctuation, spelling, formatting, all of it mattered. There weren't that many times when I could really impress, so being sure to shine at every opportunity was key.

I wasn't allowed to trade. I wasn't allowed to do much of any-thing in terms of serious work that involved clients, because as an intern I didn't have any trading licenses. I hadn't gone through the testing and background checks and other requirements that would allow me to do the real work of Wall Street. Instead it was, "Okay. Read the *Wall Street Journal*, and then ask smart questions about what you read." It was, "Go and bind the proposals," the actual proposals that private wealth advisers would take to new clients, or the presentations in which they would review their clients' portfolios. These were clients that dealt in millions of dollars at a time, so those binders were important. It just wasn't front-line, impressive work. To me, that meant I had to find ways to stand out and be impressive all on my own.

I paid attention to everything those managers said, did, and wrote, and to the material that I was tasked with binding. And every once in a while, I would speak up. "Oh, I noticed your client has a bunch of positions in this sector. Here is the latest research on the sector that you might want to highlight to your client."

When I noticed a particular client had a big position in a certain stock, I would go and find some news about that stock and tell the private wealth adviser, "I printed out this article for you to read on the way to your meeting, because the client has a big holding in this."

Not everyone was going to get an offer at the end of the summer. I simply wanted to do whatever I could to make sure I was one of the chosen few. I only had four weeks with each group. That was not a lot of time to stand out and make an impression.

Every day was packed full and moved so quickly. I spent from morning until late at night at the office, and then in the all-night revelry of New York City. Meanwhile, my personal life was about as unsettled as it could be.

One night, Robert told me, "There's this girl in Indiana that I met over spring break freshman year."

Out of blue, he told me they'd been staying in touch.

"Okay, so?" I asked. He kept quiet, so I pressed him: "Well, is she your girlfriend or something?"

"Kind of," he said.

"What the...?" I was fuming. I started pacing. In a long, angry monologue, I asked him a million questions: "Why have you never told me? We've been hanging out almost every day for months. You never brought this girl up. What's wrong with you? Why are you just now, after we kissed, telling me about this girl?"

"I'm sorry," he said. "Can we just not…Can we just…Can you just forget about it?"

"No, I can't forget about it! Are you crazy?" I said.

The thing was, I *did* kind of forget about it. Robert had issues, and that other relationship certainly couldn't be anything serious, because the girl lived in Indiana, and he and I were spending the whole summer together in New York. As a result, our relationship developed into a constant back-and-forth: "I never want to talk to you again. Don't call me anymore," followed one day later by, "I love you. I miss you. Come over."

There were all sorts of interesting, good-looking, and smart guys in SEO and in New York City in general, and since Robert had some girl in Indiana and wasn't my "boyfriend," I didn't stop myself from getting to know any of them. But I never let anything get too serious, either, because that would have forced me to stop seeing Robert altogether. I sometimes wondered if that was holding me back from finding a real relationship.

Honestly, it drove me nuts. Who had time to wonder about such things when I had a job offer to land? The summer was flying by so quickly that I was shocked when I learned it was almost time for my midsummer review. Word on the street was that if your midsummer review sucked, you were toast. There would be almost no point in continuing for the second half of the internship. Goldman was a place where they expected results, and there wasn't a whole lot of room for second chances.

CHAPTER 13

The Offer

Walking into the intern manager's office, I was pretty confident that I had done well, but I couldn't help but be a little nervous. Everybody's nervous when walking into a review like that, aren't they? What if I was toast?

Despite the nerves, I was poised and professional. I just desperately hoped that I'd made a good impression.

Apparently, I had. The intern manager spent a solid twenty minutes telling me what a good job I had done. Then he made one comment about how one of the managers said I needed to "pay more attention to detail," which I found really disturbing, because I thought I *had* paid attention to detail at every turn. But overall, he didn't give me any of those dreaded areas that I "could improve on." So I asked him: "Am I missing something? What can I do to improve for the next four weeks that I'm here? What can I be doing better?"

"Just keep doing what you're doing," he said. "You're doing well. Keep it up."

"Okay," I said. I stood up, shook his hand, and immediately started obsessing over the fact that at some point I'd failed to "pay attention to detail." I should have been happy that I had done such a good job, but I couldn't let go of that one small comment. *Where*

did I make a mistake? When? Did I forget to put a page number some-
where?

It bothered me.

Eventually I calmed down and realized that what mattered most
was my work ethic. I really was the first one in that office every
morning and the last one to leave. I would sit there and work until the last private wealth adviser went home. Even if I didn't have
anything to do, I would sit there and find something to do, and
it was in those times when I would find an article to highlight or
some new potential client that I might have missed had I gone
home early. Remembering how I used to take a ninety-mile bus
ride to San Antonio to sell funnel cakes, being on my feet all day,
being hot, greasy, and sweaty, I would think, *This is nothing. I get to*
sit in an air-conditioned office. I get to take a car home if I work late,
and they even buy my dinner. This is fantastic!

I was thankful for the opportunity to be there, so the hard, long
work hours didn't faze me. Neither did the work itself ("Sure, I'll
get your coffee. I'll staple this thing for you. I'll go pick up your
laundry. Whatever you need me to do, I'll do it") because I had
done things that were a lot harder.

I also felt a responsibility to the people who'd helped me get there,
like Rafael, the SEO recruiter who'd fought for me to get into SEO.
I felt like I had a personal responsibility to *him* to get an offer at the
end of the summer.

After four weeks, I was pretty sure that private wealth management was not where I wanted to be. Frankly, it was a little slow and
boring. It didn't take a lot of mental capacity to put together the
PowerPoint presentations, which was what a lot of analysts spent
their time doing. I heard some other interns say, "I'm not really
going to try for an offer here, because I don't want to work in this
division," and all I could think was, *Are you crazy?* I knew I had to

get an offer so that I could use that as leverage to try to get a job where I really wanted to work, which at that point was in the markets coverage group, something that was more fast-paced. PWM was like a baseball game, and I wanted to play basketball.

It just seemed to me that it would be hard to get a job anywhere else if you didn't have an offer on the table. At any other division, or even at another investment bank, when a recruiter asked you about your internship and whether you got an offer, if you said no, you would then have to explain why. How do you explain why someone who tried you out for eight or ten weeks would not want to hire you? How would that make you look in the eyes of someone who has barely met you? No matter what, I wanted to be able to say, "Yes, I got an offer. However, these are the reasons why I'm interested in working for you and not for them."

My second rotation was a whole lot more exciting. All of the private wealth advisers on the new team were women: two white women, Marla and Chris, and a black woman named Nicole. They had clients that were much more trading oriented, so it was more fast-paced. We all had to keep up with the markets every day because the clients were into short-term, tactical trades and not just long-term strategic planning. It felt amazing to see these really successful women totally kicking butt at Goldman Sachs!

Nicole in particular wound up being an incredible mentor. One of her clients was invested in a structured note, a flexible financial product that allowed clients to invest in the markets while protecting their principal, or getting leverage, or a combination of the two. It was the first time I had heard about structured notes and derivatives outside of a classroom, and Nicole was more than happy to walk me through it and let me see it all from the inside. Learning about structured notes and how they worked and how creative you could be in putting them together and the components of the deal was thrilling to me. My mind was racing. I ate it up. I wanted to learn everything there was to learn about derivatives, and she encouraged me to do whatever I could while I was there to accomplish that.

"You should go sit down with a derivatives team. Talk to them," she said. Then she took it a step further. She introduced me to some people who worked on the derivatives trading desk. It was like sitting down for face time with the Apollo astronauts if you were interested in NASA, or meeting with movie stars on your first day of acting class. These were the guys who did the work, who were actually out there making this stuff happen and making millions upon millions of dollars for their clients, the firm, and themselves.

Some of this stuff was random, right? I didn't ask to be put on that team. Interns were placed wherever they got placed. So maybe I wouldn't have learned about derivatives if I'd been placed somewhere else, but because of what I was able to learn during that last half of my summer internship at Goldman, I decided: "That's what I want to do."

I made time to sit at the markets coverage desk and soak it all up, and then I made more time to meet with the man in charge, Dave Coquilette. I also met with a number of managing directors (MDs) and even partners at Goldman, but I did it strategically. I thought to myself, *I am not the only intern trying to meet with these people. I can imagine if this really busy person is going to meet with five different people for coffee they might not give any of us their full attention.* So I started organizing the interns myself: "I'm going to meet this person. Do you want to come?" Then I would e-mail the MD or partner and say, "I and three other interns are really interested in learning more about what you do. Do you have thirty minutes to spend with us?"

A lot of people wouldn't do that because they would think, *Oh, I just want to meet this person one-on-one. I don't want some other intern to outshine me in the meeting.* But that was never my attitude. My attitude was, "I'm the one who's taking the initiative to set up the meeting. I'm already standing out just by doing that."

When I got my feedback toward the end of that second half of the summer, the feedback included comments saying, "Julissa is really proactive and helpful and efficient with her time."

I wasn't perfect, of course. I was young. I was green. I still had a lot to learn. And during my time with the all-female-led team, I didn't have to wait until the end of the four weeks to learn where I was coming up short in my attention to detail. I made a mistake on a presentation. It was nothing more than a typo. But it mattered. One of the women on the team sat me down and showed me the mistake herself. "This can't happen again," she said. "You've been so good the whole summer, but people will remember the one mistake you made."

Then she added something. She told me that as women, we are under a microscope. *As women, we get a lot less slack than men do.* There simply wasn't room for mistakes of any kind.

That's a lot of pressure. At a place that's already as pressure filled as Goldman Sachs, that's an *extraordinary* amount of pressure. And the thing that I realized in that moment was that the pressure was even greater for me as a Latina. It really hadn't dawned on me that there weren't very many Latinas in PWM. As hard as I'd worked and as driven as I'd been, if I were going to make it at a place like Goldman Sachs, I had to step it up even more.

That said, my final review was even better than the first. In fact, I was allowed to participate in Goldman's "internal mobility" program, which gave me the opportunity to interview with other divisions within the firm. I was given clearance to come back for

Goldman's "Super Day," when a whole bunch of interviews would be done all at once for new recruits in the securities division.

Once again, I was flying.

I hand wrote thank-you notes to everyone I worked with that summer, including some of the assistants and client advisers whom I probably didn't need to thank but wanted to anyway. I realized the success I'd had and those glowing reviews were not just about me. They were a product of a group effort.

As a rule, Goldman Sachs doesn't make any postinternship offers until September. They make their interns wait it out and sweat. So even though I felt good about where I stood, I wasn't 100 percent positive that I'd get an offer at the end of my stay. I hated that. I wanted to know. I felt such a nervous buzz inside as I went around to say my good-byes to everyone. I tried not to think about it, but those uneasy pangs were torturing me: *What if this is the last time I see these people? What if I don't get an offer? What if I don't get to come back here? Ever?*

The private wealth management division was on the forty-first floor. The fortieth floor was home to alternative investments and the markets coverage group and a bunch of the other teams. Between them was a staircase. After saying good-bye to everyone on forty, including Dave Coquilette, I headed for the stairs. By that time I had already interviewed with everybody on Dave's team. I'd had coffee with them. I'd made the rounds. I'd made my presence known. All I could do was hope and wait until September to get the news I so desperately wanted to hear.

There was all sorts of construction going on that summer, with scaffolding and plastic sheeting blocking the view of the fortieth floor, so I was surprised when I heard Dave's voice behind me. I hadn't seen him coming.

"Julissa!" he said. "Let me walk you out."

"Great!" I said.

Halfway up that staircase, he stopped me. "Julissa, come September, you can expect some good news."

"Oh, that's really wonderful to hear," I said. I realized my smile was all the jumping up and down I needed to do. I could feel it. It was huge. "I really look forward to hearing from you in September," I said.

I did it. I actually did it. His words meant only one thing: I was getting an offer.

I walked out into the streets of Manhattan, feeling the swirl and energy of the bustling streets, ready to go home and to tackle my senior year at UT knowing full well that I would be coming back here the very next year—and coming back to a full-time job at Goldman *effing* Sachs.

When I called my parents to share the good news, it struck me that I had now gone almost three full years without seeing them. Three full years without seeing my mom's face or giving her a hug. Three full years without a moment spent listening to one of those old José Alfredo Jiménez cassette tapes in the car with my dad, and without helping Julio with his homework. *How have three years passed already?*

They knew it was a big deal that I had a job offer, but I wasn't sure they really understood just how big an accomplishment it was to be hired at Goldman Sachs. As much as I didn't want to admit it, our daily lives were becoming worlds away from each other. I tried to stay in touch as much as possible, but there were times when it was so painful to talk to them that I found it easier simply not to talk to them at all. At times, I would go weeks without a conversation with my mom, dad, or Julio.

It seemed as if every new achievement was met with a bitter-sweet taste of how much I had given up, and how much they had given up, just so I could walk down this road. I did my best to push the sad feelings down and instead focus on everything positive that had happened.

I spent a couple of extra weeks in New York City after the internship ended. I had to give up my dorm room, so I crashed on the couch of Jessica and Antonia, whom I'd met through HBSA and who were now living and working in the city.

I stayed that extra time so I could have a few interviews around town. Even though I basically had an offer from Goldman in hand, I still wanted to know what my options were. I wanted to land offers elsewhere if I could, just so I would know without a doubt that the best offer of all was from Goldman. I interviewed at JP Morgan Chase and at UBS and at Lehman Brothers. It was such an amazing thing to be able to say to them, "I don't have an offer from Goldman yet because they don't give offers until September, but the MD told me to expect good news." That made all of my interviews so much better, and I interviewed for almost everything, including investment-banking positions. I knew that I didn't want to be involved in IPOs and mergers and acquisitions, but I took those interviews anyway, and I was asked to come back on their Super Days. At that point, I turned them down. I knew those were spots that I was potentially taking away from one of my fellow SEO colleagues who actually wanted those jobs, and I didn't want to hamper anyone else's chances.

Instead, I went back to UT with the full confidence that I'd be getting a call from the recruiter at Goldman come September.

Back at school at the start of that semester, Robert and I were, for all intents and purposes, in a relationship.

"Well, it's obvious he really, really likes you," friends would say. "Maybe. I don't know. We're just friends!" I'd insist.

One of our mutual professors kept asking me if we were a couple. She invited the two of us over for a group dinner at her home one night, and afterward she told me, "If you two aren't together, you should be."

The two of us threw a barbecue on Labor Day Weekend, and it was one of the most relaxed, fun times I'd had in ages. Just watching Robert dance around with a tequila bottle in his hand while he made our guests margaritas made me feel like there was something special between us.

Then his parents came for parents' weekend, and he invited me to meet them. "You should come with us to dinner," he said. I'd never had anyone to spend parents' weekend with, but I was unsure about taking that step. I still wasn't sure what we really were to each other.

"Come on. You should come," he insisted. So I did. I met his parents and his brother at dinner.

I finally resolved to myself that it didn't matter what we called each other. We were together in our own way, and we were both just rolling with it. *Whatever*, I thought. *I'm not asking questions anymore. This is us.*

What I didn't realize is that stuffing my discomfort over the status of our relationship down deep inside somewhere and not addressing it was just one more stressful situation I was adding to my life. I wouldn't fully grasp the ramifications of that kind of stress until years later. I wasn't able to connect the dots while I was going through it all.

It was mid-September when my phone rang and I saw it was a 212 area code—a call from Manhattan. My stomach filled with butterflies as I pressed the Talk button. It was Jen, the recruiter from Goldman Sachs, officially offering me a job as an analyst in the Markets Coverage Group.

"Thank you so much," I said. Once again, my SEO coaching kicked in. I knew not to accept the offer on the spot. I wanted to be professional—excited, but not overly excited. I was jumping up and down on the inside but all I said was, "Thank you so much. I'll give this some thought. As you know I'm going back for Super Day, but I'm really excited to have gotten this offer and this opportunity. I will be in touch."

As soon as I got off the phone I screamed and jumped up and down with pure joy. Besides my parents, Robert was the only other person I really wanted to tell. He was so excited for me, too—even though I think it made him a little uneasy about not receiving a job offer for himself quite yet. (His would come a couple of weeks later.) We were both just so excited about what this would mean for my future, and—I thought—*our* future.

It wasn't until things quieted down that night that I felt a panic: *Oh. How am I actually going to take this offer? How am I actually going to be able to have this job? I'll have to go through background checks, and I have to go through all of these government agencies just to get my licenses. It's never going to work.*

My stomach stayed tied in a knot for the next couple of days as a deep sense of angst ran over me. I kept thinking, *How the heck am I supposed to do this?*

The only solution I could come up with was to stuff my worries away and put them in a little mental closet. Like always, I retreated back into my little bubble where everything was all right. I moved forward with blind faith that somehow it would all work out. I was sure I'd have to deal with it eventually, but there was nothing I could do about it at the moment. So nothing was exactly what I did.

CHAPTER 14

Big Time

I flew off to New York for Goldman Sachs's Super Day and aced my morning interviews with the structured equity solutions (SES) desk. The SES team structured derivatives for corporate clients rather than private clients, which sounded really exciting to me. My interviews went well enough to get me invited back for the second round of interviews that afternoon, while a bunch of my competitors were sent packing before lunch. I felt I was on my way to having a whole range of choices at my fingertips. I was confident that by day's end I would have my pick of whichever group I wanted to work for at that firm.

That was when my phone rang.

"Hi, Julissa, it's Eric Lane calling."

I couldn't understand why Eric Lane, Goldman Sachs partner, Dave Coquilette's boss, a true Wall Street star—a legend, basically, who became a partner at Goldman by the time he was twenty-seven—was calling me.

"Hi," I said, nervously. "How are you?"

"Good," he said. He wasn't one for small talk. "I heard you're back for Super Day. You should stop by. I really think you should take our offer," he said.

"I can come by right now if you want," I said.

"That'd be great. See you soon." He hung up.

Five minutes later I was in Eric's office, where once again he uttered the phrase "I really think you should take the offer," meaning the offer I'd received from Dave, through the recruiter Jen, over the phone a couple of weeks earlier. I'd wanted to keep my options open, to seem professional, to do what I'd been taught—but at that point, my instincts overrode all of that: if a partner at Goldman Sachs tells you to take the offer from his team, you *take the offer!*

"Yes," I told him right there on the spot. "I'd be thrilled to come work for the markets coverage desk."

"Good," he said.

My head was spinning as I walked out. I like to know how and why things happen, and I started thinking back over the conversations I'd had with Eric. Most had been so short they didn't even amount to real conversations. He was always going, always on the move, always on to the next subject. He was operating at such a high level he didn't have time for chitchat with interns. *Why had he remembered me? Why was he calling me? Why did he want me on his team?* I was sure Jen had asked him to make the call, but still, he wasn't calling every intern to accept their offer.

Then it hit me: This power player of a guy had actually taken time on more than one occasion to talk to me about the Texas Longhorns, and our rivalry with Oklahoma University, and I'd been able to give it right back, talking stats and players like any guy might on a Sunday afternoon. I had done good work. I know I impressed the private wealth advisers I worked for and had great reviews, but everything in life is about the personal connections we make on some level.

Eric Lane moved so quickly that our sports conversations had likely given me more face time with him than any other intern had received, and the thought of that made me smile. That wasn't anything I'd learned from SEO. It wasn't a ploy or a strategy for me. It was as natural for me as breathing. I talked sports with the guys on the trading desk, too. I talked sports with anyone who cared to listen! Sports had always been my way in—the unifier that brought everyone together—and I was pretty sure that one simple thing had helped me out in the biggest career move of my life.

As I stepped out into the sunshine in the city where dreams are made, I shook my head and smiled. I picked up my phone and shared the news with Robert. Then I bought a calling card and dialed my parents in Taxco to share the good news with them—knowing that as soon as the school year was over, I'd be starting a job with a salary that I was pretty sure was more than they'd managed to take home in profits since back at the height of my mom's silver-trade success in the mid-1980s. And I'd be doing it from an air-conditioned office in New York City.

As pumped as I was about everything when I got back to UT, my body began telling me something was wrong. I wasn't feeling as good physically as I was in my heart and mind.

I'd developed some back pain during my freshman year. I was pretty physically fit and I certainly wasn't getting old, so I didn't understand why it was happening, especially after I'd closed up the funnel cake stand. The pain actually started to grow worse after I took the job at the call center and got behind a desk, and it continued to plague me all the way through my internships. I went to see a chiropractor, and I tried making all of the ergonomic adjustments that everyone tells you to make when you're working at a desk and typing all day, but nothing seemed to help. When I got back from New York after landing the position at Goldman, new symptoms started to pop up, too. I had joint pain all over. I seemed to get tired easily.

Robert kept bugging me to see a doctor, but I was worried. One, I was afraid there might be something serious going on. Two, I was always nervous walking into a situation that might require me to show some form of ID.

It was getting harder and harder to hide my secret from Robert, too. He didn't understand why I kept working so hard to pay for tuition instead of just getting a student loan and enjoying our senior year together. It drove him nuts that I didn't have a better phone plan. "Sprint sucks!" he said. But Sprint had given me a phone plan without a social security number, and I remain a loyal customer because of it. He wanted to know why I drove so slowly and why I was so overly paranoid every time there was a cop behind us on the road. Other friends just thought I was kind of a square, but Robert was with me all the time. With him, my excuses and cover-ups felt more like lies. Well, they *were* lies.

One night after a three-hour study session, I got a craving for Jim's Tacos. "That sounds like exactly what we need right now," Robert said. We were both pretty sure there was a Jim's on IH-35 right outside of Austin. We hopped into his sporty red car and drove. I stared at him. He had one hand on the wheel and one on the stick shift and he looked so sexy. I realized how in love with him I truly was. We drove and drove until finally we found the Jim's in San Antonio, over an hour away. It was worth it. We ate tacos, drank sweet tea, laughed and made plans for our new lives in New York.

On the way back to Austin we got stuck in bumper-to-bumper traffic thanks to the never-ending construction on that freeway. We were stuck in a car with no place else to go. As we sat in that little private bubble, I finally felt inspired to face the facts. Robert was my best friend. He had just driven me an hour to eat tacos and even then refused to let me pay. I'd met his family. We were both set to move to New York City to start our lives after college. If there was anyone in the world I should be able to talk to about how terrified I was that I might get deported for using fake papers, or how much I missed my family, or that I was tired of all the tiny little lies I had to tell, it was *him*. The parking lot incident seemed so far away. *I can trust him now*, I thought. After two years of friendship, his sad eyes told me again and again: *I can trust him.*

So I took a deep breath and told him everything. I told him my parents had brought me to live in San Antonio when I was eleven, and that my visa had expired when I was fourteen, which sent me into a state of limbo. I told him about purchasing fake papers from a strange woman in town. I told him how I applied to the internship with those same fake documents. I explained all of the weird things I did: why I never went on spring break, why I drove so slowly, and more.

"I thought that might be the reason," he said.

"What do you mean?"

"All of that stuff. I thought there had to be a reason, you know? And with your family not being around and everything else, I wondered. That's all."

I had always been sure I had hidden my secret perfectly. If Robert guessed what my secret was, perhaps other people suspected it as well. I needed to do a better job of hiding it. I made a mental note to work harder to keep my secret under even tighter wraps than I'd kept it all along.

As we sat there staring at a sea of red taillights, I told him about of all the Christmases and birthdays I had spent alone. I told him about my little brother, and how much I missed him. I told him how much I missed my grandmother. I told him how terrified I was that at some point this could all just end—that everything I'd worked so hard to achieve could be taken from me.

That's when Robert took my hand, kissed it, and put it on the stick shift under his. "Don't worry," he said. "We're in this together."

We drove the rest of the way home with our hands intertwined. He never let go. He had told me that we were in it together, and I believed him.

For weeks, I'd been going back and forth between feeling ecstatic about my future life in New York, and agonizing about whether or not I should *really* move forward with the offer from Goldman. It was one thing to verbally accept the offer, but once the background check paperwork came in the mail, it felt like a different story. If I took the offer, I'd be breaking the law *again*. If I didn't take the offer, I'd be giving up on everything I, and my parents, had ever worked for. I wasn't afraid because I thought I was doing something wrong. I had earned that offer. I *was* afraid of getting caught or having to live with the embarrassment of the Goldman recruiter telling me that I didn't pass the background check.

I sought the advice of a lawyer who told me—not as a lawyer, but more as a mother—"If you don't at least try, you'll regret it for the rest of your life."

My back pain and migraines became unbearable as the second semester moved along. I couldn't take it anymore and I finally went to see a doctor. He listened to my symptoms. He ran all sorts of blood tests, and he told me I was suffering from fibromyalgia. He explained that the widespread musculoskeletal pain, my occasional migraine headaches, my trouble sleeping, were all symptoms. He also told me that there wasn't any known cause, and there wasn't any known cure. It was something that tended to happen more in women than men, but he couldn't explain why or how. He said I could take medicine to reduce the symptoms—pharmacological Band-Aids, basically—but that otherwise I basically had to learn to live with it. He also told me I should see a therapist. *A therapist?* I thought. *I am not some crazy person.* In my culture, we didn't see shrinks; we just sucked it up and buried our emotions. Shrinks were for rich people with rich-people problems.

"Oh, and try to get more rest. Try to relax and de-stress. That might help," he added, as if that were even a remote possibility for a Latina woman headed for a career on Wall Street.

The diagnosis didn't feel right to me. I worried that there was something more going on, and my worrying probably caused me to feel more stress than ever. Then one day Ade, whom I'd known since back in my Greek and Latin Club days, told me, "No *real* doctor would ever make that diagnosis." *So maybe I just need to wait this out,* I thought. *Maybe a real doctor in New York City will be able to get to the bottom of it.* After all, New York was home to some of the finest hospitals and doctors in the world. I'd have access to all of that once I was there. So in the meantime I resolved myself to do my best to suck it up and get on with my life.

Before I knew it, graduation day was upon us. I graduated cum laude from UT, one of the top five business schools in the whole country. *Me.* A Mexican immigrant. The youngest daughter of Luisa and Julio Arce. I had no idea if any other students in my graduating class were undocumented. I had no connection to any sort of support group or networking organization for people in my situation. I had only kept up with immigration policies from the sidelines. I was embarrassed by the fact that I wasn't showing more support to those who were fighting for my rights, but more than being embarrassed, I was afraid to come out as an undocumented immigrant.

I had good friends, I had Robert, I had HBSA and SEO and was about to become a part of the Goldman Sachs family, too. Yet, in many ways, I was entirely alone. I felt as if I knew no one in the world who could really validate my feelings of angst and panic. I was a young woman who wasn't supposed to be here but who'd somehow managed to overcome that obstacle and make the most of the opportunity. I was one of the very first students anywhere to benefit from the passing of a bill in Texas that allowed me to pursue my dreams. I would imagine the legislators who passed that bill could have gotten a lot of mileage out of showing off a bright young graduate who benefited from their good work—especially a graduate who had done so well. I should have been a gold star in their political careers. Rick Perry, who signed HB 1403 into law, who supported it during his 2012 presidential bid, who posed for a picture with me as I received the Texas Conference for Women Scholarship, should have been thrilled to stand with me. But in a post-9/11 world full of anti-immigrant rhetoric, that simply wasn't to be.

Since my job in New York wouldn't start until the end of the summer, I moved in with my sister in San Antonio for a few weeks after school was out. Robert was also from San Antonio, and we spent a lot of time together and with his family. We took a long-weekend vacation together with a few of his friends down in Corpus Christi. I even spent the night at his parents' house a bunch of times.

"This is weird," I said as he closed the door to his bedroom. "Don't your parents care? My parents would never allow this!"

"No, they're fine," he said.

Not that his parents had anything to worry about. We still

weren't sleeping together. I wanted to, but he repeatedly told me he was saving himself for when he got married.

"Okay," I said, and the strangeness of our relationship continued.

We always seemed to be surrounded by other people during those early weeks of summer, be it family or friends. It was fun playing basketball and hanging out, but I was really longing for some alone time with him, and I started to get really excited about our planned trip to New York. To save some money on airfare, we decided to rent a Penske truck and make the move ourselves. We were planning to take our time and make a real road trip out of it. I was thrilled at the prospect of traveling with him in the cab of that bright yellow truck, stopping at random restaurants, seeing the sights along the way.

Then all of a sudden at the last minute, Robert offered to take some of his friend's furniture in our truck. And apparently, it was urgent for the furniture to get to New York. The whole trip got pushed up and shortened. And then Robert's roommate wound up making the trip with us, too. We drove almost straight through without stopping. No back roads. No retro diners. No sights that couldn't be seen from the highway. Just me and Robert and Mr. Third Wheel. How romantic.

It was a huge disappointment to me, but I did my best to get over it. After all, this was it. This was the big time. We were moving to New York City, and we'd both managed to find apartments in the very same building at 45 Wall Street—directly across from a Trump building and just up the block from the New York Stock Exchange. Right in the heart of everything.

The simple act of walking into the lobby of 45 Wall made me feel like I'd made it. It was all dark wood paneling and marble, with beautiful light fixtures and good-looking people in business suits walking in and out with a rapid, nonstop pace that exists only in Manhattan. There were doormen behind a desk who were there to assist with whatever I needed. And while Robert and I weren't sharing an apartment, it felt amazing to know that we were just an elevator ride away from each other: him on the fourth floor, me on the tenth.

Goldman Sachs had provided me with a signing bonus—a little upfront money to help with the moving costs and settling in. So as soon as I got to the city I decided to update my wardrobe. I had some professional clothing. I'd worn skirt suits to every HBSA meeting starting freshman year, and I stepped it up even more when I became president. But after spending the summer interning at Goldman the year before, I knew I had to buy more heels and collared shirts and just kick it up a notch all-around. As I'd learned through Dale Carnegie and all of my time spent in HBSA: "Dress for the job you want, not the one you have."

I was very conservative at that point. My wardrobe was mostly black skirts and tailored shirts. But being at Goldman showed me just how fashion forward a businesswoman could be. I could wear black dresses, I could wear colors, and I could even wear florals, not that I ever did. But it didn't have to be black all the time. Women at Goldman were *fly*. Their outfits were flawless. It seemed like every one of them wore the most beautiful, red-soled, Christian Louboutins. Those who were married or engaged were blinged out in the most amazing diamonds, too.

There was no way I could bring myself to spend $600 on a pair of shoes. Most of my clothes growing up had come from Goodwill or Target. But I also knew that something from H&M wasn't going to cut it in the Goldman Sachs world. As a first-year analyst, I certainly wasn't on a Saks or Barney's budget, either. Luckily, I found a store that seemed tailor made for me: Club Monaco. I loved everything about that store. It was so well lit, the space so minimalistic, it smelled good, and the salespeople were so incredibly helpful and friendly to me from the moment I stepped through the doors. Almost anything I grabbed off the rack looked nice and professional. It wasn't cheap, but it wasn't so outrageous that I wouldn't be able to buy groceries. If I wanted to, I could splurge on a $150 shirt at that store, and although that still felt like a gigantic leap to take given what I'd been accustomed to all my life, I found that I could do it and feel good about the purchase. After all, I was a Goldman Sachs analyst now. Tyler, one of my SEO friends, and I joked that we were spending based on the present value of our future earnings. Not quite the smartest way to think, but it made sense to us at the time. In a couple of weeks, I'd be walking through the GS doors and, I thought, making bank.

That was when the panic attack hit: sitting in Robert's apartment, just two weeks to go, surrounded by moving boxes and that third-wheel friend, drinking ice-cold beers and watching TV. The pain in my chest, the numbness in my arm, the rush to the hospital, the distinct feeling that I was going to die, the confusion over the diagnosis (Panic attack? *Me?*), and the silent walk back to 45 Wall Street at dawn—all of it swirled into a shocking realization that I in fact had every reason to panic.

My body was finally doing what my mind refused to do: to admit that my life was so incredibly abnormal, that hiding my truth and constantly ignoring the potential consequences of being found out had taken a toll.

CHAPTER 15

Setting Sail

I was barely recovering from the scare and embarrassment of the panic attack when I got a surprise call from Dave Coquilette.

"Eric and I have decided to put you on a different team," he said. "We know that you were really interested in derivatives. Actually, we hired this guy, Ted, to start a derivatives team within private wealth management. I think you'll really like him. I think this will be a great fit."

Derivatives? This sounds interesting. But who is this Ted guy? I thought.

Dave kept talking Ted up, though, and I started to get a little excited: "Goldman doesn't hire people from the outside as managing directors, and we hired him as a managing director. You'll really like him."

I was an intern who'd been hired as a first-year analyst, and this managing director was calling me in advance to convince me that the new position they were putting me in was going to be okay. Realistically, they didn't even need to tell me, let alone check to see how I might feel about the whole thing. By the time we finished that phone call, I was blown away. At what other company would a managing director take the time to do that? At what other company, on Wall Street especially, would a boss show that much care and attention to a junior employee who hadn't even walked through the doors yet? I already had a good feeling about the culture at Goldman while I was an intern, but now I was sure that Goldman was the place where I was supposed to be.

The caring didn't stop there. A week before I was set to start, my new managing director, Ted, took me to lunch. Let me reiterate: I hadn't even started yet, and a newly hired managing director at one of the most powerful financial firms on earth took me to lunch to introduce himself to *me*.

The moment I sat down with Ted, I knew that Dave's assessment was right. We were going to get along just fine. Ted had spent years working in Latin America, and even though he was a white man from Maine, I didn't consider him culturally white. I mean, he called himself El Rey del Mambo (The King of Mambo). When he wasn't making millions for himself and others, he had a passion for salsa dancing. He owned a sailboat and had a passion for the sea, too. He seemed to be a man who loved life and lived it to the fullest, truly enjoying all of the benefits that came along with a successful career in the financial world that provided his fulfillment of the American dream.

Ted spent that lunch reassuring *me* that everything was going to be okay, reassuring *me* that even though I didn't know him and we had never worked together, he thought it would be a great career opportunity for me. The entire team was just him and me, and we'd be working to build a new team, figuring out the best ways to market derivatives to private wealth clients. He made it clear to me that he wanted me to bring ideas to the table. He would be looking for my input and creativity. The best part about the unexpected change was that I would be working directly for him.

First-year analysts don't get to work with a managing director.

Landing a job at Goldman Sachs was the fulfillment of a dream, but the job Ted laid out for me was something far beyond what I'd imagined. I felt that God had led me down a path and bestowed me with gifts far greater than I ever could have expected.

I was so excited to get started that I woke up in a complete panic on my first day of work. There's no other way to put it: I was terrified. All of the new analysts across the firm, from every office around the world, came for training in New York. There were hundreds of us. We all had to trek over to Jersey City that year, to the same building where I'd gone for my initial intern training the prior year. The company had planned to move all their trading floors to that Jersey City building, but the traders revolted and refused to be moved away from lower Manhattan. So now the Jersey building was used mostly for technology and these sorts of training activities while Goldman built a shiny new headquarters at 200 West Street—basically across the street from where the Twin Towers once stood. That state-of-the-art building wouldn't be finished for another six years, and in the meantime, Goldman had offices in a number of buildings in the Wall Street area.

I was glad I had plenty of prior experience figuring out which trains to take and how to get to Jersey City, because my nerves were just plain raw that morning. They gathered us all into one big conference room where we were started on a diet of Goldman Kool-Aid by a senior executive. We were also given a long overview of what to expect during the training seminars that week. At some point they passed out those familiar IRS W-4 forms to everyone in the room: name, address, social security number, and signature. That's all those forms asked for. Simple. Easy. *Terrifying.*

I filled out the form as I listened.

"We'll need photocopies of your government-issued IDs to file with the W-4s, and since there are a lot of you, what we'd like everyone to do is to leave their IDs on the desk. We'll photocopy them while you're at lunch."

My heart sank. I could barely breathe. I pulled out my fake green card and social security card and placed them on top of the W-4 on the table.

On my way to lunch I ducked into a bathroom stall, closed the door, and puked. It took everything I had just to breathe.

You already passed the background check, Julissa. You worked for them all last summer. Get a grip. It's going to be okay. I kept worrying about all of the other new analysts in that room who'd come from other countries. What if my green card looked glaringly fake when held up next to theirs? My mouth was dry. My armpits were soaked. *Thank God for my suit jacket.*

God, please let my documents work, I prayed. I had to believe that God had a plan for me and that this job was still part of His plan. I had to believe no matter how awful I felt. *God, give me peace.* That was my prayer. I know for some people it's hard to believe in God, but it's hard for me *not* to believe in God. Even in times when I've wanted to think that maybe God doesn't exist, I couldn't do it. I always come back to the thought that God has a big plan for my life. It's something I feel. Something I know, deep down. I don't know what God's plan is, but it was clear to me ever since I was a little girl that I was meant for something.

Praying to God in that bathroom stall calmed me down for the time being.

As I came back into the room after lunch, one of the women who'd been checking people in was positioned near my table. She looked right at me. I tried to avoid eye contact but as I walked past her she spoke to me.

"I put your documents under the paper," she said.

"Oh," I said. "Okay. Thank you." I sat back down in my chair and found my green card and my social security card hidden underneath my copy of the W-4 instructions. My panic went into overdrive. *Did she look at them and suspect something and put them under the paper to hide them? Is she going to report me?*

I closed my eyes and took a deep breath and tried to think of another reason why she might have done that. *Maybe she was just telling me because it wasn't right on top of the desk, so I wouldn't think they got lost or something. Or maybe she just didn't want me to stick out, since most people on my row had U.S. passports.*

Everything that happened the rest of that day was a haze. I put my documents back into my purse and tried to just blend into the crowd of suited-up men and pearls-and-heels-wearing women. I could not stop thinking about it. *Did she know? Did she know and just dismiss it? Did she know but then think to herself, "Well, she passed the background check. She interned here last summer. She must be okay"?*

I tried to focus on the many reasons no one had ever questioned my papers before that day. I speak English well. I have good credentials. I went to college in the United States. It made sense that I had a green card because my parents had lived here for a long time, and I must have come here on a student visa and my parents petitioned me in. I knew what to say if anyone questioned me. I knew enough about how the system worked to feel confident about anything except those actual physical documents that I'd been carrying since the latter half of my freshman year at UT.

I also thought about the fact that anyone who questioned a Latina woman about her "papers" in a high-class, highly educated environment like that wouldn't just *seem* racist, but *be* racist. Heck, if he or she were wrong, a person could sue for discrimination.

When no one escorted me out of the building by the end of that first training day, I let myself breathe a big sigh of relief—for about five minutes. On the train ride back to Manhattan, I panicked again. I still had a whole series of license tests to overcome in the next few months in order to allow me to work with clients in the financial industry. I'd read that I would have to get fingerprinted and go through yet *another* background check, and come in with photo ID, which meant using my Mexican passport with no visa.

I just kept reminding myself of the good things that had already happened. I had already passed step after step after step, so each test would just be one more step. I told myself over and over, *It will work out. It will be okay.*

When those panicky feeling arose on any given day, I forced myself to take deep breaths and think about the worst-case scenario. If I got caught, I wasn't going to die. I might get fired, but there was always a chance that they wouldn't report me and I'd be free to get another job—albeit a much less interesting job—somewhere else. Even if they did report me and I did get deported, I had my whole family in Mexico. I had a degree. I would survive. My life wouldn't end. The worst part about deportation would be the ten-year ban on reentering the United States—a policy that I learned had passed during the Clinton years, of all times. That might come close to killing me, I thought, but I was pretty sure I would survive that, too. After all, I'd now survived almost a decade of exile from the country of my birth. Thinking through all of that made my fear a little easier to swallow. *I won't die*, I thought.

I realized that I was one of the fortunate ones. There are thousands of immigrants to this country who aren't so fortunate, who *do* face death if they are deported to more-dangerous countries.

I sailed through training without another tense moment, and one week later I was finally ready to start my new career in earnest. Robert and I had taken the time to map out our routes to work. He and I rode the subway to midtown at different times of day to see how long it would take him to make it to the shining Lehman Brothers headquarters just north of Times Square where he would be working. We also timed the walk from our apartments at 45 Wall Street to One New York Plaza, down on the edge of the East River—the building where I was about to spend more hours per day than I would spend in my own apartment.

I got up that first morning particularly early. Ted had told me that he usually got in at 7:00 a.m., and I wanted to be sure to get there before he did, to really start things off on the right foot. I left my apartment at 6:30 a.m. and power-walked the ten-minute trip in my best heels. (It would take me a few weeks before I realized I could wear flats on the way in and change into heels at my desk.) The sidewalks were still quiet at that hour, and I maneuvered those crooked old streets with ease: making the right on William, bearing left at the crossroads in front of Delmonico's Steak House, a nineteenth-century landmark, passing the original, unmarked, brown-brick Goldman headquarters at 85 Broad Street, in the center of all of that history, and finally making it to my silver skyscraper on the edge of the greatest city in the world. Goldman didn't announce itself with bright electronic signs on the outside of a building the way Lehman Brothers and other firms did. There was no indication on the building that the most powerful financial firm in the country was inside. I liked that. To me, that inconspicuousness was a symbol of strength.

There wasn't much flash on the inside, either, except on certain floors. Clients never visited the fortieth floor where I was about to set up shop with Ted, and even after the previous summer's construction it seemed a little dark and dingy as I stepped out of the elevator into that quiet, still-empty space. The carpet was old. There was nothing flashy about the furnishings whatsoever. The fortieth floor was a place where work got done, period.

I didn't want to come off as the wide-eyed newcomer, but after making that walk and stepping foot in that office, having it all to myself for the first few minutes of the day, I kept thinking, *I can't believe I work at Goldman Sachs. I can't believe I live in New York City. I can't believe this is my life!*

Moments later, other employees started filing off of the elevators. I was welcomed with a steady stream of, "Hey! Welcome back!" and "Good to see you again!" and as soon as Ted arrived, we got to work. When he said we'd be working together, he meant it: he placed me in a seat right next to his, at the head of the long table that we called pods, full of colleagues from other teams, at the front of our little corner of the Goldman Sachs world. Eric Lane, the Goldman partner who insisted I take the offer, sat right behind us. I could literally swivel my chair around and ask him a question. He could get my attention without even raising his voice. In a place like Goldman, where you sit matters, and I couldn't have been placed in a better position.

The PWM division at Goldman isn't the Wall Street you see in movies. I wasn't on a trading floor. But our little corner on the fortieth floor was more of a trading floor than was the polite PWM division on the forty-first floor. We might not be screaming with every tick of the Dow, but I definitely had to learn how to block out the constant noise of ringing phones, hollering, and personal phone calls.

Ted and I started talking about goals and ambitions, about which private wealth advisers were most likely to recommend our products to their clients, and even on that very first day he started to teach me everything he knew about derivatives and more. Even though I arrived at the office before him, it became clear to me that Ted had been up since 5:00 a.m., running on a treadmill while he read the papers. He already knew all the big news stories of the day before he came in. He'd been in touch with international markets and overseas trades that happened while the rest of the world was still asleep. I would have to work extra hard to bring him information he hadn't already read. Yet he didn't wield any of that over me or try to make me feel bad for not being up to speed on everything the way some bosses might. Instead, he spent the whole day teaching me. He took me to lunch. He walked me through everything. Not just about work, either. He taught me never to order sushi on Mondays, which was a pretty big thing for me, because I had never even eaten sushi at all before I moved to New York. (The first time I tried it, I ate a whole mouthful of wasabi, thinking it was avocado.) In the course of the first few days, he started calling me J. Sometimes he called me sweetie pie, too, which for some reason wasn't offensive when he said it. If anyone else had called me sweetie pie, we would have had words. But I trusted Ted, and he quickly became my mentor, not just my boss.

In time, Ted would teach me how to stand up to traders, when to ask for a raise, and all the ins and outs of not only doing the job but turning my job into a successful career. Even in my very first week he taught me to get out of my comfort zone, to interact in a wealthy world, and to dream big.

Ted threw a party on his sailboat on the evening of my third day in the office, and he invited me to come along. I'd never been on a sailboat before. I'd never really seen one in real life—at least not a big boat of that type. It was more like a sailing *yacht*, like you'd see in *Vanity Fair* or an '80s music video. It was the sort of gorgeous piece of floating architecture that celebrities might be seen on at Cannes. There I was, the little girl from Taxco, out on the Hudson River on a yacht full of attractive, well-dressed people with the Statue of Liberty as the backdrop to the most gorgeous sunset ever. The boat had a kitchen on it, and a private chef. With the wind in my hair and a garlicky fragrance wafting from the galley, the wondrous Manhattan skyline bobbed up and down in front of my eyes.

And I started to get seasick.

God, please, no. Don't embarrass me like this. I ducked into the little head down a short flight of stairs and told myself, *I will not puke. You are not doing this. Not here. Not now!* And I didn't. I somehow regained my composure and rejoined the party just in time to see the sun go down on that beautiful, late-summer day.

Stepping from a yacht into my closet-sized apartment was jarring. I realized I had a long way to go before I was really a part of that world. In fact, in the coming weeks I would realize that my "big" $55,000-a-year paycheck wasn't actually big at all. New York City is an expensive place to live, and after taxes, my salary barely covered all of my bills.

Yes, I paid taxes. Like millions of undocumented immigrants in America, I had taxes taken out of my paycheck every single week. Those taxes went to Washington under the social security number I supplied. Where they went from there was up to the government. My taxes, along with $100 billion paid into the social security fund over the last decade by undocumented workers, all went into the system. I, like so many others, knew that I would never see the benefit of those dollars when it came to actually receiving a social security check in my retirement or many other government benefits that citizens and those with legitimate green cards can access. In a way, the U.S. government was basically taking massive amounts of money from millions of undocumented—and therefore unrepresented—people in this country. I wondered sometimes how to reconcile that with the idea of "no taxation without representation," which I'd been taught in my American history classes.

I don't remember exactly when the first letter came from the IRS saying there was a discrepancy with my social security number. I filed my income tax with a number called an ITIN—individual tax identification number—which was different from my fake social. I do remember that the letter said they had also sent a copy to my employer. No matter how hard I was working, or how well things were going, there was always a reminder that I wasn't really supposed to be there, that I didn't really belong among those Wall Street types.

I stuffed that letter in a drawer and did my best to forget it ever existed. I would do the same with subsequent letters year after year. Like so many other things, I ignored it and just hoped for the best. I later realized that these letters weren't necessarily an immigration red flag. Most of the time, "no match letters" go out to people who have misspelled their name, or haven't updated a name change with the Social Security Administration. There wasn't a reason for Goldman to question my immigration status based on these letters.

Even with this prestigious job, I quickly found myself living paycheck to paycheck. I was once again worried about money all the time. My tiny apartment was $1,200 a month, plus utilities. My clothing budget was larger than it had ever been. I was sending money to Mexico to help my family, and within a few weeks I found I could barely keep up. Meanwhile, a lot of my peers seemed to be living the high life in New York City, going out to fancy restaurants and clubs, and having the time of their lives. I wondered what I was doing wrong. I soon discovered that many of my peers in the firm had wealthy parents who were paying their rent for them, leaving them with plenty of discretionary income from their paychecks. Not to mention that those who did or didn't have rich parents had something important that I didn't: credit cards. I couldn't get a credit card even if I wanted to. I was lucky just to have a bank account and a debit card.

I thought about the joke Tyler and I would throw around, that we were spending based on the present value of our future net worth. But to me, it really was just a joke. I simply didn't have the means to prespend against my future income. Looking back on it, it was probably a very good thing.

I also didn't have the time. Two weeks into my new job, Ted and I got hit with a nuclear-size disaster. Before either of us arrived, the Investment Strategy Group, which was the team that made recommendations to all private wealth clients, had recommended that clients put a small percentage, 1 to 2 percent, into short-term structured notes on corn. Trading commodities isn't like trading stocks. It's not as simple as if the price of corn goes up and you are long corn, you win. There are other factors, such as the price of insurance, storage, and transportation. All of that is priced into the future prices of commodities, including corn. A lot of private investors went into those investments on the recommendations of their advisers, but didn't really understand the nuances of how they worked. So when the price of corn took a sharp nosedive, lots of clients panicked—and somehow, the responsibility to sort it all out fell almost entirely on new-guy Ted, which meant it also fell on me.

Suddenly we were tasked with trading millions and millions of dollars in corn notes on a daily basis for hundreds upon hundreds of clients. I had to put together spreadsheets every morning for these incredibly complex trades that I had never worked with before, all while trying to placate the clients themselves, who wouldn't stop calling.

I don't know how, but I didn't make a single mistake on any of those hundreds of orders. I was very professional and reassuring to even the most belligerent clients when they called. I was so well organized about it all that I developed my own system to make the process of making those trades more efficient, which would make it easier for myself and others to deal with this sort of situation in the future. The bosses were impressed with my spreadsheet system.

I was organized and willing to put in the work. Honestly, those were the most stressful, never-ending hours of work I'd ever put in anywhere. I don't even know how I got up every morning, especially with all the pain I was in. But it was all a blessing in disguise. I am positive that the impression I made during that crisis situation validated me in the eyes of Eric and Dave and everyone else who had taken a chance on me. My bosses knew from the start they could count on me when the chips were down. I was sure that my performance in that two-week panic moment was setting me up for a very bright future at Goldman Sachs.

And I could not wait to rush into that future, which I hoped would involve a big raise. Because I was already tired of feeling pinched.

That year, not only could I not fly home to see my family for Christmas because of my secret immigration status, but I couldn't even fly to Texas to spend Thanksgiving with my sister. When Ted asked me why I wasn't leaving the city for that rare long weekend, I told him I simply couldn't spend $700 on a plane ticket.

"Well," he said. "Keep doing what you're doing and one day $700 won't matter to you."

I believed him. I looked ahead to what the future could bring and doubled down in my efforts to get ahead. As always, I believed that if I made enough money I could somehow solve all of my problems.

I knew that getting to the top wouldn't be easy. I saw who the big bosses were at Goldman, and they were all men. White men. White men who had parents and grandparents who had walked those corridors or similar ones before them. I knew from my intern experience how much harder I'd have to work just because I was a woman. I knew by looking around that I'd have to work harder still as one of the only Latina women on the floor.

The hard work didn't faze me. And luckily I didn't experience too much of the Wall Street cutthroat culture. It was there. It existed within Goldman Sachs, but in a lesser way on the PWM floors, and during my first year, I'm pretty sure Ted sheltered me from it. He really took me under his wing. He kept me from the rat race. He gave me special assignments, letting me fly out to Chicago and other cities to meet with clients. Those were unheard-of responsibilities for a first-year analyst, but he told me again and again that he thought I was smart and driven, and that he believed in me. I'm sure there were times when he sent me to meet with clients simply because he had no choice: we didn't have a big team to rely on, and if one of us didn't meet the clients in person, those clients might have slipped through our fingers. But I always rose to the occasion, and we built our client roster faster than anyone at Goldman expected we possibly could. Of course, I was nervous before every single one of those flights. I still only had my Mexican passport to get me through TSA. I didn't have a driver's license, which meant I couldn't rent a car. Every trip to the airport was like a spin at the roulette wheel. But somehow I pulled it off, again and again and again.

As we turned the calendar from 2005 to 2006, the stock market was on fire—and derivatives were the hottest thing going. I could not have asked for a better position at a better time, and I could not have asked for a better boss and mentor.

On Friday nights, lots of analysts and interns and traders would gather on Stone Street, a cobblestone pedestrian way filled with a dozen or so bars and restaurants, all lined up side by side on both sides of the street with a sea of outdoor seating in between. It was

a place where single women came to seek moneyed Wall Street future husbands in the bars (a phenomenon we Wall Street women
would sit back and watch and laugh at). It was also a place where
you could grab a fantastic slice of pizza from Adrienne's and throw
back a few beers to blow off a little steam at the end of the week.
Even there I had to be careful. If I were carded, the only photo ID
I had was my Mexican passport. If they asked me for ID at the
table, I'd usually say something like, "Oh, I lost my license! Sorry,"
and other people at the table would vouch for me and I'd wind
up getting a drink anyway. Or I'd go into the bar, away from anyone who knew me, and order a drink with my passport in hand.
It wasn't easy; I wanted to be a part of the culture, and I definitely
needed to blow off a little steam by the end of those weeks.

I rarely ever worked fewer than eighty hours a week in that first
year. And just as I did when I was an intern, I would stay until my
bosses were gone. I would make myself useful. I wanted everyone
on the floor to know that I worked hard and accomplished a lot.
On most of those late nights I would take advantage of a late
dinner courtesy of the company (which saved on my food bills at
home), and sometimes I would take advantage of a late-night car
service, too, so I wouldn't have to walk alone at eleven or twelve
o'clock at night. It was only a three-minute ride, but still it made
me feel important.

Robert worked even longer hours than I did as an investment
banker. On rare weeknights, we'd drink a couple of beers on the
couch in front of the TV. That was as luxurious an indulgence
as we could muster. We were both exhausted all the time as we
got our footing in the big city. I couldn't tell sometimes whether
my level of exhaustion was normal, or something related to the
fibromyalgia or whatever it was that was still plaguing me. I managed to see some "real" doctors and chiropractors in New York, but

none of them seemed to be able to find an answer, either—to my back pain, fatigue, joint pain, or the increasing stomach problems and headaches that seemed to be getting worse week after week.

"Eventually you'll find the right doctors and they'll help you feel better," Robert told me. It was good to have his reassurance, and in many ways, he seemed to be more by my side than ever.

We went shopping together one day, and I'll never forget the look on his face when I tried on one particularly nice shirt. It cost over a hundred dollars. But it hugged me just right and the color was really flattering, and he insisted: "Julissa! You *have* to get that shirt!"

That night we went out with some friends. Robert didn't really dance, but that night he danced with me. I wore the turquoise shirt he insisted I buy. We went back to my place, and he stayed over like he had on dozens of other occasions. We started kissing instead of just rolling over and passing out from exhaustion. It wasn't long before I could tell by the way he looked at me that this was finally it. We were finally going to have sex.

"Are you sure?" I whispered.

"Yeah," he said.

"But I thought you wanted to wait until you were married," I said.

"Nah," he said with a sexy shy smile. "What I said was I wanted to wait until I was *with* the girl I want to marry."

Oh my God, I thought. *He wants to marry me.*

CHAPTER 16

Seasons of Change

My dreams of marrying Robert soon faded. Our relationship went back to being as strange as it always was, and totally undefined. We would go from zero to sixty and then back to zero all in a week's time. And yet I couldn't let go of him. He provided the perfect distraction to the reality of my undocumented status, and work provided the perfect distraction from my relationship with Robert.

It wasn't uncommon for me to be in the office until 2:00 a.m. in that first year. If I was in the office until two, that usually meant Ted was there until 1:45. That man was a relentlessly hard worker, and he inspired me to want to work just as hard. Most senior people on Wall Street believe that crap rolls downhill. PowerPoint presentations are crap work to be done by an analyst, but Ted saw it differently. We were a team, and putting together a PowerPoint presentation every once in a while was not beneath him. Ted empowered me to feel, and therefore to think, bigger than an analyst. I did research for clients and worked with the traders in the securities division to come up with new ways for clients to invest in the markets. I took even the oddest request by a client seriously; we were trying to build a business, and no request was too small.

The corn-note disaster never really left us, and for years clients and their advisers would bring it up as a reason not to invest with us. It was an uphill battle to establish ourselves as a reputable, trustworthy team, but we were relentless.

Ted believed strongly in Goldman's top business principle: Our clients' interests always come first. As such, he was very tough on the traders. The traders worked for the firm; we worked for the client. He started every conversation from the point of view of the client: *How am I going to get screwed?* I listened intently to every phone conversation, took notes, and asked questions. I started to emulate Ted, asking the same questions he asked the traders, taking on the same attitude. The private wealth advisers began to recognize we were on their side. But the attitude of mistrust didn't leave us with the best relationships with our own colleagues in the securities division. Ted was a managing director, and *he* could be demanding. I was a first year analyst, a *female* first-year analyst. We could use the exact same words, in the exact same tone, and they did not have the same effect.

Ted once told me: "Let me be the hardball, because you still have to work with the traders. You don't want to burn any bridges. You want to have a good relationship with them. So let me be the hardball, and then it's my fault, not yours."

I didn't listen to Ted's advice quite soon enough.

There was a managing director named Paul Humphreys, a self-described ginger, from the London office. We didn't get off on the right foot after I rubbed him the wrong way with my many questions about the pricing of a trade. He gave me the benefit of the doubt and suggested I come spend some time in the London office to meet him and his team. I immediately said, "Yes!" and then thought, *Oh no, I can't go to London.*

My fake papers were good enough to get me to Goldman Sachs, but they would not be good enough to get me through customs at the airport. I stalled, coming up with excuse after excuse, week after week, until the opportunity faded. I know that was a move that hurt my career, and my relationship with Paul was never quite fixed.

I brushed it off and kept soaking everything in, making my way up the steep learning curve. The pure physical exhaustion of working such long hours made me doubt that I could keep going. If it wasn't for Ted's mentorship and understanding I might not have made it.

One morning, I missed my alarm clock and when I finally opened my eyes and looked at the clock it was already 7:00 a.m. "Crap!" I yelled, flying out of bed and rushing to work more disheveled than I'd ever looked.

I debated the whole run over whether to apologize for being late or just walk in and pretend like nothing had happened. Ultimately, I decided that it was better not to bring extra attention to the fact that I was late. I sat down next to Ted and started going through e-mails. A couple of hours went by. *Phew, Ted didn't notice.* Then Ted glanced over at me and said, "Was it at least a good night?"

"I'm so sorry I was late this morning. It won't happen again."

"J, it's okay to be out late with the boys, but you have to come in with the men the next morning." That was it. He didn't need to say more. I got it.

I could barely keep up with work, but Ted was not only trying to build a business within Goldman, he was also the chairman of an organization called Change for Kids. Change for Kids provided after-school music programs to low-income schoolchildren. They had a series of private concerts and charity fund-raisers, and Ted would often invite me to come along.

My worlds finally collided when Ted invited Robert and me to join his birthday celebration. We celebrated by watching a Paul

McCartney concert from Goldman Sachs's private box at Madison Square Garden. Ted's wife was there, and a few friends, and it was just an incredible, luxurious evening that was far above my pay scale.

I had been so happy about Robert meeting my boss, but as was so often the case, important relationship milestones meant very little in our roller-coaster relationship. Robert worked every weekend. I sometimes managed to get Sundays to myself, and one day he asked me if I wouldn't mind taking his laundry out of the dryer and up to his apartment for him. I said, "Sure." I actually liked doing things like that. I liked to cook for Robert. I liked it when he did the dishes. There was something wonderful about the normalcy of those moments that made the nonnormal part of my life fade further into the background.

I decided I'd do Robert an even bigger favor that day: I would fold his clothes and put them away for him. I thought he'd appreciate it. I opened one of his dresser drawers and saw a collection of letters. They were from a woman. *In Indiana.* I couldn't help myself. I had to look. I took one out. It wasn't just *a* woman. It was *the* woman—the girl he'd mentioned one time that was "sort of" his girlfriend. The girl I'd managed to let myself forget about before it all came flooding back at that very moment.

I started reading. The letters weren't just casual correspondence between friends. They were serious. They made Robert sound less like a distant former boyfriend and more like a husband.

I sat on the edge of the bed, and I kept reading. I read them all. My jaw dropped farther with every line. *Oh my God.* In one of the letters, this girl talked about buying a house in Indiana—she'd finally decided she was never moving to New York.

This girl had been planning to move to New York?

I couldn't understand it. I didn't understand how I could have let myself be so delusional.

I confronted Robert and, of course, he got mad at me for going through his things. He tried to deflect it. He tried to change the subject. He tried to tell me those letters were from a while ago and it wasn't like that now. He tried to tell me all sorts of things and I just wasn't having any of it. I told him I didn't want to talk to him ever again.

Then I called the girl in Indiana.

She was almost as shocked as I was.

"Robert told me you were just a friend," she said. "He told me that once in college you guys kissed and he was really grossed out by it."

The conversation went downhill from there. I took jabs at her; she took more at me. Even then, I still felt like I was incapable of walking away from him. I felt incapable of not having Robert in my life. He was the only person in my life now who knew my secrets. He was the only person in my life who knew everything.

For weeks, I cried every night in my apartment. There were times when I had to step away from my desk to cry in the women's bathroom at Goldman Sachs, and then come back as though nothing was wrong. I turned to a friend named Jeff, whom I'd known since college and who lived in the city now; he became my shoulder to cry on. He was such a good guy, and I was glad to have Jeff when at times I felt like I had no one else.

I never talked to Ted about any of my relationship problems, but it wasn't long after that when he noticed that I wasn't myself.

"Are you okay? What's going on?" he asked me.

"Oh, nothing. Robert's a cheater," I said.

We went for a short walk and Ted said, "Forget him! You are so great. It's his loss."

That same afternoon, the phone rang at our desk and Ted picked it up himself.

"Goldman Sachs," he said. (He did that often.)

"Hi, Ted. It's Robert!" I could hear Robert's voice through the phone. "Is Julissa free?"

"No," Ted told him. He just wasn't having it. "She won't be available." He hung up on him! Ted had my back.

In the middle of it all, I started hearing rumors about an expansion in the London office. I got nervous. When I heard chatter about the possibility of Ted being tapped to head up that expansion, I was filled with dread. And one day, after an out-of-office meeting somewhere, when I felt like my always forthcoming and open boss was holding something back from me, I decided to push and simply ask the question.

The two of us were in the backseat of a black car on the FDR highway, traveling south along the East River toward the office. He was stuck on a phone call for most of the ride, but when he finally got off the phone, I said, "Ted, can I ask you a question? Are you moving to London?"

He hesitated for a second, and that was all it took for me to know the answer.

"Well, it's not decided yet. It's not for sure," he said.

"You're going to London," I said flatly.

I was so upset about it, for a million different reasons. First of all, I didn't want to lose him as my boss and mentor. Second, there was a good possibility that when he went he would ask me to join him—and I knew I would have to say no. I would have to turn down an amazing opportunity because I wouldn't be able to get a work permit to work in London with my Mexican passport with no visa, or with my fake U.S. papers. At Goldman, international experience can be pivotal in someone's career. I was furious that I couldn't pursue the opportunity. I was equally crushed by the fact that I didn't have Robert anymore. He would have been the only person who really understood my dilemma. As much as I hated him for lying about Miss Indiana, I also missed him desperately.

Ted and I had finally started to make inroads with a number of private wealth advisers, and there simply were not enough hours in the day to keep up. We needed to expand our little two-person team. We made an offer to a man named Raphael, a Brazilian guy, and I was immediately wary. Not because we didn't need the help, but because Raphael was being hired as a vice president. I was afraid Raphael would see me as just a first-year analyst and treat me as one.

When Raphael came in to sit for interviews, I grilled him. I asked him all sorts of technical questions about derivatives, just to prove that I knew more than might be assumed by my title.

Raphael got the job, and he turned out to be a really amazing friend, colleague, and mentor. We're still friends to this day. But he later told me, "Julissa, you were the toughest interview I had that entire day!"

Shortly after Raphael was hired, Ted's transfer was confirmed. There was good news. Ted would still be our boss. He would still head up our team from London. But I worried about how long that would last.

Things had been going so well, I just didn't want them to change. When they rearranged the tables and moved me from my spot within earshot of Eric Lane, I threw a fit. It made no sense to me that I wouldn't be sitting next to Raphael the way I sat next to Ted, and it felt like a demotion to me. I knew I needed to get a grip. Change is inevitable. I had to adapt.

Months had gone by and I hadn't spoken to Robert. Then he called me out of the blue. He told me the relationship with Miss Indiana was over, and in my desperation I went back to him. It was just like before. It was awkward. I never knew where I stood. I felt I couldn't lose him. When things got really bad, I tried dating someone else for a while, but I never allowed that relationship to get close. I never let that other person in. I certainly didn't tell him I was in the country illegally. So I wound up going back once more to the only place I thought was safe: Robert's arms.

He had moved to the Upper West Side by then. I was firm. I told him we needed to date and actually call it dating, and he agreed. We did that for about a week. He seemed really into it. In fact, one day he called me up and declared his love for me, fully, like he'd never declared it before. A few weeks later, we were back to being distant. I'd had it; I told him to never call me again.

Then the phone rang on New Year's Day. I picked up.

I was so frustrated by the conversation that I had to see him in person. I ran downstairs, jumped into a cab, and went all the way up to his apartment. The doorman recognized me by that point and I walked right into the elevator. I knocked and there was no answer. I turned the doorknob and the door was open. I saw Robert's roommate, Mr. Third Wheel, sleeping in his bedroom.

I walked into Robert's room. He wasn't there. I noticed a cute stuffed-animal puppy dog sitting on top of his dresser. It had a pink ribbon. It was a gift from Victoria's Secret. I got excited thinking he'd picked up a little something for me. Then I saw the note underneath that stuffed puppy. A note from Robert—to some other woman. I looked around the room and finally saw with my eyes wide open: his closet was open, and in it I saw another woman's clothes.

I thought I was going to die. I could not believe how much it hurt. I felt so stupid. I wanted to tear the room apart and throw everything he had out the window and onto the street below. But I stopped myself. I couldn't. *He's not worth it*, I thought. I couldn't risk his roommate or anyone else calling the police on me in my broken-hearted moment of insanity. I had to be the bigger person, even though I really didn't want to be. I wanted to be angry and let him see the true meaning of a woman scorned. But I had to stay on the straight and narrow. I did not have the leeway to act out emotionally like normal people do when they're hurt more than they ever imagined anyone could hurt them. My immigration status dictated every aspect of my life, even how I should react to a shattered heart. Not having documents robbed me of my ability to feel whatever it was I needed to feel that night.

I looked at the note again and rifled through his things. I found the woman's full name—and her phone number. I stormed out. I got into a cab and headed toward Jessica's apartment, my college friend from HBSA, dialing Robert on the way.

"Who is this girl!" I screamed into his voice mail.

I called again and again and again until he finally called back.

He tried to get me to calm down.

"No," I said. "Who is she, Robert? Forget it. I've got her number. I'm going to call her right now and get the truth!"

Then he said the one thing that I could not imagine anyone, let alone the man I loved and who had declared his love for me, ever saying.

"If you call her," he said, "I'll call INS."

I fell silent. I went numb. I realized he didn't care about me. Maybe he never cared about me. I realized that maybe he wasn't a virgin all that time he swore he was saving himself for marriage. Maybe everything he'd ever said was a lie. He had threatened my very life. With one phone call he could have ruined me. He was willing to destroy me, entirely, to protect what he really wanted: a woman who wasn't me.

I felt ashamed that it took Robert's saying something that disgustingly awful for me to finally get a grip, to realize how wrong that relationship was, and that it was time to move on with my life.

As the snow-covered streets of New York City blurred through the back window of that cab, my anger and hatred over all of Robert's lying and cheating drained from my body through a hole somewhere in the bottom of my soul.

For years I would question why I had held on so long, why I gave him the benefit of the doubt, even after I found out he'd been living a lie and essentially leading a double life behind my back.

Yet as much as it hurt, even in that moment, even as I rode in the back of that cab in the blurry moments of the blow, I felt something unexpected: a little glimmer of happiness.

I was finally free.

CHAPTER 17

Concrete Jungle

Hi, Ted, how are you?" I said.

Seeing his international number pop on my cell phone on a Saturday was a surprise. And, fittingly enough, he had a surprise in store for me.

"Hey, I just wanted to give you a heads-up that Kate from the securities division is coming over to our team," he said.

"What?"

I knew Kate. In the tense divide between private wealth management and the securities division at Goldman, I thought of her as one of *them*. Not one of *us*.

"Is she going to be my new boss?"

"No, no," Ted assured me. "I'll still be the boss here in London. She'll just be joining the team."

It had been less than a year since the last transition, so I knew that Ted was just trying to make me feel at ease. I was grateful that he was still looking out for me from the other side of the pond. I knew he didn't need to do that. I was still just an analyst. It was amazing of him to give me a heads-up.

Kate was maybe eight years older than me, with supermodel looks and a killer wardrobe, and I was totally intimidated by the power-woman attitude she displayed. I didn't trust her, and I think she could probably read that on my face the moment she stepped her Prada heels on the fortieth floor. Everything in me told me that she was still a part of the other team.

She made it clear that PowerPoint presentations were done by analysts. I let her know that Ted (who was *her* boss now) did his own PowerPoint presentations. I was a total witch. I felt bad about being so unwelcoming, especially because she was a woman. I didn't want to be one of those women that see other women as threats instead of allies.

Less than two weeks in she said to me, "Hey, we should go to the spa this weekend."

I decided to give her a chance. "Okay. I've never been to a spa before," I said. We made plans for a Saturday—and then she showed up an hour late.

I was furious.

One part of Goldman culture that bothered me immensely was that our meetings never, ever started on time. One of the ways executives showed their seniority and rank was by being the last person to show up to a meeting. The unspoken rule was that the last person in was the most important person—the person without whom the meeting could not start. So showing up late wasn't an accident. She was sending me a signal: "I want us to be friends, but don't forget who's boss."

All I kept thinking was, *Are you kidding me? I'm sitting here for an hour on my Saturday? This is not going to go well. At all.*

The changes and pressures of my office and personal life were so all-consuming that I often went weeks without worrying or even thinking for one second about my immigration status. Then something would come up that would throw it right back in my face, and the panicked feelings would overwhelm me all over again.

I wanted to get whatever edge I could to advance my career, and one way to do that was to become a CFA. The CFA (Chartered Financial Analyst) is a highly regarded designation in the financial world that takes a minimum of two and a half years to obtain. It takes a series of three six-hour exams. Level 1 is offered twice a year, while levels 2 and 3 are offered only once a year in June. The odds of passing the tests are incredibly low: 30–40 percent for level 1, 30–45 percent for level 2, and 50 percent for level 3. So getting your CFA designation is really a game of endurance: How long can you maintain the discipline it takes to study for all those months leading up to the exam?

The exams weren't cheap, either. I knew that Goldman Sachs would pay the nearly $2,000 in test fees and study materials, but only if I passed the exam. If I failed, I would be out $2,000 on top of the countless hours spent studying. It was hard to imagine when I would find the time to study when I was already working eighty-hour weeks.

My biggest worry about the exam, though, wasn't the difficulty of the test, or the weekends I would give up to study for the test, or the money I would lose if I failed. What really scared me about the test was my ID. The CFA website clearly stated a government-issued photo ID was necessary on the day of the exam, and I had no clue if my Mexican passport would suffice.

A couple of good friends from my analyst class signed up right away in our first year, and I knew in my heart that if I didn't sign up, I would fall behind in my career. But what if I showed up and the CFA staff didn't accept my Mexican passport as ID? What would I tell Kate and Ted? The worst-case scenario, as I imagined it, was that my cover would be blown; the CFA would contact

Goldman and tell them I was using a Mexican passport without a visa. But the thought of my friends from work witnessing the whole thing go down was almost as frightening.

I decided I couldn't do it. I couldn't risk blowing my cover, even if it meant falling behind. When people asked why I didn't sign up, I simply said, "I'm working too much." The statement was true enough. And part of me thought that maybe I could get away without it, since I was building great relationships with our clients.

Finally, in early 2007, with Ted in London, Raphael on his way out, and Kate on her way in, knowing that two of my good friends had passed Level 1 and moved on to Level 2, I decided I had no choice but to sign up for the test. I had to or I might not be on the fast track anymore. So I nervously filled out the registration form, bought the books, and began months of weekend study. My favorite place to study was Financier, a French pastry shop not far from my apartment. I woke up at 7:00 a.m. every Saturday and walked straight there. I ate a croque madame for breakfast while I dove into my books straight through noon. Then I'd take a short lunch break and go right back to studying until 4:00 or 5:00 p.m.

I kept up that routine straight through early June, gaining ten pounds in the process, which only exacerbated my already terrible back and joint pain.

I took two days off for some last-minute cramming just before the test, and as I picked up my bag to leave work on that Wednesday, everyone wished me luck, including Kate. All I kept thinking was how much I needed it—not because of the content of the test, but because of my passport situation.

At home I knelt down and prayed about it more than once, but the worry never left me. In between studying I tried working out, but my stomach still turned. So I ate some cake. I drank some wine. Nothing worked. I had no one to talk to, no one to share it with, no one who understood or could simply allow me to vent in order to calm myself down. I sat in my apartment wishing Robert was back in my life. I hated that I still missed him. I hated that I was struggling to start a new relationship with someone else because I couldn't let anyone get too close and couldn't open up about my secret. How long did I need to keep my secret before I could trust a man with it? And how could he trust *me* once I confessed that I had been hiding something so important from him?

On the night before the exam, I kept staring at the clock as the hours ticked by, wondering if everything I'd worked for might just come to a screeching halt the next morning.

Outside of the test site, I said another prayer: "God, please be with me." Then I stepped inside and put on the smiling face that had so often seen me through.

"Good morning!" I said, cheery as can be to the group of nameless individuals behind a folding table who held my life in their hands. "How are you? I don't know how you deal with all these people!"

It's amazing to think just how much my life depended on the fragility of cordial small talk. Setting people at ease, seeming familiar to them, fitting in—lessons learned in *How to Win Friends and Influence People* were truly like a compass for me.

I didn't want to make eye contact. I wanted to disappear into the crowd. I held my passport, test ticket, and calculator together in my hand and extended it forward. Someone took them. I was so nervous that to this day I cannot remember if I gave my passport to a man or a woman. I looked down, trying to hold myself as anonymously as possible. I noticed a long sheet of paper with names on it. Someone made a checkmark. My heart raced. They handed my things back to me. I was too afraid to move. A voice said, "You're all set."

"Thanks," I said finally, smiling and moving away as quickly as I could. It wasn't until I was a good ten feet from the table that my hands started shaking. I had to take deep breaths to calm down. As I stepped through the door and found a seat, I prayed again in silence: *Thank you, God.*

It would be a few weeks before the results came in, and results day was always a big day around Goldman. Everyone who took the test knew that date was coming. My girlfriend, Erin, who had passed Level 1 on her first try and was waiting for her Level 2 results that same day, planned a results-day outing so everyone who had taken the test could either celebrate or drown their sorrows.

I spent most of that workday hitting Refresh on the CFA website every few minutes. I was so anxious. Every time I refreshed the page it came back looking exactly, frustratingly, the same. Over and over and over, until finally I hit Refresh and the results popped up and I saw the word I wanted to see: *passed.*

"Yes!" I whisper-shouted. I e-mailed all of my friends. I ran to Kate's office to tell her the good news, and then I texted Erin one word that said everything: "Celebrating!"

Kate sent an e-mail announcement to my whole team—by that time we had added two more analysts to the team—and the congratulatory e-mails started pouring in. I was so happy.

Erin texted me back: "Me too!" she wrote. "Woohoo! Table reserved. See you on Stone Street at 5!"

It was a perfect summer day to sit outside, drink, and celebrate. I could finally rejoice with my friends, basking in the fact that, just like them, I had passed that incredibly difficult exam on the first try. I wanted to sprint from the building and start drinking with them the moment the clock struck five. But the thought of pulling out my Mexican passport at a bar in front of my colleagues cast as big a shadow as ever. So I stayed behind at work, hoping that by the time I showed up everyone would be drunk, or maybe the waitress wouldn't bother to ask for my ID. It was nearly 7:00 p.m. by the time I got there. There were a dozen or more people all piled around a picnic table covered with multiple pitchers of beer. Some of the people I'd expected to celebrate with had already gone home, but as soon as I walked up someone handed me a beer and a shot. "Congratulations!" somebody shouted.

"Thank you!" I yelled. "Woooo!" I downed that shot to a round of cheers and swallowed half my beer in one gulp.

No one asked for an ID. I was free to celebrate, and I did. I laughed so hard that I cried. I didn't know everyone at that table, but we quickly bonded over shared stories of missed weekends and long nights after work spent studying. I felt normal—just another drunk Wall Street analyst on Stone Street on a Friday night.

By the time midnight rolled around, the bill was at least thirty inches long and the damage was somewhere around $2,500. I threw my hard-earned dollars on the table just like everyone else, as if I didn't have a care in the world.

I never could have imagined just how much the world was getting ready to throw at me.

The next couple of months offered nothing but validation that I was on the right path. I got my first big raise. I was religious about saving money, something I learned from my grandmother, but I also sent more money home to my parents and splurged a little bit here and there. I made reservations at Michelin-rated restaurants for my friends and me. I treated once or twice for bottle service at Marquee, a celebrity and sports-star haunt on Manhattan's West Side that played host to the hottest party in town every Thursday night. I used my Goldman connections to get impossible reservations. I even upped my Wall Street wardrobe a bit at Kate's request. I wanted to be a badass warrior woman, just like her. One day she looked at the nameless T.J.Maxx bag that I always carried and said, "That is not a purse. You can't go in front of clients with that thing." I didn't take it as an insult. It was actually one of the first moments when I felt like she was on my side. She reminded me of something that I had put on the back burner: I had to dress for the job I wanted, not the one I had. It was time to up the ante. So I went out and spent $300 on a brown leather Cole Haan bag. It wasn't a $5,000 Hermès bag, but at least it wasn't nameless.

I wasn't interested in making money to flaunt a new bag or new shoes. I actually gave much more money that year to charity and to my church. If I had wanted to flaunt anything it would have been that. But the bag was a career expense, and I knew that investing in myself was well worth the price tag. My eyes were fixed on the long-term future. I was ready to earn that CFA. I was ready to get promoted from analyst to associate. I was looking forward to the day when I'd walk in Kate's shoes—although I could never imagine spending $600 on Louboutins.

As Kate settled in, I realized how wrong and unfair I had been. She was smart and she could command any room. She could sell. I started to love going to meetings with her and seeing her in action. I knew I had much to learn from her. She also took the time to get to know me and knew how much I loved sports, an interest we did not share. She received courtside tickets to a Knicks-Celtics game as a gift from a friend and gave them to me. "You'll enjoy these a lot more than I will," she said. She figured out the way to my heart!

With Kate as the new boss, our team was rocking and rolling. The markets were hotter than I'd ever seen them, and the derivatives we were marketing were making more money than ever for our clients. I honestly didn't think anything could stop me at that point.

One night, after coming home from the bars at 3:00 a.m., feeling on top of the world, I got the urge to call home to Mexico. My dad picked up. It was the middle of the night, and he wasn't sleepy, wasn't slurring any words, and wasn't angry. I told him about all of the good things that were happening in my career, and he said he was proud of me. I told him I was proud of him, too, and thankful for everything he'd done to help me get here.

I'm not sure how it happened, but we wound up having a long heart-to-heart that night. We forgave each other for some of the heartbreaks of our past. I forgave him for his drinking and, more important, for the way he acted when was drunk. He apologized and said he never meant to hurt Mom, Julio, or me. He was truly sorry. I then reminded him of the time I called the cops on him and wound up getting him deported. I still felt so guilty about it, and, on that phone call, I apologized to him. He said, "I'm really sorry that I ever put you in a position where you *had* to call the cops."

He forgave *me*. I cried really hard. It was such a release. It felt so good to have that peace with him that I can hardly put it into words. I got off the phone that night looking forward to the start of a whole new relationship with my father. I dreamed of flying him and the whole family up for a visit at some point. I dreamed of a time when maybe, just maybe, the DREAM Act would be revived and would put me on a path to finally being able to stop living so much of my life in the shadows, and to be able to fly to Mexico to see my family. It frustrated me beyond belief that I couldn't just hop on a plane and spend time with my father right then and there.

I felt like I had my dad back—the dad who was fun, loving, and kind. My brother had the good fortune of knowing him that way. Because my mom was still recovering and he had mostly stopped drinking, my dad stepped up and basically acted as both mother and father to Julio after they moved to Mexico. My father would wake him up and make him breakfast and take him to school and make him dinner and make sure he had money for lunch; he even washed his uniform. He had done that for me, too. But for Julio, the days didn't end with anger. He was such an amazing dad to my little brother. I was ready to experience a little of that myself, and I felt extremely sad that I couldn't make it happen yet. I began to feel like I was living in a very nice, very glamorous cage. Maybe going back to Mexico wouldn't be such a terrible loss. In America, I had financial resources but not much else. Even though I was twenty-four years old, I felt old and worn out. The small wrinkles under my eyes were proof.

I began questioning what I was doing staying in New York, alone, when I could just as easily go back to Mexico with the experience I had under my belt and land a job at a bank or an investment firm down there. I found myself seriously considering the possibility of going home.

CHAPTER 18

The Call

It was a quiet, early September morning up on the fortieth floor of One New York Plaza when my phone rang. It was my sister Nay calling. From Mexico. I was immediately alarmed.

"Hi, Julissa, how are you?" she said.

"What happened?" I responded. "What happened?"

"Dad is in the hospital. It all happened so fast. Two days ago he just started peeing blood. He's losing his sight."

"I have to call you back." I could feel the tears swelling up in my eyes. There is no crying at the desk, not even if your father might be dying.

We hung up and I walked down the hall. I opened the door to the bathroom and locked myself in a stall.

"Do not be anxious about anything, but in every situation, by prayer and petition, with thanksgiving, present your requests to God." I prayed, as tears ran down my cheeks. I prayed over and over and over again:

> Rejoice in the Lord always. I will say it again: Rejoice!
> Let your gentleness be evident to all. The Lord is near.
> Do not be anxious about anything, but in every situation, by prayer and petition, with thanksgiving, present your requests to God.

And the peace of God, which transcends all understanding, will
guard your hearts and your minds in Christ Jesus.

I could barely function the rest of that day. A series of phone calls with my sister and mother confirmed that my father was really ill, possibly dying. I should have gotten on a plane immediately, but how would I come back into the United States? I had risked getting deported for much less before, like that time I went to the party with Chris, or every time I drank in college before I was twenty-one. I reminded myself that sometimes I just had to live, no matter the consequences. But the stakes were so much higher now. I had a career. I had a life in the United States. *Everything I had worked for, everything my parents had sacrificed for.*

I kept going to the bathroom to cry. I told Kate my father was very sick, and she asked if I wanted to go home early. I said, "No. At least here I can keep my mind on work. There's nothing I can do from home."

"Well, why don't you go to Mexico, then?"

"No, no, my mother insists it's not that serious," I said. "And I've got to close this deal. I'm okay."

I wasn't okay. I felt the stress in my stomach, in every muscle of my body. I stayed at work until 10:00 p.m., calling back and forth to my mother and sister constantly for updates. They kept saying he was *okay*. Then my aunt called me: "Julissa," she said, "your mother and sister are not being honest with you. Your father is not well. He's not okay. They don't even know if he'll make it through the night."

"What? Why are they lying to me? Why have they hidden this from me?"

I was so angry. Whatever their intentions were, I was absolutely furious that they kept me in the dark. This was *my father* and it was my decision to make. I wanted to blame my mom and sister, but the reality was that I knew in my gut that my dad was sicker than they were letting on.

I made up my mind to get on a plane. *Just drop everything and go!* Then I decided to stay, because that was what my dad would want. *Can I even get on an international flight without a U.S. passport?* The border was still lax in some areas where there were frequent border crossings. It was pretty easy to drive a car across the border into Mexico and just say "American citizen," and the border patrol would just wave you through. I could fly to Laredo, and then rent a car and drive down, I thought. Getting back would be the tricky part. If I couldn't make it by driving, maybe I could use some of my hefty new salary to pay a mule to smuggle me across. Even if I pulled something like that off, I'd be setting myself up for misery in the future. If the DREAM Act ever passed, I wouldn't be able to be a part of it. The DREAM Act required that you'd been in the United States since the age of sixteen or younger. As soon as I crossed the border into Mexico, I was giving myself a ten-year penalty. If it was ever discovered that I left the United States then crossed back in illegally, I wouldn't be able to fix my status, even if I married a U.S. citizen. Even if, in the future, I had U.S.-born citizen children.

"Julissa! You are not risking your life! If something happens to you, I'll die," my mother said.

I went home wondering if maybe all of this was a sign from God. Maybe it really was time for me to leave. Maybe it was time for me to just fly home and leave my American life behind me. I agonized over it for hours.

At 6:00 a.m. I called my sister.

"Is he awake?" I asked.

"Sort of," she said. "He's all hooked up to so many machines that he can't talk or anything."

"Let me talk to him. Please. Just put the phone up to his ear for me, okay? Please?"

My sister put her cell phone up to my father's ear.

"Daddy," I said. "You'll be okay. Everything is okay. You'll be okay . . ." I could hear him gasping for air. I told him he didn't need to say anything. I knew he loved me and that was all that mattered.

Could this be it? Is my father really dying? I couldn't make sense of it. *This can't be happening. This can't be happening now. It isn't right.*

I struggled with what to say, knowing that there was a chance I would never be able to say anything else to him ever again.

"You remember that conversation we had a couple of months ago, right?" I said. "Remember when I forgave you. Don't forget that. I love you. I forgive you, Daddy."

I couldn't take it. I started bawling. *This is stupid! I should have left as soon I got the first phone call from my sister. I should be in Taxco.*

"Daddy? I'll be there soon," I said. "I'll be there soon. I'm almost there. Please, hang on, Daddy. Okay? Please, hang on. I love you so much."

My dad died two hours later.

My sister explained that she left his bedside for a short while to take a shower. Mom was there the whole time, she said, but when Nay came back, she walked into the room and said, "Daddy, I'm here."

Seconds later my father took his last breath and died.

"*Daddy, I'm here,*" she said. And then he was gone.

I am positive that he thought that voice was mine. I had told him to hold on. I had told him I would be there soon. I think he thought that was me walking into his hospital room. He waited for *me*.

I would never get a chance to have a new relationship with my father. I would never have a chance to hug him ever again.

I couldn't stop thinking about what he must have felt in that last moment. What was it like for him to take that last breath? Did he know it was his last breath? Was he scared? I obsessed over it for weeks.

I didn't get to say good-bye. I had a realization that a happy life is not necessarily a successful life full of accomplishments. I was successful, but I was alone. I started to visualize my life in Mexico, even if it meant giving up on my dreams.

That morning changed me forever. I still have not forgiven myself for not getting on a plane the moment I found out he was sick. I was angry that this country and these immigration policies had forced me to make a choice between being with my dad and abandoning my life in America. Why should any human being be forced into a corner like that? I wanted to blame everyone and everything. And then I turned it right back on myself. Was it all *my* fault? Should I have never stayed here? Should I have never gone to school? Should I have never taken this job?

I was suddenly wracked with guilt and doubts about every choice I'd ever made.

My mind raced constantly. I couldn't deal with my own thoughts. I started overeating. I stayed up late at night, holed up in my apartment watching hours of mindless television just so I wouldn't have to think. I felt anxious all the time, as if I was waiting for something to happen, but I didn't know what that something was.

I prayed every night. I prayed to the Lord to send me some sign; to tell me whether or not I should leave this all behind and go to

Mexico to be with my family. *Lord, what is best for my mother and my brother?*

I never got an answer.

I cried on my friend Jeff's shoulder more than ever. The two of us had become close over the course of the previous year. What was only a friendship managed to cross some boundaries that made us want something more. It was never all that well defined, but it wasn't tumultuous the way things were in my undefined relationship with Robert. With Jeff, everything was always good. It was always loving. We told each other "I love you" and it came from a very deep place of friendship.

Jeff couldn't understand why I didn't get on a plane immediately when I found out my dad was sick. He simply could not understand why I made that decision. So after my father died, I told Jeff everything. I told him the whole story.

He didn't get angry at me for not telling him sooner. "I just wish you could have trusted me enough to tell me sooner," he said.

I poured myself into my work during the day, giving it everything I had and using my focus there to distract me from the pain I was feeling, emotional and otherwise. Finally in 2008 my hard work was rewarded with a promotion. I became an associate at Goldman Sachs. My compensation jumped to $120,000 a year.

My dad's death forced me to reevaluate everything, again and again. As I moved to a nicer apartment, I kept asking myself whether my actions were reflective of my values and beliefs. A $120,000 salary was a lot of money, but surprisingly it didn't go very far in Manhattan. I wasn't making the *big* bucks yet. I was comfortable, but I wasn't rich. Still, I went out and wrote a $10,000 check for a scholarship fund for undocumented immigrants. I gave more money to my church. I sent more money to my family than ever before. It was my way of making up for everything I had done wrong.

A few months later, after I had proved my worth again and again, my compensation jumped to $190,000 a year. The funny thing was, I had no illusion about the fact that there were people who were making more than I was making. Not just a few thousand dollars more, or even ten or twenty thousand dollars more. Multiples of my compensation. I wasn't blind to that. No one on Wall Street thinks they're making a proper salary, of course. We all believed we were getting shafted on our salary one way or another. My team alone was responsible for billions of dollars in trades every year. At its peak, my tiny team alone made Goldman Sachs more than $150 million in revenue. But I had very good reason to believe that men who were doing the same job that I was doing were making lots more than I was. I lived with that. I accepted it as a fact of life. I kept spreadsheets of the amount of business I brought in, and the work I did, and I pushed hard for every raise that would follow. After all, the reason I was there was to get rich. That was my goal from the beginning, right?

Focusing on work couldn't keep me from my grief, though, and in June of the following year, my grandmother—my beloved Mama Silvia—also passed away. It wasn't as harsh of a blow as my father's death. I had a wonderful relationship with my grandmother. We spoke on the phone all the time. She was always home. I knew I could call her day or night and she would be there for me. So I didn't suffer that sense of lost time with her. I tried to take solace in the fact that getting hit by another death so soon didn't knock me down quite as hard. I tried to make peace with the fact that I couldn't go to her funeral, either; that once again, I was not allowed to mourn with my own family.

In the wake of her death, as the one-year anniversary of my father's death approached, I sometimes found it hard to get up in the morning. But it was less about the sadness over the losses I'd suffered, I thought. My body was simply wracked with more physical pain than ever. Still, I felt pretty good about how I was doing. I was able to look back on how sad I had been the year before with some perspective. So I once again doubled down on work—just in time to face the stock market crash of 2008 and watch as the entire financial industry fell apart.

While colleagues all around me were let go, I managed to stay on. But the crash just made me question my goals even more. It pushed me to question why I was staying in that job. I started to question my own dreams, my own ambitions, and what any of it was worth. I started to question everything.

In the middle of all of that, I sat down and read the biography of Mexican president Vicente Fox, and it made me angry about the unfairness of my situation. President Fox wrote in great detail about the contributions of Mexican immigrants to the United States, and Mexico's failure of not creating enough opportunities for talent to thrive in Mexico. He noted the massive amounts of tax revenue Mexican immigrants provided to the U.S. government even though they had no hope of receiving any of the U.S. government's services, and in fact could wind up deported if they ever found themselves in need. How was that fair? I started thinking once again, *Maybe I can move back to Mexico. Clearly they don't want me here! I succeeded in spite of a million obstacles, so maybe I should just go back and do something with my life there!*

I was so moved by that book that I sat down and wrote a letter to President Fox himself. I told him all about my story, including the following passage:

I have through many perils been able to get a great job on Wall Street, yet I can't go as fast as I'd like for fear of getting caught and getting deported. In fourteen years of living in the United States no law has passed in which I would qualify for residency. Despite all my accomplishments, I am still an "illegal alien" this country would rather dispose of.

I was fired up. No one in my life other than Jeff had any idea how far along my thought process had gone. I was ready to abandon America, to walk away from Goldman Sachs, and to see what I could do to change the world from my old hometown of Taxco. I started thinking, *Who cares about money? And who cares about having things if you can't even share them with your family?* We couldn't go on family vacations. I couldn't give them Christmas presents in person. I couldn't give them a hug for my birthday. I worked myself up into a frenzy.

"What am I doing here? This is not worth it. Forget this place. I'm going back to Mexico!" I said.

I never sent that letter to President Fox, though. Instead, I soon abandoned my plans to leave the United States behind altogether. That was because something totally unexpected happened: I got married.

My mom, dad, and me with my beloved Mama Silvia at a family gathering at my grandmother's house. Growing up, most special occasions, including my birthdays, took place at Mama Silvia's. I am cheesing super hard because this was the first time I was seeing my parents in almost a year.

With my cousins and sister Nay on a road trip across the United States, living out my house-on-wheels dream. It was one of the most memorable summers of my life. We had just visited Elvis's house in Memphis.

After making a deal with my mom that I would make *la escolta* (the Mexican version of the honor roll), I studied super hard and kept my mouth shut during class. Making *la escolta* meant my mom would come visit me in Taxco. This picture was taken in the dining room of our second-story apartment.

After a series of unfortunate circumstances, my mom missed me marching in *la escolta*. I was so sad that I marched on the wrong foot. I may have also cried the entire time.

Posing with my dad for the camera when I was in the seventh grade in our apartment in San Antonio, Texas. This was a good day, and I was so proud to be my father's daughter.

I was bad at a lot of things in the sixth grade, especially English. But when we got to perform a Mexican folklore dance, I was the only one with a real outfit. No leotard with ruffles for me!

At my high school graduation with my mom, Uncle Mike, my sister Aris, my nephew, Victor, and my brother, Julio. As excited as I was to graduate high school, a shadow was cast over me since my college plans were still uncertain.

After my mom's accident, I took over the funnel cake stand. In this picture, my mom is looking much better after months of physical rehabilitation. She never ceases to amaze me!

Ivan, me, Delma, and Kevin (from left to right) at a college party. These are some of my best friends in the world. Together with Israel and Annie, we made up the six-pack.

The Hispanic Business Student Association is where I first felt like I belonged. Becoming president of the organization in 2003 is still one of the greatest honors of my life. This picture was taken after a meeting with the rest of the 2003 officers.

To earn extra cash during my unpaid Chicago Fire internship, I dressed up as the Monarcas mascot. I was the shortest mascot in Major League Soccer history, but it paid the bills.

After getting my green card, all I wanted to eat the first time I set foot in Mexico was quesadillas from this stand that sits under a bridge. I try to eat at this place each time I visit Mexico.

My mom and Nay floating in Xochimilco during my first visit to Mexico in 2009. I was truly happy that day. While money doesn't buy happiness, on this occasion it definitely facilitated it.

Here I am at my grandparents' family business, Metales Aviles, in 2009. Growing up I loved spending time there, imitating my grandmother, Mama Silvia.

I am second from the right in this photo with the 2014–2015 Ascend Educational Fund (AEF) scholarship recipients. Cofounding AEF has been one of the greatest accomplishments of my life. Being able to help students who are walking in the shoes I walked in brings me great joy.

Addressing our guests during the 2016 Ascend Educational Fund Gala, I was happy and redeemed. I told them, "You are the difference between a student achieving her full potential and a student's talent being wasted." We raised some good funds that night.

I put the finishing touches on *My (Underground) American Dream* during Christmas break 2015, surrounded by generations of my family. This book isn't just mine; it belongs to all of them. It was their sacrifice, their encouragement, and their unconditional love that allowed me to live through the fire and embark on this new journey.

PART III
Redeemed

CHAPTER 19

The Proposal

I was a ticking time bomb, and all Jeff could do was listen. For weeks I'd been walking him through *every single one* of my thoughts. "Look. This is what I'm thinking. The time to go is when my lease is up." I had moved to a nicer apartment on Gold Street, with big, beautiful windows in my bedroom. It was still small. All my bedroom could hold was my queen bed with no other furniture. I had one tiny, makeshift closet from Bed Bath & Beyond. It didn't have much of a view, either, but it was definitely a big step up from the closet-sized space of my first apartment at 45 Wall.

"Actually, I should probably stay until at least February, when we get our bonuses, or maybe even till the following year when my bonus might be bigger, and then I'll have more money to take with me," I said.

I couldn't figure out how I would take large sums of money to Mexico, so I kept trying to work that out by talking it through with Jeff. I didn't have a bank account in Mexico. I couldn't wire more than $10,000 at a time because I didn't have a social security number. I didn't want to lose massive amounts of money in fees by making wire transfers or using Western Union. The banks and wire services might as well be highway robbers with masks and guns given the percentages they take for those transactions. It's predatory. Then I'd lose more money on the exchange rate turning those dollars into pesos. I couldn't seem to come up with a solution that made sense. But I didn't let that stop me. *Maybe I would just take suitcases full of cash money.* My plan making continued.

"I'll have to tell my friends. I'll have to come clean and just tell them why I'm leaving, and that I'm basically never going to see them again unless they come visit me in Mexico," I said. I just kept going through the whole thing over and over again.

Jeff listened patiently. He also kept asking, "Are you sure? Are you sure that's what you want to do?"

I could tell he wasn't comfortable with the things I was saying, but he knew when to listen and when to give advice. That was one of the things I most loved about him.

"I miss Julio," I told him. "My brother was eight the last time I saw him. He's fifteen now, Jeff. *Fifteen!* I miss my mom. I miss everyone. I'm sick and tired of living in this golden cage, you know? I just don't see any other way."

We were sitting on my bed listening to music one night with the sounds of the city and the lights from the apartment building across the way streaming in through my big, beautiful windows, when out of nowhere, in the sweetest voice, Jeff said, "What if we get married?"

"What?" I laughed. "You're being crazy."

He turned to me, took my hands, looked into my eyes, and said it again: "Marry me."

I didn't laugh that time.

"Look," he said. "If we get married, you don't have to leave. I don't want you to leave."

Hot blood filled my head. Ten million thoughts ran through my mind in an instant. *Is this is the right thing to do? Are we rushing into something to fix this problem?*

"You are my best friend," he said. "I love you. I know you love me. So why not?"

Why not?

Those simple words felt like a crane that came along and lifted the weight of a car off of my shoulders. I swear I felt physically lighter.

"Okay then," I said. "Why not? Let's get married!"

A couple of weeks later, we made our way to City Hall to apply for a marriage license. We told both of our families all about it, and they were incredibly supportive. We actually sat down with Jeff's mom and dad and told them the whole story. I opened up to his amazing parents and told them every detail of my background. It felt like another weight lifted just knowing that his family approved and supported our decision to get married. It felt so good to know that I had a few more people in the world who knew what I had been through.

Because my father was no longer there to walk me down the aisle and because I couldn't get married in front of my family, we decided to have the wedding with no family at all. We agreed: "Let's get this done quickly and get my green card so we can go to Mexico. We'll figure out the rest later!"

We got married one year and one day after my dad passed away. We hired a cute old lady to officiate the ceremony in the backyard of Antonia's apartment. Antonia was one of my best friends since back from my HBSA days, and our only witness. The ceremony was very short, but I held a little bouquet of flowers, and we each read our own vows. I was so nervous that I found myself laughing as Jeff read his vows to me.

"Oh, how cute. You're crying," the woman said. I thought, *No, I'm laughing. Wait, but there's tears coming out of my eyes. Maybe I am crying.* I honestly couldn't tell the difference.

"I now pronounce you man and wife," the nice lady said, at which point we both thought, *What do we do now?*

Antonia joined us for champagne at a wine bar in the Lower East Side.

Our next stop after that was an immigration lawyer's office where we started the process of filling out the application for my green card. I learned that I would have to apply for an "adjustment of status," because I was "out of status"—meaning my visa had expired.

I had been "out of status" for a very long time.

One of the biggest hurdles to overcome would be establishing when my last entry into the country occurred, and then having proof that it truly was the last time I exited the country and came back. Plus, we would have to bring all sorts of stuff to the table to prove that our marriage was for real.

Just like way back in high school, when I first went to the INS (which had since been renamed United States Citizenship and Immigration Services, or USCIS) with Troy and learned about the process of getting a green card through marriage, we had to show that my new husband stood on solid financial ground. Easy enough—Jeff had a big shot job on Wall Street. But, of course, it was never that simple.

In the aftermath of the 2008 crash, right in the middle of this whole process, my new husband got laid off. We couldn't believe the terrible timing. It was an awful blow to Jeff, and I worried about him and his career and what he would do. It was also a major blow to our application process.

God forbid someone from another country happens to fall in love with someone poor. First of all, we had to sign a $10,000 retainer with a lawyer, which was a lot more money than many people have. Then there was no way around that income requirement on the application process. With Jeff out of work, the lawyer informed us in no uncertain terms that we wouldn't get approved—unless we found a sponsor. So Jeff turned to his parents. Without hesitation, he asked his mom and dad to get involved, and his parents stepped right up and became my sponsor. That meant they had to share all of their financial information in the application and agree in a legally binding contract that they would support me in the case their son couldn't. I was so blown away. Once again, when the chips were down, there were angels who showed up in my life.

All of the fears I had about whether we were doing this for the right reasons faded away as we went through that process, because it was not easy, and Jeff was down with everything. Nothing scared this man—no amount of paperwork, and no amount of applications. He never backed off. He never flinched. He never once complained. He truly, truly wanted this for me. For *us*. And he was doing all of this while also diligently looking for a new career opportunity.

As we went through it all, gathering all of our documentation and laying out photos to prove our relationship was real, our attorney told me he was impressed with how meticulous and detail oriented I was. I felt as if I had spent my whole life preparing to not mess this up. I didn't let anything slip. Not one thing.

At that point we had some house bills that were in both of our names, and that was really important to show our connectedness, but I couldn't find one month's cable bill and I really freaked out. The attorney said, "It's okay, it's just one month," but I was like, "No! We have to be perfect!" and I kept digging everywhere until we finally came up with a copy to provide to USCIS. I didn't want to take any chances. I didn't want anything to be missing. *Nothing.* For instance, we didn't wear wedding rings. Our marriage wasn't something we announced to the whole world, so why wear rings? We didn't change our Facebook status. But I went out and bought us rings so we could wear those rings to the interview. I didn't want anyone having to stop to ask us why we weren't wearing rings.

A couple of months after submitting our application, I was summoned to a biometrics appointment—one very long day in which my picture and fingerprints were taken. A couple of months after that, we received notice that our application had been reviewed, I had passed the criminal background check, and that we were ready to move on to the final step in the process: the USCIS interview.

I couldn't really tell Kate that I had to take time off for my green-card interview; I was supposed to already have a green card. I had set a longtime precedent of never, ever, missing work. I couldn't tell anyone what I was really up to, of course, so I kept making excuses about my health, saying I was going to see a string of doctors. In between appointments with lawyers, I was still seeing doctors for my continued ailments. I knew for a fact that there were rumblings on the floor about me. People wondered if I was interviewing at other firms. I just hoped and prayed that being gone so much wouldn't hurt me after all I'd been through.

Trying to secure my green card wasn't the only distraction that kept me from focusing on work. I learned from my mom and my sister, Nay, that Julio had been struggling in school ever since our dad died. Julio was just fourteen when we lost our dad, and he had taken it really hard. He didn't really care about school anymore. Nay told me he was making friends with older kids who were known to be involved with selling drugs, and a horrifying thought kept me up at night: *My baby brother could get caught up in a drug gang and wind up dead.*

I couldn't allow that to happen. I had money. I was on my way to getting my green card now. It was time for me to use my resources for the benefit of my brother.

Jeff and I made the decision to bring Julio to live with us in New York, and it quickly turned into a nearly all-consuming task. Julio was born in the United States. He was a U.S. citizen. But he moved when he was eight, and my parents never got him a U.S. passport. The only real ID he had as a teenager was his birth certificate, but when he took it to the U.S. embassy in Mexico City, they told him it wasn't enough to prove his citizenship.

So I spent all sorts of time and money trying to track down the proof they needed. They wanted hospital records, which most hospitals dispose of after ten years, so we hit a dead end. I flew to Texas and went to his old school to get old report cards and transcripts as a substitute "proof" that he was born and lived in the United States for a long period of time before moving to Mexico. Then they wanted proof that our mother was actually living in the United States when she gave birth to him. This was beyond infuriating, because a few years earlier they had stripped my mother of her visa and banned her from entering the United States for ten years precisely *because* they knew she had been living in the country during that period!

When all of that was finally done and we managed to get him a passport, I then had to worry about getting him covered by health insurance, which was not the easiest thing to do in America. It's a matter of course in most countries but not here. A child like Julio who fell between the cracks could suffer horribly if he became ill without insurance, and the only way I could get him covered under my insurance policy was for me to become his legal guardian. So I set about accomplishing just that—another bureaucratic red tape nightmare that kept me in and out of the office for long stretches on a daily basis.

I was thrilled that I would finally be reunited with my brother, but it wasn't lost on me that he had mixed feelings about it. He knew it was the best thing for his future to come live in the United States with me and Jeff, but I knew he felt guilty about leaving my mom in Mexico. In many ways, Julio and I would have to get to know each other all over again. The last time we lived together, he was eight years old, and now he was a teenager who had lost his dad. Ours would be a complicated relationship at the start. There were times when I wanted to be his friend, but he saw me as a parent figure. Other times, I wanted to be a parent figure and he would remind me that I wasn't his mom. It would take time to find our rhythm.

⚬⚬⚬

Our attorney came with Jeff and me as we carried a box full of all of our paperwork into the Federal Building in lower Manhattan, right on the edge of Chinatown, across the street from a McDonald's. We'd spent time in that attorney's office going through mock interviews for weeks prior to that moment.

"These are the types of questions you can expect," he would say. So Jeff and I stayed up late preparing for anything they might throw at us. We had heard that these interviews could be brutal, and there was so much on the line. As nervous as we were, I was also very confident. We had crossed all of our *t*'s and dotted all of our *i*'s. We were prepared. We were ready.

We sat for what felt like an eternity in a jam-packed, standard-issue, drab federal-office waiting room full of other couples that early morning. Finally, they called us in. We entered the office of a short, chubby, balding white guy who was super nice and cordial to us. He didn't seem cold and official at all—and that made me wary. *He's being too nice.* Our lawyer had told us, "Sometimes they pretend to be nice and then try to slip you up with a random question." I felt myself sitting up straight on the edge of my chair, perhaps looking just a little too intense.

The funny thing was that when we sat down, the interviewer mistakenly thought that I was petitioning Jeff.

"Oh, no," I said. "Actually, he's petitioning me."

"Wow. How did you get *her*?" the officer said.

We all laughed at that, and I felt myself relax a little. Then I worried about relaxing too much.

"Oh, man," Jeff responded. "You know. I had to lock it down!"

Jeff's trust antennae apparently weren't up at all. Once he realized he had permission to joke around with this guy, he started joking around. That was just his personality. And you know what? It was perfect.

The officer asked us how we met, when we met, what I liked about Jeff, what Jeff liked about me, and it all went smoothly. He asked us about what we liked to read, and why we got married. All good.

Then he started reading something and making some notes, and I got really nervous. He looked up at me and said, "Do you work?"

I said, "Yes."

He said, "Where?"

Our lawyer had warned us about that. "If he asks you about your work, you tell him. Straight up," he said. "You cannot lie." The biggest potential hurdle in my case was the fact that I had used fake documents to get work. My application could be denied because of that one fact alone. But our lawyer explained that it really would be up to the officer. It's essentially an arbitrary process, because if we happened to get someone who wanted to make my life miserable, he could. If we got denied, there would be an appeals process we could go through, but it could take months, even years, if we didn't make it through on the first try. The possibility of deportation was right there, hanging in the room right in front of me now, dangling over me like a giant rock about to come tumbling over the cliff onto my head.

"I work at Goldman Sachs," I said.

The man looked at me. He seemed to pause. "Okay," he said. I couldn't tell what he was thinking. He kept looking at those papers and making notes to himself. I felt my heart pounding in my chest. But I kept a straight and confident face.

I was prepared to answer whatever questions came next. He could ask me about the documents themselves, where I got them, how much they cost, how many times I'd used them. I was ready to tell him everything.

I thought about all of the couples we'd seen in the waiting room. It was packed full. I wondered if it was packed full like that every day of the week. There were Muslims in head scarves, other Hispanics, Asians, Africans, white people, seemingly every nationality and background you could imagine all gathered in that place. All nervous, like me, I was sure. I wondered how many of them were undocumented. I wondered how many of them had relied upon fake papers at some point in their lives. I couldn't possibly be the only one.

I waited. Holding Jeff's hand was reassuring.

I wondered why this was the only way in for me. Why did I have to get married? Why was attaching myself to a man the only way for me to make it in America? Why couldn't my accomplishments be enough to make it in this country? Why was it that a man had to rescue me from my situation? I remembered my mother telling me her only way out was to marry my dad, and she hadn't wanted that for me. We came to America so I could grow up to be successful independently of any man. The irony of my situation stung deep in my soul.

Jeff was my best friend, I loved him, and he meant the world to me. But I couldn't stop wondering, *Why did it have to come to this?*

The balding man kept writing notes, silently, and in my own silence, I prayed. *God, I am in Your hands. All good things come to those who trust in the Lord.*

Finally the officer looked up. "Well, this still has to go through review, and my supervisor will review my notes, but . . .

". . . I don't see anything that would prevent you from adjusting your status."

"Oh, my God. Thank you. Thank God!" I said.

We shook the man's hand and walked out into that waiting area beaming. I could feel the eyes of all of those hopeful couples upon us as I walked past wearing the brightest smile ever.

We said good-bye to our lawyer out in the hallway, and then we just stood there and hugged.

"Thank God," Jeff said. "You're so lucky. God loves you so much. That went as well as we could have hoped."

I could hardly believe it. After all that time, all that worry, all that fear, all that panic, all that sacrifice, all that hardship, the whole thing was over and done with before 10:00 a.m. Barring any unforeseen circumstances, I could be getting my green card— a real, actual green card—in the mail in a matter of weeks.

I had taken the whole day off, so we went back to our neighborhood and ate a celebratory lunch in our favorite hole-in-the-wall Puerto Rican restaurant. We were the only two people in the joint wearing suits.

CHAPTER 20

Going Home

I started bawling before I could even open the envelope. When I picked up our mail on that still-freezing early-spring afternoon, I could feel the shape of the card inside: *My green card!*

It was March, right before my birthday, and it was the greatest present I could imagine. I called Jeff. He didn't answer. He had picked up some temporary contract work in the city. I called him again and again until he finally called back.

"What's the matter? What's wrong?" he said, having seen my number pop up on his phone again and again.

"Oh my God, Jeff," I said. "It's here. My green card is here. I got my green card!"

"Oh my God," he said. "I'm getting in a cab right now. I'm coming home. We're going out!"

On a random midweek evening, we took a cab to Ricardo's in Harlem for the greatest steak dinner ever. I couldn't believe I wasn't here illegally anymore. I had no reason to hide. I couldn't even begin to comprehend how this was going to change my life.

I kept pulling out the card and looking at it. I was thinking over and over, *I went through all that pain for this tiny piece of paper.* My eyes were filled with tears as we ate dinner. I was so grateful the hiding was over. I was so grateful for *Jeff.* He changed my life forever. And it wasn't just my life that was changed. Because I had a green card now, I could go visit my mother and take flowers to my dad's grave. I could bring my little brother to live with me, so he would be able to go to college here, just like I'd dreamed.

"Oh my God, Jeff. This means I can travel. I can see the world. I can go anywhere in the world and be able to *come home*."

I felt like I could breathe for the first time since I was fourteen years old.

"I know, babe," Jeff said. He got a huge smile on his face. "So... where do you want to go?"

He already knew the answer: Taxco.

I would have booked my ticket that same night if I could have, but it wasn't that simple. As soon as I caught my breath, I realized, "Oh, wait a minute."

Goldman Sachs had hired me with a fake green card and a fake social security card. Now that I had a real one (a social security card would arrive a few weeks later), I needed to switch everything over. How on earth would I explain to Goldman Sachs that I suddenly had a new green card and new social security number?

Part of me wondered if I'd have to quit; if I'd have to switch to another firm just so I could start fresh with my legitimate documentation.

I was still happy. I was still filled with joy. But the notion of *How the heck am I going to do this?* plagued me for weeks.

Once again, the timing of everything worked out better than I ever could have imagined. Coincidentally, the expiration date on my fake green card was coming up early that summer. I don't know what would have happened had that expiration date come and gone. I had no idea where to buy a new fake green card in New York City. And how on earth would I get a new fake card with the same number as my old one? It would have been one more reason for me to leave the United States and move back to Mexico permanently. But that wasn't what happened.

Instead, I simply made a phone call to the HR department and said, "I have my new green card. Also, I got a new social security number." I hoped they wouldn't ask for reasons why. I didn't have a good answer. Luckily for me the woman at HR said, "Okay. Just scan and send me the copies of the new cards and we'll get them into the system."

She gave me the e-mail address to send it to. I scanned my new green card and social security card, and a couple of weeks later I checked the system and saw my new numbers were there. Just like that.

Once again, I took advantage of the stereotypes of what people think about people who are in this country illegally. I was an associate at Goldman Sachs. There was no thought in anyone's head that I could possibly be in the same category as someone who paid to get smuggled into this country on the back of a truck, or someone who crossed the Rio Grande under the cover of darkness, or who came into this country through some tunnel. That couldn't possibly be *me*, in my expensive suit and nice silk scarves.

Once that task was through, I had another big one to check off my list: going to get my first-ever driver's license. I had been driving for years and went all those years without so much as a ticket. Yet in New York State, I was required to take a four-hour class, then a written test, then a driving test. I could not believe how much time I had to take off of work just to stand in waiting lines at the DMV. But I was glad to do it.

I just wanted all of the various loose ends tied up. I wanted everything official. I wanted to be 100 percent legitimate and aboveboard in every way before I got on a plane to Mexico—a thought that after so many years of worry still absolutely terrified me. I could not shake the dread of going there, finally seeing my family, and then hitting some glitch at customs on the way back that might force me to abandon the country I love, the job I love, and the life I love.

The final checkmark on my post–green card to-do list was to file an application for a new Mexican passport. Once again: timing. My old passport, the one that had seen me through so many ID checks on this seemingly endless underground journey, was set to expire that same year, too. So I renewed it. And then?

It was time to go see my family.

Jeff and I arrived in Mexico City on a hot, late-summer afternoon. We hit customs and saw the two lines: the citizens' line and the visitors' line. I would always be a Mexican citizen; I would not use some visitors' line. I proudly handed the man at the counter my Mexican passport with my green card. Then we gathered up our luggage and headed for the exit. At customs, we had to press a button. If the button turned green, we would get to go through without anyone searching our bags. If it turned red, our bags would get searched. I was just so excited to get out of that airport and through those big white-glass doors on the other side of the customs area that I didn't want anything else standing in my way or holding me back. I closed my eyes and I prayed for green as I pressed on that button—and that was what I got.

"All right! We're good to go! You ready?" I asked Jeff.

"Are *you* ready?" he said.

I smiled and nodded and started walking toward the doors. They opened up automatically, splitting open slowly from the middle. I could see a crowd gathered around the barriers on the other side. There were loved ones hugging loved ones and people with signs and balloons and flowers. And as the doors spread all the way open and I finally stepped through, I saw my beautiful mother, smiling bigger than anyone in that crowd as tears welled up in her eyes. Uncle Mike stood right beside her, looking exactly the same as he did all those years ago. And my sister Nay was there to greet me, too.

I started crying before I reached them, and when I did, I threw my arms around my mom in the biggest bear hug I could muster.

"Welcome home," she said. "My baby girl."

"It's so good to see you!" I replied through tears. "And Uncle Mike!" I said, throwing my arms open and embracing him before finally turning to embrace Nay.

"Everyone," I said. "This is Jeff."

None of them had met him before that moment, yet they all gave him a great big hug. I could not believe that I was finally hugging my family, and that my family was hugging my husband.

I knew some parts of this trip would be painful. I would be going to see my father's grave and my grandmother's grave, and I dreaded those moments more than anything. But in that moment, at that airport, all I felt was pure joy.

"How's Julio?" my mother asked.

"He's fine, Mom. He's good. He's taking classes, and he's already maneuvering through New York City better than I did in my whole first year."

"You're sure he's okay there by himself?"

"Yes, Mom. I promise. He's doing great. You'd be so proud of him."

My mom was happy that Julio was living with me in New York; it was what was best for him. But I also knew that it was painful for my mother and Julio to be away from each other. It made me sad that no matter what, our family was still separated by a stupid border and unjust immigration laws. I shook off the thought. *I am in Mexico!*

Knowing we had a long drive to Taxco ahead of us, we didn't

linger at the airport very long. We piled into my uncle's tiny SUV and quickly realized there weren't enough seats for everyone, so Jeff had to ride in the back with the suitcases. We had a good laugh over that one. It was like, "Welcome to Mexico, Jeff! You're riding in the trunk!"

With our vehicle packed full we rolled straight out of Mexico City and all the way past Cuernavaca, the City of Eternal Spring, without stopping.

"Is anyone getting hungry?" my uncle asked.

"I'm starving," I said, "but I don't want to eat anything except those quesadillas under the bridge."

He knew exactly what I was talking about.

"All right," he said. "Let's get you those quesadillas under the bridge!"

It had all come rushing back to me. There was this taco stand that we would always stop at on the way back to Taxco from Mexico City, and I suddenly craved the food from that taco stand more than anything I'd ever craved in my life. I was so excited for Jeff to experience this little place on the side of the highway. We were definitely not in Manhattan anymore.

These quesadillas are not the quesadillas we have here in the United States. These are like corn tortillas with Oaxaca cheese, which is more like mozzarella cheese than the cheddar you find in most Americanized Mexican dishes. All of the salsas are homemade. The tortillas are handmade, too. When we finally pulled over to that roadside stand, I stuffed my face.

"Oh my God! This is so good!"

The food in Mexico has a unique flavor. Even if you're making the same exact thing in the United States, it's not the same. Even the eggs taste different. I cannot believe I survived as long as I did without tasting those flavors.

It was in that moment, savoring all of those flavors, that I finally felt I was home. This was where I was born. This was where I grew up. I was back in the place of my roots.

As we piled back into the car, I was increasingly excited about getting to Taxco. The sun had just dipped below the horizon when we came around the final, familiar curve in the road, after which the whole skyline opened up to the beautiful sight of Taxco's thousands of white houses, marked by the warm glow of living room and porch lights, all rising up on the side of the mountain.

"Wow," Jeff said from the back.

"It's beautiful, isn't it?" I said.

It was late enough by the time we arrived that we decided to go straight to my mother's house and settle in. We were exhausted after the long travel day, and I thought I might fall asleep quickly with the windows open, and the smell of that Taxco night air that was just as familiar to me as it was the last time I'd slept in that city. *Can it really be over a decade?* I marveled.

Then I turned the light out in the house I grew up in and realized that I was completely terrified. I'd always been afraid of ghosts. I'm a super scaredy-cat. I can't even watch a commercial for a scary movie. I have to change the channel. I've always been spiritual and religious and believed in God, and because of that, I also believe there are ghosts and spirits—good and evil.

When I was little, I made my dad promise me he would never die. Then when I got a little older, I made him promise that if he did die, he had to come back and tell me that he was okay. I didn't think about the fact that if he did that, he would be one of those *ghosts* I feared so much. That memory washed over me as I lay in my bed and I was suddenly terrified that his ghost was going to come visit me.

"Jeff, I can't sleep. He's coming back to tell me he's okay," I whispered.

"You're talking crazy talk. Nothing is going to happen. It's going to be okay," he promised. He held me as he fell asleep, and I stayed up tossing and turning. I kept waking him up: "Did you hear something? Did you hear that?"

My father's ghost never showed up, I think, because he knew I would've had a heart attack.

The next morning, we got up and went straight over to Mama Silvia's house. It was my uncle's house now, and the moment I walked past the old bougainvillea tree and up those stone steps and placed one foot inside, I lost it. For the first time I fully felt the absence of my grandmother. That wonderful house exuded a different energy. She wasn't there anymore. My uncle made breakfast for us, but the food wasn't the same as the food I always ate in that house. The light was still beautiful, and there were memories of her everywhere. But she was gone. Even her big green parrot was gone. That old bird died just a couple of weeks after my grandmother, and everyone was sure it had died of a broken heart.

"It's okay," Uncle Mike said. "Let it out. It's okay. Cry. Let it out." He hugged me tight for the longest time and just let me cry and cry.

I was so happy to be home, but being in that house meant confronting all the things I'd lost, all the connections I'd given up, all the Christmases I'd missed with my family, and all the people I would never see again with my own eyes. The fact that I was finally living and working in the United States legally didn't take away any of the years that I'd lost. No amount of money I could ever make for the rest of my life would buy back that time. No year-end bonus could bring back my father or Mama Silvia. It all washed over me in a way that made me truly understand what people meant by the phrase "drowning in sorrow."

That sorrow quickly grew into something worse when I realized where my mother and brother had lived during their first two years after leaving Texas for Mexico. While my mother recovered, before my dad went to rehab, the only place they had to stay in that house was a tiny spare room with one bed. I wanted to punch a wall, the thought of it made me so angry. *But how could I be mad when my uncle Mike had always done so much for us?*

While our six-story house rotted away because no one ever lived there, my mom and Julio were living in a spare room. My dad and sister Nay were living in our old apartment above Metales Aviles. Seeing that big house, still empty, still incomplete and crumbling, made me sick. That big, unfinished house was a physical reminder that my parents' dream was still not complete.

Once again I found myself questioning every choice I'd made. I wondered if anything I'd done had been the right thing. I was positive had I known, I would never have allowed my mother and Julio to live like that.

I cried in bed that night, wondering how I could ever make it up to them.

CHAPTER 21

Happy

I had a big surprise in store for the end of that week: I'd made plans to take my mother and sister to Mexico City for a five-star stay at the Four Seasons Hotel. But I had a few things I needed to do first, and the very next day I decided to face the hardest of those all by myself.

I went to visit my father's grave alone. I didn't want Jeff to come with me. I didn't want my mom. I didn't want anybody. I didn't want to have to think about anybody else while I was there. If I needed to cry, I wanted to cry. If I needed to scream, I wanted to be able to scream. If I wanted to throw things, I wanted to be able to throw them. I didn't want to have to worry about what some-body else was going to think or say. I certainly didn't want someone to pat me on the shoulder and tell me "It's okay," because it *wasn't* okay.

Cemeteries in Mexico are very different from cemeteries in the United States. Cemeteries in the United States are superuniform, organized, with a little cross or a little tombstone and that's it. In Mexico, especially in my hometown, cemeteries are crazy. People build little minichapels over their family plots. They paint these chapels different colors and go all out to make them beautiful and meaningful to their families.

My mother's side of the family had this plot for many generations, and it has a little domed chapel that we keep secured with five padlocks—just to keep the homeless people from coming in and sleeping there. There's a big beautiful bougainvillea tree right next to that chapel. I had visited the graves of my grandfather and great-grandparents back when I was a little girl growing up in Taxco. Since that time, a cousin had been buried there as well. And now, even though he wasn't a blood relative, my father was buried in that same plot, as was my Mama Silvia.

I unlocked the padlocks and stepped inside, and before I had a chance to be sad, I got angry. The chapel was *filthy*. There were old, dead flowers inside, and a layer of dust covered every surface, including the photos of all of my relatives who were laid to rest in that space. The tile floor, which basically had to be cracked open whenever someone new was buried, had been left a complete mess of cracked concrete. It hadn't been retiled like it was supposed to be after every burial. Even the candles were melted down to nubs.

My dad must be turning over in his grave right now, I thought.

I stormed off to the nearest shop and bought a whole bunch of cleaning supplies, as well as the biggest, longest-burning candles I could find. Then I got down on my knees and scrubbed the floors. I dusted everything. I organized all the pictures and lit the candles. When everything was back in order and it looked good again, I finally sat there and cried. Then, when I was finished crying, I screamed. Then I cried again.

I sat there and talked to my dad. I told him about everything that had happened. I told him all about Jeff, my green card, my promotions, and what it was like to live and work in New York City not having to worry about getting caught anymore. Finally, I talked to him about how amazing it felt to be back home and just how much I wished that he were there with me.

I went and told my uncle about the condition of those graves. He'd had a really hard time with my grandma passing away. He told me he couldn't bring himself to go visit her grave, but he had hired a woman to take care of our plot. She was supposed to light candles, and bring new flowers, and keep the place clean, just as Mama Silvia had done every week for all those years when she was alive. He was angry that she hadn't followed through, and he promised me that it wouldn't fall into that condition again.

Somehow, half my stay in Mexico had already passed by the time I felt I could breathe again. I apologized to Jeff. I told him we would have some fun soon. He said he didn't mind, and I knew he meant it. But I also meant what I said. I got everyone out of the house for a walk around Taxco. I wanted to show Jeff the old sights. We went by the Metales Aviles locations. We walked through the Mercado. I showed him where my school was, and where I took piano lessons.

"Let me carry your purse," my mother insisted as we walked.

"No, no, I'm fine," I said.

"But your back! It looks heavy. I worry about you. Let me hold it," she said, and I let her take it for a while. My back had definitely been hurting, but I don't think the purse had anything to do with it.

That evening, I went to grab something out of my bag—and I couldn't find it.

"Mom, where did you put my purse when we got home?"

My mother couldn't remember.

"Mom. My green card and my passport are in that purse! Mom, if I don't have that purse, I can't go back to the U.S. How the heck am I going to be able to go back? I just got my green card!"

We searched everywhere. I went into a complete panic. This wasn't just a small loss. This was everything. We retraced every route we'd taken, looked under every piece of furniture, called any shop we'd wandered into. We even called the local radio station and paid them to put ads on right away offering a large reward—no questions asked—for the safe return of that bag and its contents.

I started thinking three steps ahead: "Okay, so if we just go to the embassy today in Mexico City and figure out how to get a new green card, maybe we'll have it in time for the flight back."

I tried to calm myself down by thinking, *I can't be the only person who's ever lost her green card.* But I panicked nonetheless. *My first trip to Mexico and I lose my green card!*

Hours later, it turned up. The purse had somehow fallen behind the bed, but not so far down that it hit the floor. So in all that searching, even when someone looked under the bed, it simply wasn't there.

I can hardly express how relieved I was to have my purse back, along with all of its very important contents. But then I felt awful because I had been so mean to my mom. I swore to myself then and there that I would never be mean to her ever again. It felt like yet another thing I would want to make up to her forever.

In fact, my guilt made the end of our trip at the Four Seasons even more important to me. I was so used to flying around and staying at nice hotels on my business trips that it had almost become routine to me—but to see my mother's and sister's eyes light up as we stepped into that beautiful lobby was worth every single penny. I actually had a great rate for that hotel thanks to my Goldman connections, and that left us plenty of spending money for days and nights on the town.

The Four Seasons offered to drive us around in a big Suburban with security, and even have security people walk around with us just to be sure everything went smoothly. It wasn't necessary, as

Mexico City is one of the top tourist destinations in the world, but we took the Suburban around town nonetheless. It felt awesome to be able to show my mom and sister such a luxurious experience. We were riding with our guards like some kind of foreign dignitaries in our own country.

One day I took them all to Xochimilco, this beautiful spot on a river where men in gondolas sing songs for you as you float around on beautiful, brightly painted barges with picnic tables and chairs under the stars. That's right: Venice isn't the only city with gondolas! It's a magical spot where you can order drinks on the water while mariachi bands play for you. We wound up spending the whole day floating around, drinking big drinks and buying food from the smaller gondola "food carts" that floated around us as we listened to the music and laughed and shared stories with each other. At one point Jeff paid a mariachi band to play just for us, for a whole hour. I sat back with a giant michelada, the Mexican version of a bloody mary, in my hand and a big sombrero on my head watching as my mother danced with Jeff. She was so impressed that he liked to dance, and so proud that I'd chosen such a wonderful, handsome man for a husband.

I sat there and watched the two of them, and looked over at the smile on Nay's face, and I realized something: in that moment, in that place, having my family around me and enjoying the spoils of life, I was truly, deeply happy.

I couldn't believe it was almost over. A big part of me didn't want to leave. I realized that I might not have been able to enjoy that night with them at all had it not been for my career at Goldman Sachs with its sizable paychecks and bonuses. I felt so conflicted. I couldn't change the past. I couldn't change the decisions I'd made. I'd forged my way forward over every obstacle and was now finally achieving some of the dreams I'd had so many years ago, when I believed that being rich could solve all my problems.

I wasn't rich yet, but my immigration status wasn't a problem anymore. I might not have been able to be at my father's bedside in his final hours, but I had been able to help my father get the help he needed, and I was able to bring Julio to the United States. Those were all good things. There were a lot of good things that had come from my hard work and pursuit of financial success.

I thought, *Maybe what I need to do is go back to New York and work even harder at fulfilling the rest of the dream.*

Maybe it's time to go back, totally free and clear of everything that had been tormenting me, maybe even compromising my health, and to see what happens when I focus all of my energy on my career and getting rich for real.

CHAPTER 22

When It Rains, It Pours

I went back to Goldman determined to get ahead and determined to get promoted to VP as soon as possible. I went right back to the eighty-hour weeks I'd been pulling as an analyst.

I had stopped questioning Kate's loyalties by then and saw her instead as an ally, a mentor, and a trusted friend. Ted continued to be my mentor and advocate with the bosses. I never lost touch with him. But Kate's new boss, and therefore my boss, too, was a man named Mike Siegel. Mike had been at Goldman forever and was on track to become a partner. He would become a very important person in my career. The decision to promote me to VP would have to be cleared by him, and if he wanted me to be a VP, I would be.

I had taken a few trips with Mike to visit clients in Atlanta and Miami, and on one of those trips Mike asked me about my long-term goals.

"I want to be the first Hispanic woman partner at Goldman," I said. "I hope there is another Hispanic woman who makes it before I do, but if not, I want to be the first."

His response gave me all sorts of confidence: "There are people who have the drive and not the talent, others have the talent and not the drive. You have both."

People ask me sometimes about the career-defining moments, the milestones that led to my success and promotions at Goldman Sachs. There were, of course, big trades, new products that my clients were the first to trade, and projects I led that made our team an efficient machine. If I was the first to trade a new product, Eric Lane himself would send an e-mail to the entire team recognizing my efforts. My clients sent e-mails to Kate, Mike, and Eric letting them know how much they liked working with me. At one point, while still an associate, I was bringing in more than 25 percent of our team's revenues. All of those things helped, but truthfully, *every* moment was a key moment. I worked hard and did my best to shine in absolutely everything I did, day in, day out. And *that* was what led to my success. Maybe I drank too much of the Goldman Kool-Aid, but focusing on my client's needs first really did lead to my own success.

Yet even as I tried to refocus all of my energy on work, my heart kept pulling me back to my family. I now had the responsibility of caring for my baby brother, and I took it seriously.

Julio barely spoke English. He'd left the United States when he was eight years old and had stopped using the language. I enrolled him in some private English classes, similar to the ones I had taken when my parents first brought me here, hoping he would catch on quickly. I didn't want him to suffer the stigma of taking ESL courses at his high school. I wanted to do as much for him as my parents had done to set me on the right course in this country. This was his home. It was *my* home. He needed to succeed here, and outside of my work, worrying about Julio became all I could think about.

Having a sixteen-year-old kid living in a tiny apartment with Jeff and me put a bit of a damper on our relationship. I was frequently acting like a mother figure in front of Jeff, standing in front of the stove telling Julio it was time to do his homework. As giving and generous as Jeff had been through all of this, I think seeing me take on that role in our home may have pushed him past his limits. We had never talked about children; we had never even talked about what being married really meant. Now, all of a sudden, we were coparenting a teenager.

I wasn't blind. At a time when our marriage should have been aglow in its honeymoon phase, I could feel him pulling away. Even without a job he started spending longer and longer hours away from our apartment. I tried not to worry. I assumed things would get better once he found a job and once Julio settled into a routine. I was much more focused on the demands of my job and trying to be a mom, a sister, and a friend to my sixteen-year-old brother than I was on my relationship with Jeff.

In the aftermath of the 2008 crash, New York City was flooded with out-of-work Wall Street bankers. Finding a job was nearly impossible. Jeff went an entire year without finding any other meaningful work, and then, finally, he got an offer—in a faraway city, in another state, halfway across the country.

We sat on my bed that night and agonized over what to do.

"Jeff, I can't do that," I said. "Julio just got settled in school. I can't send him to another school. I'm on track to make VP in the next year. I can't leave Goldman now. I mean—"

I also couldn't ask him to stay in New York, without a job, with a sixteen-year-old, and with a relationship that was up in the air. So he took the job. Again, just like that, life tore a hole in my sails.

Jeff and I spoke on the phone every day. We couldn't fly back and forth every weekend, but we visited each other often. Still, nothing we did to overcome the distance seemed enough to make our marriage last. I quietly suffered another heartbreak even as I should have been celebrating my greatest year ever.

In 2010, Goldman Sachs promoted me to VP. I was twenty-seven. My compensation jumped to over $340,000. I moved into a higher echelon of responsibilities. I still couldn't bring myself to spend $600 on a pair of Louboutins, but I knew I *could* if I wanted to and that doing so would hardly make a dent in my bank account. I had more money to take better care of my mother. I never had to think twice about buying clothes or school supplies for Julio. I was living the American dream—the dream that I had longed to achieve ever since I was a young girl struggling to learn English in San Antonio.

So what was wrong with me?

I couldn't understand why I felt so empty. I couldn't understand why I felt so alone. I couldn't understand why I felt like there was something missing from my life. I also couldn't understand why my own body was still betraying me.

Over the course of that year my back pain, joint pain, and stomach problems all grew worse. I had already visited the best doctors. I'd managed to pay for every treatment and medicine I could find. I even went to see a therapist. I finally realized that shrinks weren't just for "rich people with rich-people problems," the way I mistakenly thought of them back in college. That attitude was a reflection of what so many people in the Latino community think. There's a real stigma attached to therapy, so walking into that office took guts. As it turned out, therapy was really good for me. I also thought I had reduced the stress I was under pretty significantly by getting my green card. But nothing helped.

No one would have known it by looking at my smiling face and my fancy clothes, but I was desperate.

With Julio's approval, my family and I wound up making the decision to send him to my sister's house in Texas to finish out his high school career. He actually thought it would be exciting to move back to his home state, and my career was simply taking up too much of my time for me to act as a good parent all by myself. I had no doubt he was on track to get into a good college and to start to pursue his own American dream in the coming years. That felt good. But as soon as he left, the loneliness of my life really set in. I had friends. I had work. But my family was still torn apart. I had gotten so used to Julio being around that as soon as he left, the hole in my soul grew bigger.

With nowhere left to turn, I turned to my faith. I realized that every time I needed him, God delivered me. I didn't think of God as a genie who gave me all my wishes, but what I had always found, in the midst of whatever chaos, was peace in God. He had also done some pretty miraculous things in my life. Every time I needed my fake papers to work, He was there for me. Each pit I fell into, He had taken me out of it. Every hurdle I had to get over, He'd gotten me over. *Why should this be any different?* I poured my heart out to God in prayer and wrote long passages of thanksgiving in my journals. Finally, I decided to talk to my pastor.

I told him about the physical ailments I was suffering, and in the course of explaining all the pain I had been through, I wound up telling him I had been undocumented. He seemed taken aback. I don't think he had ever encountered that sort of a confession before, and he didn't know what to make of it or what to do with it. He suggested that I needed to do something more to get to the root of my ailments. He suggested that I needed to see a prophet—something that's obviously far removed from the black-and-white, numbers-based world of Wall Street, but wasn't all that far removed from the Christian upbringing of my Mexican childhood. Since nothing else had worked for me, I told him I was willing.

It took some time to set everything up, but when the well-known prophet Jim Laffoon came through New York City, my pastor arranged for me to see him. My church met at the historic Lamb's Theater in Times Square. After church I made my way backstage, just behind the velvet curtains, where my pastor's wife held my hand and prayed for me before I met with Jim Laffoon.

After working for so long on Wall Street, I could confidently say I wasn't intimidated by anyone, yet I felt humbled in Jim's presence. He looked so deep into my eyes it felt like nothing in the whole world existed but the two of us in that one moment. I was ready to hear what he had to say. I was ready to do whatever he might tell me to do.

"You're very good with numbers," he said. He talked about the importance of the number 3 in my life. He spoke about things that didn't seem to offer me any direct answers at all. Finally he said, "You are going to go through a two-year period that seems like it holds so much promise, but in reality will be so much pain—and then God is going to deliver you into the greatest hour you have ever known."

I went in looking for answers and instead I got a prophecy that seemed to tell me I had a lot more suffering ahead of me. *Gee, thanks*, I thought. Still, there was something about what he said that gave me hope. That last part about God delivering me the greatest moments I'd ever known was something worth holding on to.

I tucked that prophecy away for the future. I went back to my life. And a few months later, I realized that life as I knew it had to change.

CHAPTER 23

The End

My marriage was not technically over. Jeff and I would support each other emotionally long-distance for the next few years, even as we lived separate lives. While we tried to figure out what would happen to our marriage, we decided to leave our romantic door open—and in walked Dom.

Dom was an artist, a freethinker, a filmmaker, and a man for whom I would fall head over heels. His was the best first kiss I'd ever had in my life. He was mysterious and sexy, and from the minute his lips touched mine I felt an electrical signal slide through my entire body. I could feel his kiss in my toes and my fingertips and in my belly.

Dom lived a life far different from any other man that I'd ever fallen for, and in our brief but fiery time together, he would challenge me to my core.

"You work for *the man*," he would sometimes say to me late at night, as if "the man" were the devil himself. "Look at your life! You've been willing to do *anything* to get ahead. You even got *married* as a way to get ahead!"

Had I? I didn't think so. I truly didn't believe that. What did Dom know, anyway? He went to Harvard. He was born an American citizen. He could afford to be an antiestablishment free spirit.

I would not have had the freedom to do the things I was doing if it wasn't for the money I made at Goldman, if it wasn't for the fake papers I had used.

Dom was black, so he'd had his own struggles in America. *But at least he never had to fear being deported,* I thought. And then one late night we were walking in the Lower East Side after seeing a documentary about graffiti artists, when a white homeless man began screaming at Dom, "You effing nigger, get off my street. I'll stab you in the neck." How could I expect to be treated well in a country where one of its own citizens was being called an ugly racial epithet?

I couldn't help but wonder if on some level was Dom was right. *Had I been willing to do anything to get ahead?* I hated that he questioned my marriage. Despite being separated, I missed Jeff. He was my best friend. I missed a relationship that for the first time in my life felt like a true partnership. Still, I couldn't shake it. Dom's words cut deep. I had long been questioning every choice I'd made, and he made me question my choices harder than I ever had before.

When our relationship ended, I was crushed. But I realize now that he was there for a moment and for a reason. He pushed me and pressed me to continue my quest to find my real calling in life—to find out who I really am—and for that I am eternally grateful.

Right on the heels of that breakup, one of my best friends died. Quickly, suddenly, and with absolutely no warning. Chris was twenty-nine years old. He was the life of the party.

Since moving to New York, I had become close friends with a group of Texas alumni. Some of us never met at UT, many of us were not there at the same time, but somehow we found each other in the jungle of New York City. I saw the Texans, as we called ourselves, every single weekend. When Chris died, it destroyed us all. He was supposed to go to Mexico for a long weekend with his family and come right back. Instead, he fell from a sixth-story balcony while he was in Mexico. He was the glue that kept our group together; he was best friends with each of us. Losing him was like losing a limb, and none of us would ever be the same again.

The combination of the questioning of my own true self and the pain of such a sudden loss made me think a lot about the sudden loss of my father, and before long I found myself pondering the fragility of life itself. What if I really was on the wrong path? What if monetary success and the life I'd been leading weren't actually what I wanted? What if this particular American dream I was chasing wasn't *my* dream? Was the never-ending pain in my body trying to tell me something? Was my never-ending series of heartbreaks trying to tell me something, too? *What if I'm running out of time? What if my own life is fleeting? What would happen if I died tomorrow with this feeling in my gut, this doubt, this hole, this emptiness that keeps telling me I have a different purpose?*

In the midst of all of my obsessive worrying, I realized that the latter half of that last question wasn't really a question at all. I had *always* felt that God had something in store for me. God had a purpose for my life. I realized the emptiness I felt, the hole I felt, was because I wasn't living out that purpose.

I didn't know what that purpose was, but I certainly wasn't going to find out by working in the same eighty-hour-per-week job that I'd been grinding away at since college. I needed to break free. I needed to go out into the world and find the pieces of myself that I had never known.

By January 2011, I had made up my mind to leave Goldman Sachs. More than that, I knew I wanted to get out of the financial industry altogether. I also knew that to anyone else it would seem like a rash and possibly irresponsible decision. But to me, it was the only decision that made sense. I'd made up my mind and no one could change it. I simply had to wait for the right time to make my exit.

My love life had fallen apart twice over the course of the previous year, but I was thrilled that my boss and friend, Kate, had been promoted to managing director—and was getting married! Looking at her life gave me hope that it was possible to have a top-notch career *and* love at the same time. She was engaged to be married and planning a lavish ceremony to be held that spring in Mexico. She invited me to the wedding. I decided out of loyalty to her and not wanting to rain on her parade in any way that I would wait until after she came back from her honeymoon to announce my resignation.

I went on about my business as VP, which included a trip to the UT campus to staff a career fair and to talk to the school's administrators and various group leaders about our recruiting efforts.

A group of us had dinner together after the recruitment fair was over, and one of the administrators who was present for that dinner was the Hispanic woman who worked in the business school. We were sitting at this dinner discussing all sorts of important things, and right in the middle of it she told my colleagues, "You wouldn't believe this, but back when she went to school here, Julissa had red hair and a tongue ring. Can you believe it?"

This wasn't a comment about how far I'd come, or how inspirational it was that a young girl with little direction wound up having a successful career. It seemed to me that she wanted to put me in my place.

My colleagues all looked at me and we kind of just awkwardly laughed it off. But after dinner, I decided enough was enough.

"May I speak with you?" I asked politely. "You may think that what you said at dinner is funny, but it's not. I was nineteen years old when my hair was red and I had a tongue ring. You were an adult, and you clearly judged me then when you were supposed to be helping me. I am a vice president at Goldman now, and I really don't see the point of your bringing that up."

She seemed apologetic, and I hope my words resonated with her. I didn't wield my VP position over others very often. I knew what it was like to be treated well as an intern and as an analyst, and I worked hard to treat all of my own interns and analysts with the utmost respect and understanding. I offered advice and guidance the way Ted had with me. I soon found, though, that things were a little different when you're a woman in charge.

There was one time when I asked one of my first-year analysts to put together a presentation for me and he said, "I don't do that. I only work on things that make money." He said that in front of everyone—and he was dead serious!

"Wait a minute. You're an analyst, and you are *going* to do whatever I say you're going to do," I told him. His face went red and the whole desk got quiet.

I was that blunt because I wanted to make sure he didn't misinterpret anything I had to say. I talked to him about it in private afterward: "Just because I am cool with you and gave you advice and tried to mentor you doesn't mean you can be disrespectful to me, and especially not in front of other people."

He understood, and we're still friendly to this day. But I know for a fact that he never would have said that to me in a million years if I were a man.

The culture of male dominance on Wall Street became more and more clear to me during my last couple of years at Goldman. Wanting to play with the big boys meant going along as they hung out at the clubs after conferences and meetings. And while I don't like to dwell on it, I fended off one harassing male executive who came pounding on my hotel door after a conference in Miami. He was visiting from an international office, and he had shown me pictures of his family at dinner, and after hours he wanted to show me something else.

It got tiring after a while, and it just served as one more validation for my decision to leave.

In the months leading up to my big good-bye, I did a lot of thinking about where I came from, going all the way back to my roots. I thought about my family—who they were, what they did with their lives—and I knew that all of them were entrepreneurs. So I decided that was what I would set my sights on first when I left Goldman.

Now that I had a green card and was free to roam the world, I thought a lot about travel. There were so many places I wanted to go that sometimes the sheer number of options available felt paralyzing. I found myself wishing there was a travel site that would help guide me, a young woman who wanted to see it all. I dreamed of a site or a service where I could simply share how much money I wanted to spend, and maybe tell the computer what some of my criteria were, and then that site would give me suggestions of where I could fly and stay on my budget. People always say the best entrepreneurial ideas are the ones that fill a missing need in the world, and to me that felt like a missing need. So before I left Goldman, I started the ball rolling on the launch of my own online travel startup. I had money. I had connections. I knew investors. I had drive. I had absolutely no doubt that I could make that startup fly.

Kate's wedding was everything a top Wall Street player's wedding should be: glamorous and gorgeous and over the top, with no expense spared. Everyone had the time of their lives. I felt privileged to be there and to call Kate a friend.

That made it all the more difficult to walk into her office and tell her that I was leaving.

"What? You are resigning?" she said. She turned red whenever she felt uncomfortable.

Mike came into the office and said, "We can convince you to stay." I knew what that meant: they would offer me more money.

"No. This isn't a ploy. I'm not looking for a better offer. I'm not going anywhere else. I'm getting out. I'm launching a startup," I said.

I was as honest as I could be without revealing the secret I still held so tightly inside. There was still no one in my professional life who had any idea that I'd used fake papers to secure my employment. In 2005, when I started working at Goldman, E-Verify, the system employers use to check documents against government records, wasn't widely used. Once I passed the background check, there was no reason for Goldman to question my paperwork. I simply told Kate that I'd been soul searching. I talked to her about the loss of my father and my friend's sudden death and how all of it had taken me down a road that made me question everything. I needed to go find myself, and that was it. There was nothing anyone could do to change my mind.

When the time came, I sent an e-mail to everyone I'd ever worked with during my six-plus years at Goldman Sachs:

Over the past six years, I have sent over one hundred thousand e-mails, but this one has been the most difficult to write. Of all the e-mails I have sent, I feel the most unprepared to write this farewell message, mostly because I never thought I would be writing one.

There are times when an idea just pulls at your heart and will not leave you alone until you pay attention to it. And so it was with an idea to help people experience and see more of the world! In the next year, I will be working to launch an online travel site.

It is only because of the last six years I spent at Goldman that I am ready to take this next step. I am so incredibly grateful and humbled to have had the opportunity to be part of such an amazing organization. Every single one of you has had a lasting impact on both my professional and personal life.

I cannot find the right words to express how much I will miss this place and each of you. I hope that our paths will cross again in the future, and I hope to power your next adventure!

Attached is my contact information—please stay in touch.

Regards,

Julissa

I received hundreds of responses back on the day I sent that e-mail. Some made me laugh. Some had me tearing up. For more than six years of my life, for most of the hours I was awake on any given day, the people in that company had been like a family. My Goldman Sachs family.

Kate and Mike threw me a big going-away party. They had the whole team don sweater vests and scarfs, two of my favorite accessories, for a photo tribute. I was humbled. I had no regrets about leaving. I was ready. I had to go. But it was not easy saying good-bye, and I shed a whole lot of tears as I walked out of the office with a box full of my personal belongings, not knowing exactly where life was going to take me. I guess that's all part of the adventure. We have to take leaps now and then to see where we land.

CHAPTER 24

The Odyssey

I had money in the bank. I had freedom. I had time. And as soon as I wiped away the tears, I knew what I wanted to do first.

I traveled to Mexico and finally spent a significant amount of time with my family there. Then I decided to live out my world-traveling dreams. I traveled to Europe, the Caribbean, and South America. I took a boat trip down a river in North Carolina. I made my way all across the country to visit old friends. I headed out to UT to sit in the stands at football games and mingle with fellow alumni.

I saw a lot of beautiful places. I found myself awed. Yet I knew without a doubt that as soon as I was eligible, I would submit my application to become a U.S. citizen.

In between all of my much-needed fun, escape, and introspection, I tried to get focused on my next career move. That was when I ran into a great big problem: I had spent so many years knowing exactly what I wanted and needed to do next that having a completely blank canvas paralyzed me. Without structure, without clear guidelines, without knowing what steps I should take, I couldn't seem to find my way.

In a matter of months, my travel company completely fizzled. Then I ran into a great opportunity to join a former Goldman colleague in financing another small businesses startup, but that turned out to be a $20,000 mistake.

After not working for nearly a year and burning through about $70,000 in savings, I started to wonder if instead of taking a bold leap of faith, maybe I'd mistakenly jumped into a pit full of quicksand.

Then I received a call from Raphael, my former colleague at Goldman Sachs, with a very tempting job offer. Not just a job, but a promotion across town at one of Goldman Sachs's competitors, Bank of America Merrill Lynch.

I was feeling pretty lost—and that out-of-the-blue job offer made me feel found.

I was refreshed after my time away from the rat race, and I saw that a new job at a new company was a huge opportunity for me. I imagined how amazing it would feel to be starting as an executive with a legitimate green card and social security number. How exciting would it be to go into a job with that kind of standing and with no excuses to make; no debilitating, vomit-inducing fear to face when I filled out my W-4. The whole thing sounded like a dream. I was ready. I *wanted* this! I absolutely convinced myself that this job held all sorts of promise.

I jumped in with both feet—and soon found myself drowning. Raphael left Merrill just a few months after I joined. The structure of the entire team then changed and I was caught in a political quagmire that was impossibly difficult to navigate. In the shuffle, the revenue of the business fell by more than half. As a result, my compensation was cut by almost half, too.

Wanting to make the best of it—and not wanting to admit that I'd made a huge mistake by coming back to the financial world when I knew in my heart that I needed to find a new calling— I decided to make a major investment in an initiative that would reflect my true values. I pooled some money together with some Wall Street friends and started a scholarship fund for immigrant students, regardless of their immigration status. Documented, un-documented, it didn't matter. Students who were struggling, who needed help, were going to find it through us. We named it the Ascend Educational Fund. We would give out our first awards the following year in a teary ceremony that filled me with joy. I should have known right then what my true calling was. I should have thrown myself into finding those sorts of opportunities to help other immigrants full-time.

Instead, I tried to reorganize and give it my best try at Merrill Lynch. In some ways, the company seemed to lack the sort of loy-alty to its own people that Goldman practiced so well. In other ways, I lacked the loyalty to Merrill Lynch that I'd had for Gold-man. The organization seemed not to have any definable culture, at least that I could see. Wanting to foster a positive corporate cul-ture with best leadership practices, I found myself starting every other sentence with, "At Goldman, we..."

As it turned out, at its heart, Merrill Lynch wasn't interested in being much like Goldman Sachs at all. I never really fit in there, and to be fair, I never really tried as hard as I did when I was at Goldman. I felt like I was letting myself down every time I came to the office late, or left early. I would sit at my desk waiting for 6:00 p.m. to roll around so I could leave. I spent two whole years pretty much hating my job.

It was the first part of my prophecy come true.

When the company downsized and laid me off in May 2014, I wasn't upset in the least. I was relieved. I thought, *Maybe this is God's way of telling me to stop stalling.* I left the office, walked home at 10:00 a.m., changed into my gym clothes, and went to a noon Crossfit class with a big smile on my face. After two years of what

I thought was a new job filled with great promise, I realized it was time for the other part of my personal prophecy to come true: it was time for God to show me the greatest moments of my life.

It also helped that I got a nice severance package, so money wasn't an issue.

I reached out to Goldman Sachs and a few other firms, just to be safe, and in no time I had interviews lined up all over town. The financial recovery was well underway, and I knew there would be no shortage of jobs for the taking. With my experience and background, I figured I could keep working in the financial industry for the rest of my life if that was what I wanted. So I didn't fret over it. I didn't worry about what was going to happen next. I put it all in God's hands and decided to focus on something that was really important to me: celebrating my thirtieth birthday in style.

As the big day grew closer, I thought back to the anticipation I'd had for my fifteenth birthday and the quinceañera that never was. I had been so naive then. I couldn't have known that the real pain, the real struggle, was only just starting. Yet even as a thirty-year-old woman, I still felt sad for my fourteen-year-old self.

I wasn't that same little girl anymore, of course. My parents may not have been able to throw me a quinceañera fifteen years earlier, but I decided I could do even better: I could throw myself a splendid extended thirtieth-birthday celebration. A double quinceañera.

I spent ten days, including my actual birthday, in Japan during the Cherry Blossom season. Cherry blossoms had replaced the bougainvillea's blossoms as my favorite flowers, so seeing their magnificence on full display in their country of origin was at the top of my bucket list. I walked among those trees and I let the petals rain down over me as their beautiful scent filled up my senses.

When I got back, I let it rain in a different way: I hosted

twenty-five of my closest friends for brunch at Saxon and Parole, a trendy American eatery on the Lower East Side. The special menu made up just for me read, "Julissa's 30th Bday Celebration—Boogie Stop #1." People from every stage of my life in America came out to celebrate, including some of my best friends from college, and my former boss, Kate. Together we ate and drank, and drank some more.

"Boogie Stop #2" was my East Harlem apartment—and the whole group rode there in the back of a Hummer stretch limo. Kate couldn't make it all the way to Boogie Stop #2. She insisted she had to leave after brunch. But we insisted we give her a ride in that Hummer from the Lower East Side to her posh Tribeca apartment. I'm pretty sure she wanted to die when her doorman opened the door of that ostentatious limo. A couple of neighbors waved at her; on cue she turned red.

From there, we took a purposefully long, slow ride around Manhattan, swinging right in front of the shiny new Goldman Sachs headquarters at 200 West Street before making our way uptown. One of the benefits of a limo on steroids was room to stand up and dance. Bass was thumping and lights were flashing as my girlfriends and I took turns on the party pole, spinning around and posing for ridiculous cell phone pictures, which we all promised wouldn't wind up online.

This is what money can buy, I thought, as I sipped another glass of champagne. We dropped off a few more friends along the way, but we were still a large group when we arrived at my apartment and continued the celebration. More than once I looked around my living room and took it all in. I wanted to remember this. *Money can't buy happiness, but it sure does facilitate it.* I wanted to remember how much I had enjoyed turning thirty. I wanted to remember how much I enjoyed being celebrated by my friends.

When I woke up the next morning, I didn't remember having ordered pizza, but the pile of cardboard boxes revealed otherwise. A few friends were still asleep on the couch and on the floor. There were beer cans and champagne bottles everywhere. I thought about how long it was going to take to clean up as I tried to block the glare of light coming through the windows. I think I had more of an emotional hangover than a physical one, though. I was happy with how the party turned out. Everyone had a great time, including me. And yet, at the same time I felt joyful, I realized how much I would never get back. No party I could ever throw would make up for what I'd lost. Even on the occasion of my double quinceañera, I didn't wear the pink dress, roses weren't shipped in from a faraway city, doves didn't fly at the end of the celebration, and I didn't have any chambelanes to dance with.

On that morning, I realized why the loss of that long-ago party still haunted me. I realized that the loss of that party marked the beginning of every struggle I'd suffered for the last fifteen years. In a very real way, the loss of my quinceañera marked the loss of my innocence. And on that morning, it finally hit home for me that some things, once lost, are lost forever.

Once again, I reminded myself that no amount of money could ever buy back those moments, memories, times, and people that I'd lost. *Hadn't I learned that lesson already?* I thought. *Didn't I feel that lesson enough as I wept in my uncle's arms at Mama Silvia's house after she died?*

I knew enough not to question God's plans anymore. Once that lesson was finally learned, my redemption was just around the corner.

CHAPTER 25

Out of the Darkness

Becoming a U.S. citizen is not as easy as standing in a line waiting for your turn. It's expensive, time-consuming, and cumbersome. That is, if you are even eligible to stand in the line.

The process began when I received my green card, an expensive, time-consuming process in its own right. It continued when Jeff and I put our semi-estranged marriage aside and worked together to renew that green card in an exhaustive second round of vetting two years later.

It continued as I began the long wait in the proverbial line to even qualify to apply for citizenship. I wasn't eligible to submit my official application until December 2013. I'd already lived here and considered myself an American for twenty years as it was. Now, five years and nearly $20,000 in legal fees after I started the path to citizenship, I filled out some paperwork and still found myself waiting.

In fact, I was in the middle of all that waiting and wondering, still mired in a soul-searching state of unemployment, when a woman I met who worked at the Mayor's Office of Immigrant Affairs invited me to watch *Documented* at the Museum of the Moving Image in Queens. It was a documentary film about a man named Jose Antonio Vargas. I'd heard of him. He had become *the* voice in the immigration rights movement. He had written an article for the *New York Times Magazine* on the subject of his own struggles as an undocumented immigrant growing up in this country. It was published in June 2011—pretty much at the exact same moment I was leaving Goldman Sachs.

As I sat in that darkened theater, after putting my full faith in God that He would show me the path that I needed to take, God finally showed me the way.

Jose had a successful career as a journalist using fake papers. He even won a Pulitzer Prize. He'd come from the Philippines when he was twelve. He'd used his papers to land jobs at the *San Francisco Chronicle*, the *Washington Post*, and the *New Yorker*. He hadn't seen his mom in more than twenty years. He'd risked everything by writing that *New York Times Magazine* article and coming out while he was still undocumented. It was an astounding story to watch unfold.

Throughout the film he kept using the word *undocumented* instead of *illegal*. He made it very clear in every step that he took that he was not an "alien." He was a human being; a kid who had been sent here to live with his grandparents so he might have a shot at a better life; a kid who'd been caught up in a system that didn't allow him to fix his undocumented status, through no fault of his own. I found his use of language absolutely breathtaking. It had never occurred to me just how much shame and humiliation I'd felt thinking that anyone might call me an illegal alien. That dehumanizing phrase had seared itself into my brain when I'd first heard it used in San Antonio at the age of fourteen. I believe those words were responsible for one part of the immense fear I felt every time I faced an ID check.

Illegal alien is dehumanizing. *Undocumented immigrant* is not. A piece of paper does not define the entirety of who I am.

Everything about this man's story resonated deeply with me.

Tears streamed down my face pretty much the entire time I watched the film. It felt as if I was watching my life up on that screen. The fear he described, the emotional reactions he had when filling out the most basic forms, the way his secret affected his relationships, all of it, felt like my story. In so many ways, he was *me*.

For the first time ever, I started to consider how many other people might be out there who were just like him, who were just like me. I'd felt so alone in my struggle for so long that watching that film was like throwing open a window and seeing the world for the very first time. It was like that song by the Police, "Message in a Bottle," in which a lonely man casts a bottle into the sea. At the end of the song, he looks out one morning and sees billions of bottles just like his washed up all over the beach. "Seems I'm not alone in being alone," the song says. I wasn't alone anymore.

That one night, that one film, triggered my epiphany. There were millions of other people out there just like me. There were millions of children in America who were just starting this journey that I'd already been through.

I realized I was supposed to be doing something about that. Something else. Something bigger. Something that was focused on helping other people like me. And I finally knew why I had lived through so much pain: *I can use everything I went through to do something good.*

Jose founded a nonprofit organization called Define American on the very day that his story was published in the *New York Times Magazine*. His organization was founded to share the stories of all sorts of immigrants on a broad, national level—as a way to humanize the issue and change the conversation on immigration in this country.

I wanted to meet him. More than that, I wanted to work with

him. I wanted to work with him as badly as I'd wanted to land a job at Goldman Sachs after visiting New York City for the very first time in the summer of my junior year. I set out on a mission to get in touch with him, using every skill I'd developed in all of my years spent networking at Goldman Sachs, and eventually, I reached him. I met him. I talked to him. I made it very clear from the first time I met him that I wanted to work with him. He didn't even know he had a job to offer. But after a couple of conversations, I convinced him that he absolutely needed to hire me on as a director of development at Define American.

I had no idea how I would support myself financially by working at a small nonprofit. I had no idea how I was going to make it work. But I took a complete leap of faith and started down that road, which for me was also the start of playing catch-up on learning about my own culture—including a history of Mexicans and other immigrants in America that had been obscure to me.

Thinking back to my school days, including my American history courses, I realized I hadn't learned a thing about my people. I'm not white. I'm not black. *We don't even have a place in the textbooks on the civil rights movement.*

I had gone through my entire life thinking that Latinos had no place in American history when nothing could have been further from the truth. We had our own fight for education equality in East Los Angeles. There were massive student walkouts that led to real changes in south LA. But you'll never read about that in a textbook. *Why?*

I knew that a lot of what we call America today was actually our land that Anglo settlers took from us. This newfound connection to my own history didn't make me feel anti-American in the least.

I just don't understand why we aren't talking about the truth when we talk about this country. Latinos were here, *always*, but in so many school systems our history is ignored and forgotten.

More than our history being forgotten and ignored, why aren't we connecting the dots between our struggles and the struggles of African Americans and other minority, disenfranchised groups? Our histories, and our futures, are tied to one other.

The deeper I dove into these subjects, the more I reconnected to my own past. Being from Texas, of course we learned all about the Alamo and its heroes, including Davy Crockett. But we learned about it from a position of "We defeated the Mexican invasion."

Actually, that's not true. Texas was part of Mexico. Anglo settlers came in—invited by the Mexican government, mind you, to help populate the northern part of Mexico. Mexicans fought and died in the Alamo only to become second-class citizens once Texas won its independence.

My father had told me all about it during one of my childhood trips to visit my parents when I was maybe eight years old. I couldn't understand why I had let it all fade so far back into my memory, but I recalled my parents taking me to Austin, to the state capital, where I stood up on top of a big boulder and looked around at all of the land that used to be a part of Mexico. I wanted to reclaim it for my country. I had big dreams back then. In addition to wanting to be a singer or performer of some kind, I thought for sure that I would grow up to be the first woman president of Mexico someday. So I stood up on that boulder and I made a promise: "My name will no longer be Julissa if Texas doesn't become part of Mexico again when I'm president!" In reality, I wanted to reclaim California, Arizona, and all of that Southwest land that used to belong to Mexico. I meant it, too, because saying that phrase, "My name will no longer be Julissa," was like the biggest, most intense promise someone could make in my culture. Our name, our word, means something.

It felt really strange to recall how passionate I was about it way back when, and to think that I had stuffed all of that knowledge and pride away for all those years.

I never even learned about Cesar Chavez until I was in college, and I'm pretty sure that most college students in America don't learn about Cesar Chavez, in college.

Why?

I found myself asking why again and again.

Why had this history been hidden away? Why were we treating people from Mexico, people who were a part of this country from the beginning, as "alien"? Why were there so many awful stereotypes about undocumented immigrants in this country being dirty, filthy, poor, lazy, dangerous people? Why did I never hear stories like mine when people talked about the plight of undocumented immigrants in this country? Why did I never see faces like mine attached to the immigrant conversation?

And that's when it hit me: *I need to share my story.*

CHAPTER 26

Connecting the Dots

After I left Wall Street, I decided to tattoo my life experiences on my body. I didn't want anything cheesy or flashy at all. On this body of mine that was continuously wracked with so much pain, I wanted to inscribe something meaningful—something deeply personal to me and me alone. I spent a lot of time thinking about what that would be, and I came to some surprising conclusions.

Part of my lifelong struggle had been one of belonging. Where did I belong? Was I Mexican? Was I American? What I'd come to realize is that where I belonged was really a much deeper question than one of country or nationality. It was a question that transcended nationality and the artificial borders we humans like to draw up to keep "others" out and our own penned in. Where I belong is actually a question of what I am, and what I am first and foremost is a child of God. I *belong* to God. I had only made it to this exciting new precipice in my life because of Him. So the first tattoo I put on my body consisted of two words: "The Lord's." I had those words etched around the base of my ring finger, right where a traditional wedding ring would go.

The second tattoo was, on its surface, something very simple: a set of lines that link three tiny moles on my left arm—like a child's connect-the-dots—symbolizing to me that everything happens for a reason. One thing leads to another. I may not have always been able to see the path I was on when I was on it, but my story unfolded uniquely and perfectly just the way it was supposed to unfold. The lines between those dots didn't turn out perfectly straight. As an artist's canvas, the human body doesn't do well with straight lines. That upset me at first. It was such a simple tattoo; I wanted it to be "perfect." But I soon realized that my path itself had not been straight. I came to realize that the tattoo, like the journey itself, existed just the way it was supposed to exist.

A third tattoo would come later. The most meaningful one yet.

I would place it on my body only after I became a citizen of the United States of America.

By mid-2014, I had jumped every hurdle and passed every test and background check I needed to pass. I was finally eligible to become a citizen. The date was set for my naturalization ceremony at the Federal Courthouse on Pearl Street in Lower Manhattan on August 8.

As fate would have it, I played MC at a friend's startup launch party a few weeks before my date at the courthouse. As part of the introductory remarks, I shared that I would become a U.S. citizen in the next couple of weeks. A woman who worked as a writer and photographer for *Elle* magazine was in the audience. She asked whether I might be willing to let her document my big day for a feature story in the magazine. She had been on the hunt for a unique photo essay she could both write and shoot for *Elle*. I told her I would not only be willing, but that my story was actually a lot more interesting than she might expect. She brought the idea to her editor, and the editor loved it. This was it. I was about to go public with my story.

Julio flew in from Texas just for the ceremony. He was in college now, just starting his sophomore year at Texas Tech. He was making his way. It felt so good to have him back in the city for my special day.

I got dressed up in a black dress and pearls. We took the subway downtown. I walked into the courthouse knowing that I would be walking out an official American, after so many years of hiding. I looked around that courtroom full of tearful, smiling faces of every color, and I imagined the stories that every one of those amazing people had to tell. The judge who presided over the ceremony said it best: "What is America? Look around you. You represent fifty-seven different countries. Becoming an American citizen means accepting the world as your nation."

Every one of them had worked hard for this. Every one of them wanted to live in this country and call it home because America is still the shining beacon of the world. I kept wiping away my tears, simply overwhelmed to think that this day was finally here, and that never again would I have to live in fear of being deported from the country I loved. Never again would anyone be able to question that I was an American.

The *Elle* magazine article telling the story of my life and documenting the day of my naturalization went live on Elle.com in November. The pictures were absolutely stunning. I was so thankful that Morrigan McCarthy captured one of the most important days of my life so beautifully.

I soon reached out to a reporter at Bloomberg whom I had met the previous year through a completely unrelated story he wrote. Max Abelson would make my secret life the subject of a 3,400-word profile on *Bloomberg Businessweek*—a piece that was highlighted for the site's 24 million unique monthly visitors. The article appeared in the print version as well, under the headline "Shadow Banker," and the story was promoted as a "Top News" item on every Bloomberg terminal around the world.

That morning, I imagined my former colleagues catching up on the news, and nearly choking on their coffee because they could not believe what they had just read.

It didn't stop there. The article went viral. In the course of the next few months, my story became the subject of more than two hundred follow-up articles and interviews—and the entire trajectory of my life was transformed.

I was asked to appear on Bloomberg TV, CNN, MSNBC, Telemundo, Univision, NPR, and other major media outlets. I was asked to speak at forums all over the country. I gave a TEDx Talk at Julio's school, Texas Tech University. I attended the Forbes Reinventing America Summit, an invitation-only meeting of industrial leaders, entrepreneurs, and academics to discuss how to attract and retain the best talent in the world. I was invited to speak on a panel at the Forbes Women's Summit alongside luminaries such as Nancy Pelosi, Jessica Alba, and Gayle King, and I received countless invitations to share my story in speeches across the nation.

I went from being completely unknown to sharing my truth with the entire world. And I realized that everything I had done in my life—every business conference I'd attended, all the travel I did while I was at Goldman Sachs, all the networking and handshaking with clients, even the PowerPoint presentations I had to put together as an intern and a first-year analyst—every bit of it prepared me for the journey I was suddenly taking.

Over the course of 2015, I would have hour-long conversations with some of the most recognized producers in Hollywood and meet with some of the most iconic business leaders in the United States. Every single one of them was intrigued by my story. Every one of them wanted to learn more. Every one of them wanted to know what they could do to help my story make an impact.

I cared that such important people wanted to meet me, but I wondered if they also wanted to help others like me. The best, most rewarding part of the journey wasn't getting an audience with them, but the countless messages I got from others like me. One of the most humbling messages I received was from a young man named Mario Enrique Choto:

> A few months ago, before I read about you and all the hard work you've done, I was lost, hopeless, emotionally broken. I thought I was a defective object, another meaningless and funny wetback with a minimum wage job. I was in dream-land but my dreams could never be true 'cause I felt alone and till this day I'm still alone here. I got no family here but then I found out about this labeled "undocumented" human be-ing who was weeping over her father's death in a bathroom of a prestigious company, her world had fallen apart but she wouldn't give up. It got my attention, I fully read that article, and I found out that even successful people like you had to endure harshness and sometimes swallowed some bitterness. You lit up my hope once again and made me feel safe and part of an 11 million family members with dreams and hopes. As for now you earned your valuable citizenship but I'm more impressed by the fact that you still care for those who are on the verge and that is an act of kindness as huge as delivering the speech "I have a dream" during segregation times. Thank you, are the most honest and sincere two words I can give to you. Thank you, because what you've done is inspiring.

I've done a lot of thinking about why my story struck such a chord, and I think one of the biggest reasons is simply because America is a country full of immigrants. Native Americans are the original Americans, and we must face the ugly truth: we slaughtered them and stole their land.

Americans today often view immigration as a political issue and forget that immigration is, in fact, about human beings who have dreams, ambitions, and aspirations. Immigrants do not come to the United States to take anything away from Americans. We come to America to give our sweat, blood, and tears to pursue our dreams. We don't risk our very lives and leave behind loved ones to come to a strange land in order to get on welfare, as many people think. With no papers, we don't even qualify! For too long we have tried to win the debate about immigration through politics, but it's been decades since we've seen any meaningful reform to immigration policies. Before we can win the debate in political circles, we must win it culturally. We must look deep into the soul of America and realize that America is a country of *all* of us. We need to look at the human costs of our inaction.

In 2015 California began allowing undocumented people to get driver's licenses. According to the headlines, the new policy allowed 1.2 million Californians to get driver's licenses for the first time. That's all most people read. They read the headline and formed an opinion based on whatever preconceived notion they bring to the table. But there are actual people, like me, whose lives have been completely changed because now they can have driver's licenses. For the first time, they can drive down the street without having to worry about getting pulled over. They can pick up their kids from school and go to work without having fear in their minds as they're driving.

Some people think undocumented people are here illegally, so therefore they shouldn't have a right to get a license. And to that I say, "Well, do you think that's going to stop us from driving?" Why can't we take a more humane, practical approach to the situation? If undocumented people are here and they're driving anyway, wouldn't it be better for them to have driver's licenses and be able to get insurance and make the roads safer for everyone? There are millions of undocumented people here. Many of them came into this country perfectly legally but are just stuck in the sort of limbo that I was stuck in for two decades.

It's the same thing with education. Somebody could say to me, "Well, you didn't deserve to go to college because you were undocumented." Well, let's look at that from a different perspective. I wouldn't have gotten into UT if not for the grades I had and the extracurricular activities I pursued and the leadership positions I held when I was in high school. I earned that education.

Also, your tax dollars (and my parents' tax dollars) paid for me to go to public school. It was just two years of public school in my case because my parents sent me to private school before that, but regardless, that money had already been spent on my education. That was a huge investment. Should that education have gone to waste? Should we bar well-educated kids from going to school, getting careers, and making something of their lives so they are unable to pursue their dreams and ambitions? How does that make any sense? How much talent or potential are we wasting when we do that? Some people will argue, "Well, we shouldn't have paid for them to go to school," but we did. George H. W. Bush, in a GOP presidential debate in 1980, said this: "I don't want to see six-year-olds, and eight-year-old children, totally uneducated."

If we look at the number of undocumented immigrants who are here under circumstances like mine, it only makes sense that we should make the most of this vibrant, important part of our population. And that is exactly why something like the DREAM Act should pass: to give millions of people who are in circumstances like mine a chance to get ahead without all of the pain and agony in their lives. And because it makes sense for our economy.

My whole life was spent under an oppressive system that most people in America have never had to deal with. And to those who say that anyone who wants to come here should just get in line, the fact is, the line we offer is not practical at all.

For instance, now that I'm a U.S. citizen I could petition for my mother to come here to live. But the waiting line for some countries, including Mexico and the Philippines, is twenty years. There are twenty *years'* worth of applications backlogged in the system already. My mom is sixty. She may not have twenty years to wait.

What we have now in the United States is essentially a caste system for undocumented immigrants. I call it that because no matter what undocumented immigrants do, no matter how much we accomplish, no matter how long we're here, our entire lives are determined by where we were born, and specifically the fact that we weren't born in the United States. The way it stands now, there is no path that will change our situation. I was able to adjust my status because I didn't cross the border illegally, and because I was married and we had money. But if I had crossed the border illegally, it wouldn't have mattered if I married a U.S. citizen or had U.S.-born children. I still wouldn't have been able to adjust my status. And what is amazing to me is the fact that so many undocumented immigrants endure so much, knowing how hopeless our situation truly is. Doesn't that kind of hard work and passion and determination in the face of adversity define us as a nation?

In the wake of all of the media attention, it has become my mission to use my story to help tell the truth—the *real* truth—about immigrants in this country, and to help people to see that these issues are ones we can talk about together in an effort to help make America a better country. Not just for undocumented immigrants, but for all of us.

I realize that my work in this area has just begun. I am not alone, of course. I stand on the shoulders of people who have dedicated their entire lives to advancing immigrant rights. While I no longer work for Define American, I am part of a massive movement that is bringing all of these issues to the surface. My story is only one story; there are millions of other immigrant stories that must be told.

CHAPTER 27

Redeemed

I sat down to breakfast one morning in early 2015 and realized that my back no longer hurt. I took a sip of coffee and then sort of wiggled around in my chair just to see if I was imagining it. I bent over. I stood up and stretched. I had no pain. It simply wasn't there. I was shocked. I couldn't pinpoint exactly when the pain went away, either. I tried to remember if it hurt the day before, or the day before that. I was so used to being in pain that the absence of it must have sneaked up on me.

Then, as I lifted my cup for another sip, I realized that my joints weren't hurting, either.

I would wake up the next day and the next expecting the pain in my body to come back, but it never did. As I put the finishing touches on this book a whole year later, my symptoms are still gone. Every physical ailment that had been plaguing me since college simply faded away.

My hunger for understanding such things didn't fade, though. In the hopes of getting to the bottom of it I made a full-scale examination of my life, from diet and exercise to sleep habits and more, and as far as I could tell I hadn't altered any of those habits in any significant way before the pain went away.

There was only one answer I was able to come up with: my

symptoms were caused by stress. But it wasn't the stress of working too much. It wasn't even the stress of being undocumented and trying to get by on fake papers. It wasn't that I didn't have a green card, or that I wasn't able to visit my family in Mexico. I truly believe that the physical ailments were the manifestation of the unbelievable stress of holding on to such a big secret for so long in my life.

I believe that revealing my truth to the world released the stress that was causing the pain in my body.

Or maybe it's just another miracle from God.

Shortly after I became an official citizen of the United States, I went out and got one more tattoo.

The greatest lesson I learned through my entire journey is to always trust in God. Even in the darkest moments of my life, I know I am still a child of God, and because of that, I am redeemed. I am saved, I am forgiven, I am loved, and I am cared for. So I went out and had the word "Redeemed" tattooed in bold cursive letters on the inside of my left forearm. The way I sleep, with my left arm up on my pillow, I see that word first thing when I open my eyes every morning. I wake up every day knowing that God loves me and has already redeemed me. I wake up knowing that no matter what happens, *that* is all that really matters.

I was secretly afraid that my life might be over when I left Goldman. How would I make money? What would my career look like? Would my career be over? But by actually following my passions,

I've found that I'm happier and more fulfilled than I could ever imagine. God has delivered me into the greatest hour I have ever known. His promises, His prophecies come true.

There are still times when I think about all of the deep questioning I did, and the freedom that enabled me to take the time to do that. How many other people go through the same sort of angst but *don't* take the leap of faith and leave their jobs or change their lives in order to find their true passion? How many people simply don't have that option because of the financial situation they're in, or the fact that they have health issues and can't afford to get the care that they need?

The thought of that takes me back to my confrontations with Dom. I still get angry sometimes about his accusations that what I did to get ahead amounted to some sort of "selling out." But I wasn't selling out. I was *buying in*. Sometimes in America, buying in is a necessary part of the process. We're a capitalist society, and the fact is that without some money in the bank I might not have any of the freedoms I have now. I believe in reaping the fruits of your labor.

For the last four years leading up to and including the writing of this book, I've been taking the time I need to try to find myself. I couldn't have afforded to do that if I hadn't made the money I made at Goldman. I wouldn't have been able to go to Florence, Paris, and Rome for three weeks by myself. I wouldn't have been able to take my mom on a breathtaking trip to Costa Rica to celebrate her sixtieth birthday. I never could have purchased a car for my little brother so he could get back and forth to school and work from my sister's house in Texas. Not to mention that I never would have been able to afford the service of a top-notch immigration lawyer to help me adjust my status and become the proud American citizen that I am today.

I wouldn't have been able to do any of those things if I hadn't made money first. I am proud to be an American, and I am proud to have done everything I had to do in order to get myself to where I am today.

I am grateful that because of the hard work I put in and the money I earned, I am finally now able to help to fulfill one of the dreams my parents had for our family. Many immigrants dream of coming to the United States so they can make enough money to build a house in their homeland, and then go back to live in that home with their families. My parents had that dream and were on their way to fulfilling it when everything went wrong. For years, my parents' dream house remained unfinished, uninhabited. It sat there as a physical reminder of their unfinished dream. But just recently, we have started construction to finish the house—so my mom will finally be able to move in, and Julio and I will be able to have bedrooms of our own to stay in whenever we visit. My dad never got to live in that house, but his dream was for us, and in that regard we'll fulfill it. I may never have gotten to buy him his mechanic shop, but that house—the house my parents worked so hard for—is something I can and will finish with the grace of God.

I cannot wait to celebrate its completion with a grand house-warming party.

The plight of undocumented immigrants in this country is currently a hot topic again. It happens every few years, it seems, and the run-up to the 2016 presidential election provided some unusual vitriol from some of the candidates, especially on the Republican side of the political fence. But this isn't a strictly partisan issue. Democrats tell us what we want to hear to help themselves get elected but don't keep their promises. During the Obama administration more than 400,000 people were deported each year. That is 400,000 people who are mothers, sisters, brothers, and sons. Why were the immigrants of the 1900s, from Italy, Poland, Ireland, and other European countries given the opportunity to immigrate to the United States and seek a better life, but immigrants of today are denied that very same opportunity? I've listened to lots of talk about "rounding up the illegals," and "building a wall to keep the Mexicans out," and of course I have to wonder, *Would those politicians be saying such things if they were brutally honest about the fact that America reaps the benefits of the cheap labor undocumented immigrants provide? When they talk about rounding us up, are they really thinking about rounding up people like me, who are working on Wall Street, or even working for them?*

Reducing undocumented immigrants to stereotypes and talking about us as the enemy does not do anyone any good. The fact is the plight of the undocumented immigrant is difficult enough as it is. We aren't seeking handouts, we aren't seeking welfare, but we are seeking equal access to opportunities. What we should be talking about is how to make the great dream of American citizenship more available to all the millions of wonderful, smart, driven, hardworking people who want to prove themselves worthy of everything America has to offer. Racism and bigotry flourish here no matter what someone's immigration status might be. Shouldn't we be working to combat the hatred, rather than fueling it? Isn't that what would make America even greater than it is right now?

I know some people don't think I have a right to be here. After all, I skirted the law for many years before I gained my citizenship. But the law and justice have never been synonymous. Not too long ago, it was illegal to marry someone of a different race. Now it is legal for people of the same sex to marry. Laws can change and justice can arrive, even belatedly.

I thought I had made it when I had a green card and could travel to London for the weekend, but then my eyes were opened whenever I came back through customs and got pulled out of the line to be fingerprinted and questioned as if I were openly carrying a weapon. I thought I'd made it when I received my citizenship and a U.S passport, but then a saleswoman at the Beverly Hills branch of my favorite store, Club Monaco, snidely told me that certain necklaces I was looking at were "too expensive" for me to try on. She not so subtly reminded me that no matter what papers I had, and no matter how much money I had in the bank, I still didn't belong in her store, *off* Rodeo Drive, simply because of what I look like: Mexican.

So here's how I know I've finally made it in America. I've made it not because I assimilated, or because I have a little bit of money, or because my story made headlines. I know I've made it because I have earned the right to question the system in which I live. I've made it because I've earned the right to have my voice be heard. I've made it because I can disagree with and question what America is really all about. I've made it because I can demand more from my country.

I, like millions upon millions of other immigrants both documented and undocumented, am a part of America whether certain people like it or not—and therefore I can work hard and make lots of noise in attempting to create a system that works for *me*.

When political candidates say they will work for the American people, I want to say, *I am the American people. Will you work for me?*

As a child and teen, I loved the X-Men of comic and movie fame. They gave me hope because they walked among us, often as ghosts that just blended in. People walked by them without noticing them, not knowing that they were different. *They* knew they were different, talented, and amazing. Yet they feared being found out. They feared being known.

I feared being known. *I* tried to blend in as much as I could, and in the process I lost so much of myself, of my culture, of my Mexican-ness. In that regard, I am a recovering American elitist. I am trying to find myself, to find out about my culture in this country, about my ancestors, what they lost, and what was taken from them. Someday I want to tell my children the world belongs to them, because it does. I am tired of blending in and of being a ghost. I want to be seen. I don't want to blend in anymore.

I am most tired of being seen as the "other." I am 100 percent Mexican and 100 percent American. I love being Mexican. My culture is amazing. I love being American. America is not a white Anglo-Saxon society anymore. In fact, it never really was. Let's share the truth, let's share our history, let's get it right and stop fighting about it. Those who think that being an American means being racist, xenophobic, and narrow-minded are wrong. And thankfully, I think a lot of people in my generation—of all races and backgrounds—feel the same way.

Which means the future is coming. Quickly.

Getting over the fear I lived with for so long may take me years. What I went through was traumatic, and there are always repercussions to trauma.

Toward the end of 2015, on a drive to give a speech at the "Latino in America" tour, a convening of Latino celebrities, academics, and advocates in McAllen, Texas, I happened to witness a man being arrested by Border Patrol. He was sitting on the grass, wearing jeans and a red flannel shirt, and he was handcuffed with his head down. I was going eighty miles an hour but I quickly slowed down, made a U-turn, and watched from the highway crossing. I drove closer and parked on the shoulder, feeling almost motherly for some reason. I wanted to make sure that the man wasn't harmed. The Border Patrol officers didn't bother to come tell me to move along. They were too busy towering over that rather frail-looking man. All four of them.

As I sat there behind the wheel of my comfortable rental car, I wondered how far the man had journeyed. How much had he suffered? How much had he endured? I wondered if he was thirsty and if he had been offered any water before being handcuffed? I tried to imagine the frustration he felt at being arrested sixty miles inland from the Rio Grande, sixty miles into the land of opportunity, sixty miles into the land that saw him as disposable. I wondered if this had been his first attempt to cross. I wondered what happened to his companions. (Surely he didn't make the trip alone.) I wondered about his family. I worried that he might die if he were forced to try to cross again.

There was nothing I could do to help him. The Border Patrol officers loaded him into their van. The man would likely be deported immediately. If he'd been a woman or a child, he might have ended up in a detention center. Thousands of women and children end up in detention centers in this country, where they languish for weeks, sometimes months, in a system of for-profit jails that keep Congress-mandated quotas. It's horrific. Barbaric, even. But perhaps that's a discussion better saved for my next book.

I drove away from that scene with one thought in mind: the next day, I would cross the bridge into Mexico and back to the United States by foot. I would cross for that man, and for the thousands of men, women, and children who cannot. I would cross simply because I could, knowing that I didn't have to run, hide, be fearful, or risk my life while doing so.

The next morning, I asked the receptionist at my hotel how to get to the bridge to cross into Reynosa, the Mexican town just across the border. She ended her directions by putting her hand on my shoulder and giving me a concerned look. "Take care, please," she said.

As I neared the bridge, I could see a dozen or so people crossing the street and a bunch of cab drivers hollering at potential passengers, but it wasn't nearly as busy as I expected. I parked my rental in the parking lot closest and walked for a couple of minutes to reach the entrance. I paid $1 to cross into Mexico.

The length of the bridge surprised me. I'd imagined the Rio Grande to be wider. I remembered it being much wider and more violent in Laredo, Texas. But there, in McAllen, Texas, what divided the United States from Mexico was a short, five-minute walk.

I looked through the barbed wire fence at the Rio Grande. I thought of how many people had given their lives to that river.

Along the way, several people lined the sidewalk selling water. Others sat there with their hands out seeking charity.

I didn't have to show any ID to walk into Mexico. I simply put my purse through a scanner and the Mexican police welcomed me in Spanish: "*Bienvenida.*"

I had expected to be nervous or at least cautious on the Mexican side, especially given the warning I received at the hotel. But I didn't feel nervous or cautious at all. I felt welcomed. Mexico will always be my homeland. The Mexican air will always feel natural and light. As soon as I stepped into Mexico and heard the music emanating from the plaza, I smiled.

It wasn't immediately clear to me where the bridge back to the United States was located, so I approached a man and asked, "Where is the bridge to go back?" I smiled at my choice of words. "Going back" now meant going *back* to the United States.

He pointed me in the right direction and I was on my way.

I paid twenty-five cents to cross to the United States. Halfway across the bridge I stopped to take a couple of pictures of the river itself and of the people walking across it. Then I stopped and I gave thanks to God that I had the ability to walk back freely.

I took out my American passport while standing in the short line and, much to my surprise, my heart started pounding. I couldn't understand why.

When I finally reached a Border Patrol officer, he questioned me. "What brought you back?" he said.

"I just crossed because I can," I said.

Puzzled, he responded, "So...you didn't go into Mexico?"

My heart started pounding more rapidly. I prayed that I hadn't made a mistake. I prayed that I wasn't going to be questioned further, or detained, or worse. What was it that made my behavior suspicious to this man?

"No," I said. "I went across the bridge and turned around and came back."

Still in disbelief, he asked me where I was from. I had recently moved to Los Angeles, so I told him: "I live in LA."

He gave me one last pondering look, then he handed my passport back to me and nodded me through.

I walked back to my car, closed the door, and sat there in the parking lot crying tears of anger. I wished I hadn't been scared. I wished I had never known what that particular fear even feels like.

Pieces of paper don't take away years of fear, and clearly, the air in the United States didn't fully belong to me. *Not yet.*

As I sat in my car under the hot Texas sun, I made a promise to myself, and to God: "One day, my heart won't be scared anymore," I said. "One day, I *will* walk back without fear."

POSTSCRIPT

In the course of doing research for this book, I went back and read through all of my old journals. As I turned the page into 2009, I was shocked to discover an entry I have no memory of writing, nor do I even know how I *could* have written it. There are sentiments expressed here that I don't recall feeling until years later. Yet there it was, in my own handwriting, in the middle of a page.

I made the entry in March, apparently right after my green card came in the mail—two years before I would leave Goldman Sachs, and five years before I would watch Jose Antonio Vargas's documentary and start down the path I'm on now. Where did these words come from? How did I know to write them? What part of me understood the answer to what my true calling would be and somehow, consciously or unconsciously, wrote it down on a page in my journal way back then?

All I can say is sometimes the heart just knows:

I am so thankful that I now have the freedom and the resources to see and experience the world. I also have a great sense of responsibility to help others who don't have the same possibilities I've had. To help others see that this is achievable. It's not the shoes or the clothes. It's about leveling the wealth. It's about leveling the access to opportunities.

God—*use me.*

Today, I am just so thankful that God is answering my prayer and that I am finally living out the second half of my prophecy.

ACKNOWLEDGMENTS

God, thank You for Your grace and Your redeeming love.

This book would not be what it is without the writing, craft, and guidance of Mark Dagostino. Mark, your passion to help me tell my story in the most compelling way made this book possible. You are a true artist; you took the writing of this book to another level. I learned so much from you. Thank you.

This book is not just mine; it belongs to my parents, Julio and Luisa, my sisters, Aris and Nay, my brother, Julio, my uncle Mike, and the rest of my family, Tia Rosi, Tia Justi, Tio Alex, Tia Guille, and to my beloved Mama Silvia. It belongs to my friends, to my teachers (thank you, Mr. G—I would not be here without you), to my mentors, and to the thousands of people who fought for my right to go to college and who worked tirelessly to pass the Texas DREAM Act in 2001. Linda, I will never be able to repay you for the risks you took to help me before you even met me in person. Your heart is bigger than Texas.

Before I shared my story with the world, I shared it with Jessica and Antonia; I will forever be blessed to call you friends. Thank you for literally holding my head up when heartbreak and pain would not let me move.

Jeff, I'll always have so much love and respect for you. You changed my life forever, and I will never forget that you supported me, loved me, and were always there to hold me down.

To the Texans, thank you for your unconditional love and support. My life would not be as colorful and joyous without each of you. A special thanks to Rob King for reading every version of every chapter of this book and giving me such thoughtful comments and feedback, always in less than twenty-four hours. You are amazing.

To Max Abelson, thank you for telling my story; it transformed my world.

To Jodi Schlesinger, for all the times you walked with me and gave me advice. For proofreading my manuscript. You're a true friend.

To Jose Antonio Vargas, your courage inspired me to tell my story. Thank you.

I've always believed that it takes a village to raise a child, and in this case to get a book published. To my literary agent, Lisa Leshne, you are a badass warrior woman. Your professionalism and tenacity made this book a reality. To my team at Authentic Management (Jon, Jason, and Monica), GTN (David Buchalter, you rock!), and WME (Eric, you are simply the best): without your passion to help me pursue my dreams, I wouldn't be here. Thank you. To my editor, Kate Hartson, thank you for taking a chance on me and for believing that my story needed to be told through this book. To Alexa Smail, thank you for making everything work. To Andrea Glickson, Sarah Falter, Patsy Jones, Rolf Zettersten, and the rest of the Hachette team, I am grateful beyond words. To the superwomen on the sales team—Karen Torres, Melissa Nicholas, Nicole Bond, Jennifer Gray, and Simone Quallo—seeing all of you in one room put a smile on my face.

Finally, thank you to the millions of immigrants who have come before me, who have risked their lives, who have lost their lives, who have left their families and land behind to come to America. Thank you because without you, America would not exist.

RESOURCES

My existence as an undocumented immigrant was a lonely one. I never met other undocumented people when I was in the shadows. As I walked onto the University of Texas campus in 2001, I knew I couldn't be the only student who was undocumented and afraid, and who didn't have the same access to the full spectrum of financial aid, scholarships, or even loans that other students did. One day during my freshman year, as I was walking through our beautiful campus, I made a promise to myself: I would create a scholarship fund for immigrant students like me. Regardless of their ethnicity, national origin, or immigration status, I would help to provide an opportunity for those talented, hardworking, persevering students full of promise who have for too long stood behind closed doors. Education changed my life. It was my way out and my way in: my way out of poverty, and my way into success. I had a responsibility to pay it forward. As of the publication of this book, the Ascend Educational Fund, which I cofounded in 2012, has provided over $200,000 in college scholarships to thirty-four students. Each of those students has a unique story, but what binds them together is their achievement, work ethic, perseverance in the face of adversity, and commitment to their communities.

If you would like to support our work, please make a tax-deductible donation at http://ascendfundny.org/support-us/donate/.

While access to higher education continues to be limited for undocumented students, I am thrilled that more states have joined Texas in providing in-state tuition and that some private institutions have opened their doors to these talented students. More scholarships must be created to provide undocumented students with the financial resources to attend college and reach their full potential. The list below is not a comprehensive list, as new funds are being created and new laws are being enacted at the state level. Please visit my website at www.julissaarce.com for the latest list of resources.

SCHOLARSHIPS OPEN TO UNDOCUMENTED STUDENTS:

The Ascend Educational Fund: www.ascendfundny.org
The Esperanza Education Fund: www.esperanzafund.org
The DREAM.US Scholarship: www.thedream.us
Golden Door Scholars: www.goldendoorscholars.org

A more comprehensive list of scholarships can also be found at The Dreamers Roadmap, a mobile app created by a formerly undocumented student.

Information on in-state tuition, access to health care, labor-protection laws, and other resources for undocumented people can be found at the National Immigration Law Center's website: www.NILC.org.

The fight for immigrant rights has never been more critical, and I am thankful for the leadership of the National Immigration Law Center (NILC), where I am a board member. Since 1979, NILC has defended and advanced the rights of immigrants in the

United States. Through impact litigation, policy analysis and advocacy, strategic communications, and other strategies, NILC has been at the forefront of every seemingly small and significant moment in the immigrant-rights movement. I'll never meet or be able to thank all the people who worked tirelessly to pass HB 1403, the bill in Texas that allowed me to go to college, but at least two of those people still work at NILC. The work of the organization impacts millions of people, and I could not be prouder to play a small role in the organization now.